MODERN AMERICAN POETRY:

Essays in Criticism

MODERN AMERICAN POETRY

Essays in Criticism

Edited by JEROME MAZZARO

DAVID McKAY COMPANY, INC.

NEW YORK

MODERN AMERICAN POETRY: ESSAYS IN CRITICISM

Second Printing, October 1970

LIBRARY OF CONGRESS CATALOG CARD NUMBER: 73–82502

MANUFACTURED IN THE UNITED STATES OF AMERICA

For Hal and Ruth Mizruchi

Preface

The nature of American poetry is not easy to define. In *The Complex Fate* (1952), Marius Bewley, an American then living in England, claimed, "It is easier to admit a difference between English and American poetry than to analyse what the exact nature of that difference is." He identifies certain of its characteristics as "security and faith in one's own experience (whatever that experience may be), a reliance on will and assertion, and a feeling that one's own experience is pretty important" and concludes of the result that it forms "an ability to see-saw from cynicism into optimism and enthusiasm, and a moment later, rigorous conviction." Earlier, in his Introduction to *The Faber Book of Modern Verse* (1936), Michael Roberts had tried his hand at the difference. He saw it as the American poet's being less firmly rooted in a settled poetic tradition than the British. He was thus able to seize and digest traditions and influences from many languages and periods. The American poet, he noted, became paradoxically European, cosmopolitan, and far-ranging into the past while the Georgian British poet remained, before the "European" influence of T. S. Eliot, largely national and insular.

Building mainly on Roberts, W. H. Auden in his Introduction to *The Criterion Book of Modern American Verse* (1956) began his distinction between the two poetries with pace, pitch, and rhythm and then moved to show that even the countrysides the poets assumed were different. The English poet presupposed a nature which was mythologized, humanized, and friendly, and a society which in race and religion was more or less homogeneous and in which most people lived and died within a short space of where they were born. In contrast, the American poet was encouraged by neither the size, condition, nor climate of this continent to intimacy. He was likely, in addition, to show a tendency to move on and make a fresh start somewhere else as a reaction to dissatisfaction or failure. Impermanence was taken for granted. More recently, Allen Tate, in his Introduction to *Modern Verse in English 1900–1950* (1958), argued that in contrast to the British, the American poet saw his world "aesthetically," and by the term Tate meant a mode of controlled disorder of perception, a heightened sensitivity that was the means of rendering a direct impression of the poet's historical situation. The mode began with Edgar Allan Poe and Charles Baudelaire and produced the concentrated metaphors of a poet like Hart Crane.

This book does not attempt to elaborate on any of these distinctions, or to take sides in a dialogue between these two poetries. Rather, there follow in its pages attempts of fifteen American critics (one Canadian) to deal with American poetry from a variety of points of view. The points of view span biographical, sociological, and aesthetical frames. The techniques range from new critical to psychoanalytic, from phenomenology to stylistic, from myth to impressionistic. As such, they represent a cross section of American criticism as different as one might need today to approach American poetry. The tendency in the criticism to take creative literature more seriously than the British, to view it more as a confrontation with Truth than as a social phenomenon, and to call it to what Matthew Arnold called its "higher destinies" makes the criticism unmistakably American. The book may be read as a comment on the poetry or on criticism, or it may be read as a comment on both. I wish to thank especially Kevin McCullough for his aid in preparing some of the selections for publication.

Acknowledgments

I should like to thank the following people, magazines, and publishers for their kind permissions to reprint copyrighted material:

Doubleday & Company, Inc., for "Death Piece," copyright 1934 by Theodore Roethke; "Old Florist," copyright 1946 by Harper & Brothers; "The Lost Son" and "The Shape of the Fire," copyright 1947 by Theodore Roethke; "Praise to the End," copyright 1950 by Theodore Roethke; "Sensibility! O La!," copyright 1951 by Theodore Roethke; "Four for Sir John Davies," copyright 1952, 1953 by Theodore Roethke, copyright 1952 by The Atlantic Monthly Company; "The Waking," copyright 1953 by Theodore Roethke; "I Knew a Woman," copyright 1954 by Theodore Roethke; "Words for the Wind," copyright © 1955 by Theodore Roethke; "Meditations of an Old Woman," copyright © 1955, 1956, 1957, 1958 by Theodore Roethke, copyright © 1958 by *Botteghe Oscure;* "The Renewal" and "The Sensualists," copyright © 1958 by Theodore Roethke; "In a Dark Time," copyright © 1960 by Beatrice Roethke as Administratrix of the Estate of Theodore Roethke; "North American Sequence," copyright © 1960, 1961, 1962, 1963 by Beatrice Roethke as Administratrix of the Estate of Theodore Roethke; and "Give Way Ye Gates," from *The Collected Poems of Theodore Roethke.* Reprinted by permission of Doubleday & Company, Inc.

Harcourt, Brace & World, Inc., for "Emily Dickinson," by Northrop Frye in *Major Writers of America,* edited by Perry Miller, © 1962 by Harcourt, Brace & World, Inc.; "Poem #33," from *is* 5 and *Poems 1923–1954,* "Thanksgiving (1956)" and "Poem #1," from 95 *Poems,* and "Poem #76," from *Collected Poems* and *Poems 1923–1954* by E. E. Cummings, copyright © 1959, 1954, and 1958 by E. E. Cummings; material from *The*

Selected Essays by T. S. Eliot, copyright 1950 by T. S. Eliot; "Ash Wednesday" and "The Waste Land," from *The Complete Poems and Plays, 1909–1950* by T. S. Eliot, copyright 1952 by T. S. Eliot; "Mother Marie Therese," from *The Mills of the Kavanaughs* by Robert Lowell, copyright 1951 by Robert Lowell. Reprinted by permission of Harcourt, Brace & World, Inc.

Harper & Row, Publishers, for "Powwow," "The Lovers Go Fly a Kite," "Leaving Ithaca," "The Examination," "The Men's Room in the College Chapel," "A Flat One," and " 'After Experience Taught Me . . .'," from *After Experience* by W. D. Snodgrass, copyright 1968 by W. D. Snodgrass. Reprinted by permission of Harper & Row.

Holt, Rinehart and Winston, Inc., for permission to quote from *The Complete Poems of Robert Frost* and *In the Clearing* by Robert Frost, copyright 1923, 1928, 1930, 1934, 1939, 1947 by Holt, Rinehart and Winston, Inc.; copyright 1936, 1942, 1951, © 1956, 1958, 1960, 1962 by Robert Frost; copyright © 1964, 1967 by Lesley Frost Ballantine. Reprinted by permission of Holt, Rinehart and Winston, Inc. Hugh Kenner for "The Experience of the Eye: Marianne Moore's Tradition" by Hugh Kenner, in *The Southern Review*, I (October 1965), 754–769, copyright 1965 by The Louisiana State University and reprinted by permission of the author.

The Johns Hopkins Press for "Wallace Stevens' Poetry of Being" by J. Hillis Miller, in *ELH*, XXXI:1 (1964), 86–105, copyright 1964 by The Johns Hopkins Press; and "Hart Crane's Poetics of Failure" by Joseph N. Riddel, in *ELH*, XXXIII:4 (1966), 473–496, copyright 1966 by The Johns Hopkins Press.

Alfred A. Knopf, Inc., for "Some Lines from Whitman," from *Poetry and the Age* by Randall Jarrell, copyright © 1952, 1953 by Randall Jarrell; "Ten Days Leave," "Returned to Frisco," and "Heart's Needle," from *Heart's Needle* by W. D. Snodgrass, copyright 1959 by W. D. Snodgrass; and "The Auroras of Autumn," "Repetitons of a Young Captain," "An Ordinary Evening in New Haven," "The Owl in the Sarcophagus," "Metaphor as Degeneration," "The River of Rivers in Connecticut," "To an Old Philosopher in Rome," and "A Primitive Like an Orb," from *The Collected Poems* by Wallace Stevens, copyright © 1954 by Wallace Stevens. Reprinted by permission of Alfred A. Knopf, Inc.

Liveright Publishing Corporation for permission to quote from *The Complete Poems & Selected Letters and Prose of Hart Crane,* copyright 1933, 1958, 1966 by Liveright Publishing Corporation.

The Macmillan Company for "The Fish," "An Octopus," "The Jerboa," and "Critics and Connoisseurs," copyright 1935 by Marianne Moore, renewed 1963 by Marianne Moore and T. S. Eliot; "Melancthon," copyright 1951 by Marianne Moore, from *The Collected Poems* by Marianne Moore, copyright 1951 by Marianne Moore; "Mrs. Flood's Party," copyright 1921 by Edwin Arlington Robinson, renewed 1949 by Ruth Nivison; "The Book of Annandale," copyright 1915 by Edwin Arlington Robinson, renewed 1943 by Ruth Nivison; "Annandale Again," copyright 1932 by Edwin Arlington Robinson, renewed 1960 by Ruth Nivision and Barbara R. Holt; "Aunt Imogen," copyright 1920 and 1930 by Edwin Arlington Robinson; "The Gift of God," copyright 1916 by Edwin Arlington Robinson, renewed 1944 by Ruth Nivison; "Firelight," copyright 1920 by Edwin Arlington Robinson, renewed 1948 by Ruth Nivison, from *The Collected Poems* by Edwin Arlington Robinson, copyright 1937 by The Macmillan Company. Reprinted by permission of The Macmillan Company.

New Directions Publishing Corporation for permission to quote from *The Literary Essays* by Ezra Pound, copyright 1918, 1920, 1935 by Ezra Pound; *Personae* by Ezra Pound, copyright 1926 by Ezra Pound; *The Cantos* by Ezra Pound, copyright 1934, 1937, 1930, 1938, © 1956, 1959 by Ezra Pound; *Paterson* by William Carlos Williams, copyright 1946, 1948, 1949, 1951, © 1958 by William Carlos Williams; *Collected Earlier Poems* by William Carlos Williams, copyright 1938, 1951 by William

Carlos Williams; and *Collected Later Poems* by William Carlos Williams, copyright 1944, 1948, 1949, 1950, © 1963 by William Carlos Williams. Reprinted by permission of New Directions Publishing Corporation.

Oxford University Press, Inc., for "Ezra Pound: The Poet as Hero," from *The Modern Poets: A Critical Introduction* by M. L. Rosenthal, copyright © 1960 by M. L. Rosenthal. Reprinted by permission of Oxford University Press, Inc.

Random House, Inc., for "The Purse Seine," "Unnatural Powers," "Shine, Perishing Republic," "Return," "The Cruel Falcon," "November Surf," "Rearmament," from *The Selected Poetry* by Robinson Jeffers, copyright 1938 by Robinson Jeffers. Charles Scribner's Sons for "How Annandale Went Out," from *The Town Down the River* by Edwin Arlington Robinson. University of California Press for "Eliot: The Transformation of a Personality" by George T. Wright, in *The Poet and the Poem,* copyright © 1960 by the University of California Press and reprinted with their permission.

University of Washington Press for "Theodore Roethke: The Poetic Shape of Death" by Frederick J. Hoffman, in *Essays on the Poetry of Theodore Roethke,* edited by Arnold Stein, copyright © 1965 by the University of Washington Press and reprinted with their permission.

Contents

MODERN AMERICAN POETRY:

Essays in Criticism

Some Lines from Whitman

RANDALL JARRELL

Whitman, Dickinson, and Melville seem to me the best poets of the 19th Century here in America. Melville's poetry has been grotesquely underestimated, but of course it is only in the last four or five years that it has been much read; in the long run, in spite of the awkwardness and amateurishness of so much of it, it will surely be thought well of. (In the short run it will probably be thought entirely too well of. Melville is a great poet only in the prose of *Moby Dick*.) Dickinson's poetry has been thoroughly read, and well though undifferentiatingly loved—after a few decades or centuries almost everybody will be able to see through Dickinson to her poems. But something odd has happened to the living changing part of Whitman's reputation: nowadays it is people who are not particularly interested in poetry, people who say that they read a poem for what it says, not for how it says it, who admire Whitman most. Whitman is often written about, either approvingly or disapprovingly, as if he were the Thomas Wolfe of 19th Century democracy, the hero of a de Mille movie about Walt Whitman. (People even talk about a war in which Walt Whitman and Henry James chose up sides, to begin with, and in which you and I will go on fighting till the day we die.) All this sort of thing, and all the bad poetry that there of course is in Whitman —for any poet has written enough bad poetry to scare away anybody—has helped to scare away from Whitman most "serious readers of modern poetry." They do not talk of his poems, as a rule, with any real liking or knowledge. Serious readers, people who are ashamed of not knowing all Hopkins by heart, are not at all ashamed to say, "I don't really know Whitman very well." This may harm Whitman in your eyes, they know, but that is a

1

chance that poets have to take. Yet "their" Hopkins, that good critic and great poet, wrote about Whitman, after seeing five or six of his poems in a newspaper review: "I may as well say what I should not otherwise have said, that I always knew in my heart Walt Whitman's mind to be more like my own than any other man's living. As he is a very great scoundrel this is not a very pleasant confession." And Henry James, the leader of "their" side in that awful imaginary war of which I spoke, once read Whitman to Edith Wharton (much as Mozart used to imitate, on the piano, the organ) with such power and solemnity that both sat shaken and silent; it was after this reading that James expressed his regret at Whitman's "too extensive acquaintance with the foreign languages." Almost all the most "original and advanced" poets and critics and readers of the last part of the 19th Century thought Whitman as original and advanced as themselves, in manner as well as in matter. Can Whitman really be a sort of Thomas Wolfe or Carl Sandburg or Robinson Jeffers or Henry Miller—or a sort of Balzac of poetry, whose every part is crude but whose whole is somehow great? He is not, nor could he be; a poem, like Pope's spider, "lives along the line," and all the dead lines in the world will not make one live poem. As Blake says, "all sublimity is founded on minute discrimination," and it is in these "minute particulars" of Blake's that any poem has its primary existence.

To show Whitman for what he is one does not need to praise or explain or argue, one needs simply to quote. He himself said, "I and mine do not convince by arguments, similes, rhymes, / We convince by our presence." Even a few of his phrases are enough to show us that Whitman was no sweeping rhetorician, but a poet of the greatest and oddest delicacy and originality and sensitivity, so far as words are concerned. This is, after all, the poet who said, "Blind loving wrestling touch, sheath'd hooded sharp-tooth'd touch"; who said, "Smartly attired, countenance smiling, form upright, death under the breast-bones, hell under the skull-bones"; who said, "Agonies are one of my changes of garments"; who saw grass as the "flag of my disposition," saw "the sharp-peak'd farmhouse, with its scallop'd scum and slender shoots from the gutters," heard a plane's "wild ascending lisp," and saw and heard how at the amputation "what is removed drops horribly in a pail." This is the poet for whom the sea was "howler and scooper of storms," reaching out to us with "crooked inviting fingers"; who went "leaping chasms with a pike-pointed staff, clinging to topples of brittle and blue"; who, a runaway slave, saw how "my gore dribs, thinn'd with the ooze of my skin"; who went "lithographing Kronos . . . buying drafts of Osiris"; who stared out at the "little plentiful mannikins skipping around in collars and tail'd coats, / I am aware who they are, (they are positively not worms or fleas)." For he is, at his best, beautifully witty: he says gravely, "I find I incorporate gneiss, coals, long-threaded moss, fruits, grain, esculent roots, / And am stucco'd with quadrupeds and birds all over"; and of these quadrupeds and birds "not one is respectable or unhappy over the whole earth." He calls advice: "Unscrew the locks from the doors! Unscrew the doors from their jambs!" He publishes the results of research: "Having pried through the strata, analyz'd to a hair, counsel'd with doctors and calculated close, / I find no sweeter fat than sticks to my own bones." Everybody remembers how he told the Muse to "cross out please those immensely overpaid accounts, / That matter of Troy and Achilles' wrath, and Aeneas', Odysseus' wanderings," but his account of the arrival of the "illustrious emigré" here in the New World is even better: "Bluff'd not a bit by drainpipe, gasometer, artificial fertilizers, / Smiling and pleas'd with palpable intent to stay, / She's here, install'd amid the kitchenware." Or he sees, like another Breughel, "the mechanic's wife with the babe at her nipple interceding for every person born, / Three scythes at harvest whizzing in a row from three lusty angels with shirts bagg'd out at their waists, / The snag-toothed hostler with red hair

redeeming sins past and to come"—the passage has enough wit
not only (in Johnson's phrase) to keep it sweet, but enough to
make it believable. He says:

I project my hat, sit shame-faced, and beg.

Enough! Enough! Enough!
Somehow I have been stunn'd. Stand back!
Give me a little time beyond my cuff'd head, slumbers, dreams,
    gaping,
I discover myself on the verge of a usual mistake.

There is in such changes of tone as these the essence of wit.
And Whitman is even more far-fetched than he is witty; he can
say about Doubters, in the most improbable and explosive of
juxtapositions: "I know every one of you, I know the sea of
torment, doubt, despair and unbelief. / How the flukes splash!
How they contort rapid as lightning, with splashes and spouts of
blood!" Who else would have said about God: "As the hugging
and loving bed-fellow sleeps at my side through the night, and
withdraws at the break of day with stealthy tread, / Leaving
me baskets cover'd with white towels, swelling the house with
their plenty"?—the Psalmist himself, his cup running over,
would have looked at Whitman with dazzled eyes. (Whitman
was persuaded by friends to hide the fact that it was God he
was talking about.) He says, "Flaunt of the sunshine I need not
your bask—lie over!" This unusual employment of verbs is usual
enough in participle-loving Whitman, who also asks you to
"look in my face while I snuff the sidle of evening," or tells you,
"I effuse my flesh in eddies, and drift it in lacy jags." Here are
some typical beginnings of poems: "City of orgies, walks, and
joys. . . . Not heaving from my ribb'd breast only. . . . O
take my hand Walt Whitman! Such gliding wonders! Such
sights and sounds! Such join'd unended links. . . ." He says to
the objects of the world, "You have waited, you always wait,
you dumb, beautiful ministers"; sees "the sun and stars that
float in the open air, / The apple-shaped earth"; says, "O suns—

O grass of graves— O perpetual transfers and promotions, / If you do not say anything how can I say anything?" Not many poets have written better, in queerer and more convincing and more individual language, about the world's *gliding wonders:* the phrase seems particularly right for Whitman. He speaks of those "circling rivers the breath," of the "savage old mother incessantly crying, / To the boy's soul's questions sullenly timing, some drown'd secret hissing"—ends a poem, once, "We have voided all but freedom and our own joy." How can one quote enough? If the reader thinks that all this is like Thomas Wolfe he *is* Thomas Wolfe; nothing else could explain it. Poetry like this is as far as possible from the work of any ordinary rhetorician, whose phrases cascade over us like suds of the oldest and most-advertised detergent.

The interesting thing about Whitman's worst language (for, just as few poets have ever written better, few poets have ever written worse) is how unusually absurd, how really ingeniously bad, such language is. I will quote none of the most famous examples; but even a line like *O culpable! I acknowledge. I exposé!* is not anything that you and I could do—only a man with the most extraordinary feel for language, or none whatsoever, could have cooked up Whitman's worst messes. For instance: what other man in all the history of this planet would have said, "I am a habitan of Vienna"? (One has an immediate vision of him as a sort of French-Canadian halfbreed to whom the Viennese are offering, with trepidation, through the bars of a zoological garden, little mounds of whipped cream.) And *enclaircise*—why, it's as bad as *explicate!* We are right to resent his having made up his own horrors, instead of sticking to the ones that we ourselves employ. But when Whitman says, "I dote on myself, there is that lot of me and all so luscious," we should realize that we are not the only ones who are amused. And the queerly bad and merely queer and queerly good will often change into one another without warning: "Hefts of the moving world, at innocent gambols silently rising, freshly exud-

ing, / Scooting obliquely high and low"—not good, but *queer!*
—suddenly becomes, "Something I cannot see puts up libidinous
prongs, / Seas of bright juice suffuse heaven," and it is sunrise.

But it is not in individual lines and phrases, but in passages
of some length, that Whitman is at his best. In the following
quotation Whitman has something difficult to express, something that there are many formulas, all bad, for expressing; he
expresses it with complete success, in language of the most
dazzling originality:

The orchestra whirls me wider than Uranus flies,
It wrenches such ardors from me I did not know I possess'd them,
It sails me, I dab with bare feet, they are lick'd by the indolent
    waves,
I am cut by bitter and angry hail, I lose my breath,
Steep'd amid honey'd morphine, my windpipe throttled in fakes of
    death,
At length let up again to feel the puzzle of puzzles,
And that we call Being.

One hardly knows what to point at—everything works. But
wrenches and *did not know I possess'd them;* the incredible *it
sails me, I dab with bare feet; lick'd by the indolent; steep'd
amid honey'd morphine; my windpipe throttled in fakes of
death*—no wonder Crane admired Whitman! This originality, as
absolute in its way as that of Berlioz' orchestration, is often at
Whitman's command:

I am a dance—play up there! the fit is whirling me fast!

I am the ever-laughing—it is new moon and twilight,
I see the hiding of douceurs, I see nimble ghosts whichever way
    I look,
Cache and cache again deep in the ground and sea, and where it
    is neither ground nor sea.
Well do they do their jobs those journeymen divine,
Only from me can they hide nothing, and would not if they could,
I reckon I am their boss and they make me a pet besides,
And surround me and lead me and run ahead when I walk,

To lift their sunning covers to signify me with stretch'd arms, and
    resume the way;
Onward we move, a gay gang of blackguards! with mirth-shouting
    music and wild-flapping pennants of joy!

If you did not believe Hopkins' remark about Whitman, that
gay gang of blackguards ought to shake you. Whitman shares
Hopkins' passion for "dappled" effects, but he slides in and out
of them with ambiguous swiftness. And he has at his command
a language of the calmest and most prosaic reality, one that
seems to do no more than present:

The little one sleeps in its cradle.
I lift the gauze and look a long time, and silently brush away flies
    with my hand.
The youngster and the red-faced girl turn aside up the bushy hill,
I peeringly view them from the top.

The suicide sprawls on the bloody floor of the bedroom.
I witness the corpse with its dabbled hair, I note where the pistol
    has fallen.

It is like magic: that is, something has been done to us without
our knowing how it was done; but if we look at the lines again
we see the *gauze, silently, youngster, red-faced, bushy, peeringly, dabbled*—not that this is all we see. "Present! present!"
said James; these are presented, put down side by side to form
a little "view of life," from the cradle to the last bloody floor of
the bedroom. Very often the things presented form nothing but
a list:

The pure contralto sings in the organ loft,
The carpenter dresses his plank, the tongue of his foreplane whistles
    its wild ascending lisp,
The married and unmarried children ride home to their
    Thanksgiving dinner,
The pilot seizes the king-pin, he heaves down with a strong arm,
The mate stands braced in the whale-boat, lance and harpoon are
    ready,

The duck-shooter walks by silent and cautious stretches,
The deacons are ordain'd with cross'd hands at the altar,
The spinning-girl retreats and advances to the hum of the big
    wheel,
The farmer stops by the bars as he walks on a First-day loafe and
    looks at the oats and rye,
The lunatic is carried at last to the asylum a confirm'd case,
(He will never sleep any more as he did in the cot in his mother's
    bed-room;)
The jour printer with gray head and gaunt jaws works at his case,
He turns his quid of tobacco while his eyes blur with the
    manuscript,
The malform'd limbs are tied to the surgeon's table,
What is removed drops horribly in a pail; . . .

It is only a list—but what a list! And how delicately, in what
different ways—likeness and opposition and continuation and
climax and anticlimax—the transitions are managed, whenever
Whitman wants to manage them. Notice them in the next quotation, another "mere list":

The bride unrumples her white dress, the minute-hand of the clock
    moves slowly,
The opium-eater reclines with rigid head and just-open'd lips,
The prostitute draggles her shawl, her bonnet bobs on her tipsy
    and pimpled neck. . . .

The first line is joined to the third by *unrumples* and *draggles,*
white dress and *shawl;* the second to the third by *rigid head,*
bobs, tipsy, neck; the first to the second by *slowly, just-open'd,*
and the slowing-down of time in both states. And occasionally
one of these lists is metamorphosed into something we have no
name for; the man who would call the next quotation a mere
list—anybody will feel this—would boil his babies up for
soap:

Ever the hard unsunk ground,
Ever the eaters and drinkers, ever the upward and downward sun,
Ever myself and my neighbors, refreshing, wicked, real,

Ever the old inexplicable query, ever that thorned thumb, that
    breath of itches and thirsts,
Ever the vexer's hoot! hoot! till we find where the sly one hides and
    bring him forth,
Ever the sobbing liquid of life,
Ever the bandage under the chin, ever the trestles of death.

    Sometimes Whitman will take what would generally be con-
sidered an unpromising subject (in this case, a woman peeping
at men in bathing naked) and treat it with such tenderness and
subtlety and understanding that we are ashamed of ourselves
for having thought it unpromising, and murmur that Chekhov
himself couldn't have treated it better:

Twenty-eight young men bathe by the shore,
Twenty-eight young men and all so friendly,
Twenty-eight years of womanly life and all so lonesome.

She owns the fine house by the rise of the bank,
She hides handsome and richly drest aft the blinds of the window.

Which of the young men does she like the best?
Ah the homeliest of them is beautiful to her.

Where are you off to, lady? for I see you,
You splash in the water there, yet stay stock still in your room.

Dancing and laughing along the beach came the twenty-ninth
    bather,
The rest did not see her, but she saw and loved them.

The beards of the young men glisten'd with wet, it ran from
    their long hair,
Little streams pass'd all over their bodies.

An unseen hand also pass'd over their bodies,
It descended tremblingly from their temples and ribs.

The young men float on their backs, their white bellies bulge to the
    sun, they do not ask who seizes fast to them,
They do not know who puffs and declines with pendant and bending
    arch,
They do not know whom they souse with spray.

And in the same poem (that "Song of Myself" in which one finds half his best work) the writer can say of a sea-fight:

Stretched and still lies the midnight,
Two great hulls motionless on the breast of the darkness,
Our vessel riddled and slowly sinking, preparations to pass to the
   one we have conquer'd,
The captain on the quarter-deck coldly giving his orders through
   a countenance white as a sheet,
Near by the corpse of the child that serv'd in the cabin,
The dead face of an old salt with long white hair and carefully
   curl'd whiskers,
The flames spite of all that can be done flickering aloft and below,
The husky voices of the two or three officers yet fit for duty,
Formless stacks of bodies and bodies by themselves, dabs of flesh
   upon the masts and spars,
Cut of cordage, dangle of rigging, slight shock of the soothe of
   waves,
Black and impassive guns, litter of powder-parcels, strong scent,
A few large stars overhead, silent and mournful shining,
Delicate snuffs of sea-breeze, smells of sedgy grass and fields by the
   shore, death-messages given in charge to survivors,
The hiss of the surgeon's knife, the gnawing teeth of his saw,
Wheeze, cluck, swash of falling blood, short wild scream, and long,
   dull, tapering groan,
These so, these irretrievable.

There are faults in this passage, and they *do not matter:* the serious truth, the complete realization of these last lines make us remember that few poets have shown more of the tears of things, and the joy of things, and of the reality beneath either tears or joy. Even Whitman's most general or political statements sometimes are good: everybody knows his "When liberty goes out of a place it is not the first to go, nor the second or third to go, / It waits for all the rest to go, it is the last"; these sentences about the United States just before the Civil War may be less familiar:

Are those really Congressmen? are those the great Judges? is that
  the President?
Then I will sleep awhile yet, for I see that these States sleep, for
  reasons;
(With gathering murk, with muttering thunder and lambent shoots
  we all duly awake,
South, North, East, West, inland and seaboard, we will surely awake.)

How well, with what firmness and dignity and command,
Whitman does such passages! And Whitman's doubts that he
has done them or anything else well—ah, there is nothing he
does better:

The best I had done seemed to me blank and suspicious,
My great thoughts as I supposed them, were they not in reality
  meagre?
I am he who knew what it was to be evil,
I too knitted the old knot of contrariety . . .
Saw many I loved in the street or ferry-boat or public assembly, yet
  never told them a word,
Lived the same life with the rest, the same old laughing, gnawing,
  sleeping,
Played the part that still looks back on the actor and actress,
The same old role, the role that is what we make it . . .

Whitman says once that the "look of the bay mare shames
silliness out of me." This is true—sometimes it is true; but more
often the silliness and affection and cant and exaggeration are
there shamelessly, the Old Adam that was in Whitman from
the beginning and the awful new one that he created to keep
it company. But as he says, "I know perfectly well my own
egotism, / Know my omnivorous lines and must not write
any less." He says over and over that there are in him good and
bad, wise and foolish, anything at all and its antonym, and he
is telling the truth; there is in him almost everything in the
world, so that one responds to him, willingly or unwillingly,
almost as one does to the world, that world which makes the

hairs of one's flesh stand up, which seems both evil beyond any rejection and wonderful beyond any acceptance. We cannot help seeing that there is something absurd about any judgment we make of its whole—for there is no "point of view" at which we can stand to make the judgment, and the moral categories that mean most to us seem no more to apply to its whole than our spatial or temporal or causal categories seem to apply to its beginning or its end. (But we need no arguments to make our judgments seem absurd—we feel their absurdity without argument.) In some like sense Whitman is a world, a waste with, here and there, systems blazing at random out of the darkness. Only an innocent and rigidly methodical mind will reject it for this disorganization, particularly since there are in it, here and there, little systems as beautifully and astonishingly organized as the rings and satellites of Saturn:

I understand the large hearts of heroes,
The courage of present times and all times,
How the skipper saw the crowded and rudderless wreck of the
    steam-ship, and Death chasing it up and down the storm,
How he knuckled tight and gave not back an inch, and was faithful
    of days and faithful of nights,
And chalked in large letters on a board, Be of good cheer, we will
    not desert you;
How he follow'd with them and tack'd with them three days and
    would not give it up,
How he saved the drifting company at last,
How the lank loose-gown'd women looked when boated from the
    side of their prepared graves,
How the silent old-faced infants and the lifted sick, and the
    sharp-lipp'd unshaved men;
All this I swallow, it tastes good, I like it well, it becomes mine,
I am the man, I suffered, I was there.

In the last lines of this quotation, Whitman has reached—as great writers always reach—a point at which criticism seems not only unnecessary but absurd: these lines are so good that even admiration feels like insolence, and one is ashamed of anything that one can find to say about them. How anyone can dismiss or accept patronizingly the man who wrote them, I do not understand.

The enormous and apparent advantages of form, of omission and selection, of the highest degree of organization, are accompanied by important disadvantages—and there are far greater works than *Leaves of Grass* to make us realize this. But if we compare Whitman with that very beautiful poet Alfred Tennyson, the most skillful of all Whitman's contemporaries, we are at once aware of how limiting Tennyson's forms have been, of how much Tennyson has had to leave out, even in those discursive poems where he is trying to put everything in. Whitman's poems *represent* his world and himself much more satisfactorily than Tennyson's do his. In the past a few poets have both formed and represented, each in the highest degree; but in modern times what controlling, organizing, selecting poet has created a world with as much in it as Whitman's, a world that so plainly *is* the world? Of all modern poets he has, quantitatively speaking, "the most comprehensive soul"—and, qualitatively, a most comprehensive and comprehending one, with charities and concessions and qualifications that are rare in any time.

"Do I contradict myself? Very well then I contradict myself," wrote Whitman, as everybody remembers, and this is not naïve, or something he got from Emerson, or a complacent pose. When you organize one of the contradictory elements out of your work of art, you are getting rid not just of it, but of the contradiction of which it was a part; and it is the contradictions in works of art which make them able to represent to us—as logical and methodical generalizations cannot—our world and our selves, which are also full of contradictions. In Whitman we do not get the controlled, compressed, seemingly concordant contradictions of the great lyric poets, of a poem like, say, Hardy's "During Wind and Rain"; Whitman's contradictions are sometimes announced openly, but are more often scattered at random throughout the poems. For instance: Whitman special- izes in ways of saying that there is in some sense (a very Hegelian one, generally) no evil—he says a hundred times that evil is not Real; but he also specializes in making lists of the evil of the world, lists of an unarguable reality. After his min- ister has recounted "the rounded catalogue divine complete," Whitman comes home and puts down what has been left out: "the countless (nineteen-twentieths) low and evil, crude and savage . . . the barren soil, the evil men, the slag and hideous rot." He ends another such catalogue with the plain unexcus- ing "All these—all meanness and agony without end I sitting look out upon, / See, hear, and am silent." Whitman offered himself to everybody, and said brilliantly and at length what a good thing he was offering:

Sure as the most certain sure, plumb in the uprights, well entretied,
    braced in the beams,
Stout as a horse, affectionate, haughty, electrical,
I and this mystery here we stand.

Just for oddness, characteristicalness, differentness, what more could you ask in a letter of recommendation? (Whitman sounds as if he were recommending a house—haunted, but what foundations!) But after a few pages he is oddly different:

Apart from the pulling and hauling stands what I am,
Stands amused, complacent, compassionating, idle, unitary,
Looks down, is erect, or bends an arm on an impalpable certain rest
Looking with side curved head curious what will come next,
Both in and out of the game and watching and wondering at it.

Tamburlaine is already beginning to sound like Hamlet: the employer feels uneasily, "Why, I might as well hire myself. . . ." And, a few pages later, Whitman puts down in ordinary- sized type, in the middle of the page, this warning to any *new person drawn toward me:*

Do you think I am trusty and faithful?
Do you see no further than this façade, this smooth and tolerant
   manner of me?
Do you suppose yourself advancing on real ground toward a real
   heroic man?
Have you no thought O dreamer that may be all maya, illusion?

Having wonderful dreams, telling wonderful lies, was a temptation Whitman could never resist; but telling the truth was a
temptation he could never resist, either. When you buy him you
know what you are buying. And only an innocent and solemn
and systematic mind will condemn him for his contradictions:
Whitman's catalogues of evils represent realities, and his
denials of their reality represent other realities, of feeling and
intuition and desire. If he is faithless to logic, to Reality As It
Is—whatever that is—he is faithful to the feel of things, to reality
as it seems; this is all that a poet has to be faithful to, and
philosophers have been known to leave logic and Reality for it.
   Whitman is more coordinate and parallel than anybody, is
the poet of parallel present participles, of twenty verbs joined
by a single subject: all this helps to give his work its feeling of
raw hypnotic reality, of being that world which also streams over
us joined only by *ands,* until we supply the subordinating conjunctions; and since as children we see the *ands* and not the
becauses, this method helps to give Whitman some of the freshness of childhood. How inexhaustibly interesting the world is in
Whitman! Arnold all his life kept wishing that he could see the
world "with a plainness as near, as flashing" as that with which
Moses and Rebekah and the Argonauts saw it. He asked with
elegiac nostalgia, "Who can see the green earth any more / As
she was by the sources of Time?"—and all the time there was
somebody alive who saw it so, as plain and near and flashing,
and with a kind of calm, pastoral, Biblical dignity and elegance
as well, sometimes. The *thereness* and *suchness* of the world
are incarnate in Whitman as they are in few other writers.

They might have put on his tombstone WALT WHITMAN: HE HAD HIS NERVE. He is the rashest, the most inexplicable and unlikely—the most impossible, one wants to say—of poets. He somehow *is* in a class by himself, so that one compares him with other poets about as readily as one compares *Alice* with other books. (Even his free verse has a completely different effect from anybody else's.) Who would think of comparing him with Tennyson or Browning or Arnold or Baudelaire?—it is Homer, or the sagas, or something far away and long ago, that comes to one's mind only to be dismissed; for sometimes Whitman *is* epic, just as *Moby Dick* is, and it surprises us to be able to use truthfully this word that we have misused so many times. Whitman *is* grand, and elevated, and comprehensive, and real with an astonishing reality, and many other things—the critic points at his qualities in despair and wonder, all method failing, and simply calls them by their names. And the range of these qualities is the most extraordinary thing of all. We can surely say about him, "He was a man, take him for all in all. I shall not look upon his like again"—and wish that people had seen this and not tried to be his like: one Whitman is miracle enough, and when he comes again it will be the end of the world.

I have said so little about Whitman's faults because they are so plain: baby critics who have barely learned to complain of the lack of ambiguity in *Peter Rabbit* can tell you all that is wrong with *Leaves of Grass*. But a good many of my readers must have felt that it is ridiculous to write an essay about the obvious fact that Whitman is a great poet. It is ridiculous—just as, in 1851, it would have been ridiculous for anyone to write an essay about the obvious fact that Pope was no "classic of our prose" but a great poet. Critics have to spend half their time reiterating whatever ridiculously obvious things their age or the critics of their age have found it necessary to forget: they say despairingly, at parties, that Wordsworth is a great poet, and *won't* bore you, and tell Mr. Leavis that Milton is a great poet whose deposition *hasn't* been accomplished with astonishing ease by a few words from Eliot. . . . There is something essentially ridiculous about critics, anyway: what is good is good without our saying so, and beneath all our majesty we know this.

Let me finish by mentioning another quality of Whitman's— a quality, delightful to me, that I have said nothing of. If some day a tourist notices, among the ruins of New York City, a copy of *Leaves of Grass*, and stops and picks it up and reads some lines in it, she will be able to say to herself: "How very American! If he and his country had not existed, it would have been impossible to imagine them."

From "Emily Dickinson"

NORTHROP FRYE

At her death Emily Dickinson was the author of seven published poems, all anonymous, some issued without her authorization, six of them at least in what she would have considered garbled versions, altered by editors to make them more conventional. Her friends knew that she wrote poetry, but nobody, not even her sister Lavinia who had lived with her all her life, had any notion that she had written close to eighteen hundred poems. She left instructions to Lavinia that her "papers" were to be destroyed, as was customary at that time, but no instructions were given about the piled-up packets of verse that Lavinia, to her astonishment, discovered in her sister's room. Lavinia took the packets to Sue, with a demand that they be transcribed and published immediately, meeting all complaints about the length and difficulty of the task with: "But they are Emily's poems!" Sue proved to be indolent, and perhaps jealous, and after a long wait Lavinia took them to Mrs. Mabel Loomis Todd, wife of an Amherst professor of astronomy, an attractive and highly accomplished young woman, who knew Emily, so to speak, by ear, having played the piano in the Dickinson house while the poet sat invisibly in the dark hall outside and commented on the music.

Higginson's help was enlisted. At first he felt that it would be a mistake to publish Emily Dickinson, perhaps thinking of an appeal she had made to him to talk Helen Jackson out of publishing "Success." But he gradually became, first interested, then fascinated, by what he found, and helped publicize her by writing articles about her. The two editors, Mrs. Todd and Higginson, produced *Poems by Emily Dickinson* in 1890, where a selection of her poems was distributed in various categories labeled "Life," "Love," "Nature" and the like, with titles for individual poems supplied by Higginson. A second and a third selection appeared in 1891 and 1896, respectively. Although Mrs. Todd's original transcripts were accurate, the poems were systematically smoothed out in punctuation, meter, grammar, and rhymes. Higginson took the lead in this at first, but as he went on he began to realize that the poet's liberties were not those of carelessness or incompetence. When the second selection was being prepared, he wrote to Mrs. Todd: "Let us alter as little as possible, now that the public ear is opened," including his own ear; but by that time Mrs. Todd had caught the improving fever. Mrs. Todd also went through the laborious task of collecting and publishing two volumes of Emily Dickinson's letters, where she had to engage in a long tactful struggle with the owners, and prevented a good many of them from being irreparably lost. Through no fault of hers, some of them, notably those to the Norcross sisters, survive only in mutilated versions.

Some highly unedifying family squabbles stopped further publication. Sue had been alienated by the giving of the manuscripts to Mrs. Todd; then Lavinia, for reasons too complicated to go into here, turned against Mrs. Todd after Austin Dickinson's death and brought suit to recover a strip of land willed to Mrs. Todd by Austin. Nothing further was done until the next generation grew up, in the form of Sue's daughter, Martha Dickinson Bianchi, and Mrs. Todd's daughter, Millicent Todd Bingham, who produced a series of editions of both poems and letters between 1914 and 1950. Finally, the bulk of the manuscripts came into the possession of Harvard. With Thomas H. Johnson's definitive edition of the poems (1955) and letters (1958), Emily Dickinson achieved publication on her own uncompromising terms.

When Mrs. Todd's volumes appeared, there were, despite her editorial efforts, some hostile reviews and some complaints about the poet's lack of "technique," by which was meant smooth rhymes and meters. The complaints came mainly from such minor poets as Andrew Lang in England and Thomas Bailey Aldrich in America, who naturally ascribed the greatest importance and difficulty to the only poetic quality they themselves had. Against this, we may set the fact that the first volume alone went through sixteen editions in eight years, and was constantly reprinted thereafter. Mrs. Todd gave dozens of lectures on the poet, and could have given far more. It is inconceivable that the first volume of an unknown poet today could achieve such a success, unless fortified by pornography. *Somebody* wanted Emily Dickinson's poetry, and we cannot avoid the inference that in the 1890's she was a genuinely popular poet who found her own public in spite of what the highbrows said. When she reappeared in the 1920's, her reputation was curiously reversed. Then the highbrows took her up, hailed her as a precursor of whatever happened to be fashionable at the time, such as imagism or free verse or metaphysical poetry, and emphasized everything in her work that was unconventional, difficult, or quaint. Both conceptions have some truth in them.

The good popular poet is usually one who does well what a great many have tried to do with less success. For the thousands of people, most of them women, who make verse out of a limited range of imaginative experience in life, love, nature, and religion, who live without fame and without much knowledge of literature beyond their schoolbooks, Emily Dickinson is the literary spokesman. She is popular too in her conceptual use of language, for popular expression tends to the proverbial, and the unsophisticated poet is usually one who tries to put prose statements into verse. The Sibyl of Amherst is no Lorelei: she has no Keatsian faery lands forlorn or Tennysonian low-lying Claribels; she does not charm and she seldom sings. Mrs. Todd often spoke of encountering poems in Emily Dickinson that took her breath away, but what surprises in her work is almost always some kind of direct statement, sharpened into wit or epigram.

When she describes a hummingbird as "A route of evanescence,"
or says of the bluebird:

> Her conscientious Voice will soar unmoved
> Above ostensible Vicissitude.

she is using what medieval poets called "aureate diction," big
soft bumbling abstract words that absorb images into categories and ideas. She does not—like, for example, D. H. Lawrence—try to get inside the bird's skin and identify herself
with it; she identifies the bird with human consciousness in
herself. Many of her poems start out by making some kind of
definition of an abstract noun:

> Presentiment—is that long Shadow—on the Lawn—
>
> Renunciation—is a piercing Virtue—
>
> Publication—is the Auction
> Of the Mind of Man—

and most of her best-loved poems are in one of the oldest and
most primitive forms of poetry, the riddle or oblique description
of some object. In "A route of evanescence" there is no explicit
mention of a hummingbird, because the poem tries to catch the
essence of the feeling of the bird without mentioning it. Similarly with the snow in "It sifts from leaden sieves," and with the
railway train in "I like to see it lap the miles."

Such popular features in her work have their own difficulties,
and there are others inherent in her peculiar style. She has for
the most part no punctuation, except a point represented in the
Johnson edition by a dash, which, as the editor points out, is
really a rhythmical beat, and is of little use in unraveling the syntax. She also shows a curious preference for an indirect subjunc-
tive form of expression that appears in such phrases as "Beauty
be not caused," and she has what seems a most unreasonable dislike of adding the s to the third person singular of verbs. The
effect of such sidelong grammar is twofold: it increases the sense

of epigrammatic wit, and it makes her poetry sound oracular, as though the explicit statements of which her poetry is so largely made up were coming to us shrouded in mystery. As she says:

> Tell all the Truth but tell it slant—
> Success in Circuit lies

The result is not invariably success: sometimes we may agree with enthusiasm:

> How powerful the Stimulus
> Of an Hermetic Mind—

at other times we can only say, with the captain in *Pinafore* confronted with a similar type of gnomic utterance: "I don't see at what you're driving, mystic lady":

> Endanger it, and the Demand
> Of tickets for a sigh
> Amazes the Humility
> Of Credibility—
>
> Recover it to Nature
> And that dejected Fleet
> Find Consternation's Carnival
> Divested of it's Meat

Every age has its conventional notions of what poetry ought to be like, and the conventional notions of Emily Dickinson's day were that poetry should be close to prose in its grammar and syntax, and that its vocabulary should be more refined than that of ordinary speech. Thus Robert Louis Stevenson was outraged by the word "hatter" in a poem of Whitman's, and asserted that using such a word was not "literary tact." Emily Dickinson deliberately flouts both conventions. Her beat punctuation and offbeat syntax go with an abrupt and colloquial diction. The tang of her local speech comes out in such spellings as "Febuary" and "boquet," in such locution as "it don't" and "it is him," and in such words as "heft" for "weight." Speaking of heaven, she writes:

> Yet certain am I of the spot
> As if the Checks were given—

meaning railway checks, the guarantee the conductor gives
that one is proceeding to the right destination. Her editors
altered this to "chart," which was a more conventionally poetic
word, being slightly antique. Emily Dickinson could easily
have provided such a word herself, but preferred to form her
diction at a humorously twisted angle to the conventional expectations of the reader.

There is little in Emily Dickinson, then, of the feeling that a
writer must come to terms with conventional language at all
costs. When she meets an inadequacy in the English language
she simply walks through it, as a child might do. If the dic-
tionary does not provide an abstract noun for "giant," the poet
will coin "gianture"; if the ordinary "diminution" does not give
her enough sense of movement, she will substitute "diminuet."
Similarly the fact that there is no singular form for "grass" or
"hay" does not stop her from speaking of "every Grass," or from
writing, to Higginson's horror:

> The Grass so little has to do
> I wish I were a Hay—

A similar teasing of the conventional reader's ear comes out in
her slanting rhymes, which often have the effect of disappoint-
ing or letting down one's sense of an expected sound. At the
same time even a conventional reader can see that her commonplace stanza forms could hardly achieve any variety of nuance
without some irregularities. This is particularly true of the
sinewy rhythm that syncopates against her rigid hymnbook
meters and keeps them so far out of reach of monotony or
doggerel:

> Those not live yet
> Who doubt to live again—
> "Again" is of a twice
> But this—is one—

> The Ship beneath the Draw
> Aground—is he?
> Death—so—the Hyphen of the Sea—
> Deep is the Schedule
> Of the Disk to be—
> Costumeless Consciousness—
> That is he—

In sophisticated poetry close attention is paid to the sounds of words: vowels and consonants are carefully balanced for assonance and variety, and we feel, when such poetry is successful, that we have the inevitably right words in their inevitably right order. In popular poetry there is a clearly marked rhythm and the words chosen to fill it up give approximately the intended meaning, but there is no sense of any *mot juste* or uniquely appropriate word. In the ballad, for example, we may have a great number of verbal variants of the same poem. Here again Emily Dickinson's practice is the popular, not the sophisticated one. For a great many of her poems she has provided alternative words, phrases, even whole lines, as though the rhythm, like a figured bass in music, allowed the editor or reader to establish his own text. Thus in the last line of one poem, "To meet so enabled a Man," we have "religious," "accomplished," "discerning," "accoutred," "established," and "conclusive" all suggested as alternates for "enabled." Another poem ends:

> And Kinsmen as divulgeless
> As throngs of Down—

with "Kindred as responsive," "Clans of Down," "And Pageants as impassive As Porcelain"—or, presumably, any combination of these—as possible variants. It is rather more disconcerting to find "New" suggested as an alternate for "Old" in a poem ending with a reference to "Our Old Neighbor—God."

What we find in Emily Dickinson's poetry, then, is a diffused vitality in rhythm and the free play of a lively and exhilarating mind, crackling with wit and sharp perception. These were clearly the qualities that she herself knew were there and especially prized. She asked Higginson simply whether her verse was "alive." As a poet, she is popular in the sense of being able, like Burns or Kipling or the early Wordsworth, to introduce poetry to readers who have had no previous experience of it. She has, on the other hand, a withdrawn consciousness and an intense intellectual energy that makes her almost esoteric, certainly often difficult.

In any case she seems, after her early valentines, to have reached her mature style almost in a single bound. It is otherwise with her prose, no doubt because we have so much more of it from her early years. Her schoolgirl letters, with their engaging mixture of child's prattle and adolescent's self-consciousness, show a Lamb-like gift for fantasy and a detached and humorous shrewdness. She speaks of other girls who "are perfect models of propriety," and remarks: "There 'most always are a few, whom the teachers look up to and regard as their satellites"—which is sharp observation for a fourteen-year-old. After her writing of poetry begins, her prose rhythm moves very close to verse. The first letter to Higginson is really a free verse poem; some of her earlier poems were originally written as prose, and she often falls into her favorite metrical rhythms, as in the opening of a letter to Bowles: "I am so far from Land— To offer *you* the cup—it might some Sabbath come *my* turn—Of wine how solemn—full!", which is a short meter stanza. Her later letters show a remarkable command of the techniques of discontinuous prose: they were most carefully composed, and the appearance of random jottings is highly deceptive. Continuous or expository prose assumes an equality between writer and reader: the writer is putting all he has in front of us. Discontinuous prose, with gaps in the sense that only intuition can cross, assumes an aloofness on the writer's part, a sense of reserves of connection that we must make special efforts to reach. The aphoristic style of her later letters is, if slightly more frequent in Continental literatures, extremely rare in England or America, yet she seems to have developed it without models or influences.

> Her Grace is all she has—
> And that, so least displays—
> One Art to recognize, must be,
> Another Art, to praise.

The most cursory glance at Emily Dickinson will reveal that she is a deeply religious poet, preoccupied, to the verge of obsession, with the themes of death and of immortality—the latter being, as she called it, the "Flood subject." Even in her use of the Bible, her most frequent references are to the passages in Corinthians and Revelation usually read at funeral services; and Paul's remark, that we now see in a riddle, translated as "through a glass darkly," is echoed in her recurrent use of the words "Riddle" and "Disc":

> Further than Guess can gallop
> Further than Riddle ride—
> Oh for a Disc to the Distance
> Between Ourselves and the Dead!

Yet another glance at her letters will also show that in her evangelical surroundings she steadily resisted all revivals, all spiritual exhortations, all the solicitous and charitable heat that, at home, at school and at church, was steadily turned on the uncommitted. Like Huckleberry Finn, whom she resembles in more ways than one, Emily Dickinson had a great respect for orthodox religion and morality, did not question the sincerity of those who practiced it, and even turned to it for help. But she never felt that the path of social conformity and assent to doctrine was her path. Her resistance gave her no feeling of superiority: even her schoolgirl letters are full of a wistful regret that she could not feel what her friends all asserted that they felt. As she recalled later: "When a Child and fleeing from Sacrament I could hear the Clergyman saying 'All who loved the Lord Jesus Christ—were asked to remain—.' My flight kept time to the Words." She belonged in the congregation but not in the Church.

Her elders referred her to the Bible: she read the Bible and took an immediate dislike to the deity that she calls "Burglar! Banker—Father!"—that is, the legal providential God who seems to ratify everything that is meaningless and cruel in life. She remarked to Higginson that her family were all religious except her, "and address an Eclipse, every morning—whom they call their 'Father'." She read with distaste the stories of Elisha and the bears ("I believe the love of God may be taught not to seem like bears"), of the sacrifice of Isaac, of the drowning of the world in a divine tantrum and the corresponding threat to burn it later:

> No vacillating God
> Created this Abode
> To put it out.

of Adam who was asserted to be alone responsible for his fall:

> Of Heaven above the firmest proof
> We fundamental know
> Except for it's marauding Hand
> It had been Heaven below.

The whole "punishing" aspect of religious doctrine struck her as "a doubtful solace finding tart response in the lower Mind," and she asks: "Why should we censure Othello, when the Criterion Lover says, 'Thou shalt have no other Gods before Me'?" That is, why blame Othello for being jealous when God tells us that he is himself? She concluded that "I do not respect 'doctrines,'" and added, with a touch of snobbery: "I wish the 'faith of the fathers' didn't wear brogans, and carry blue umbrellas." In short, she took no care to distinguish the Father of Christianity from the cloud-whiskered scarecrow that Blake called Nobodaddy and Bernard Shaw an old man in the sky looking like the headmaster of an inferior public school.

The Son of God for her was also caught in this Father's

legal machinery. "When Jesus tells us about his Father, we distrust him." She has a poem in which she compares the doctrine of the revelation of the Father in the Son to the courtship of Miles Standish, and another in which she speaks with contempt of the "some day we'll understand" rationalizings of suffering:

> I shall know why—when Time is over—
> And I have ceased to wonder why—
> Christ will explain each separate anguish
> In the fair schoolroom of the sky—

At other times, she seems to accept Jesus as everything that Christianity says he is. Thus: "That the Divine has been human is at first an unheeded solace, but it shelters without our consent." It seems clear that her relation to the Nonconformist faith in which she was brought up was itself nonconformist, and that it would have violated her conscience ever to have made either a final acceptance or a final rejection of that faith. Her method, the reverse of Tennyson's in *In Memoriam,* was to prove where she could not believe. She did not want to repudiate her faith but to struggle with it. She was fascinated by the story of the "bewildered Gymnast" Jacob, wrestling with and finally defeating an angel who—according to a literal reading of the text which the poet promptly adopted—turned out to be God, and to this story she reverts more than once in her letters. When she compares the Bible unfavorably with Orpheus, whose sermon captivated and did not condemn; when she speaks of Cupid as an authentic deity and asks if God is Love's adversary, she is saying that there is another kind of religious experience that counterbalances, but does not necessarily contradict, the legal and doctrinal Christianity which she had been taught. As she says with a calculated ambivalence: " 'We thank thee Oh Father' for these strange Minds, that enamor us against thee."

This other kind of religious experience is a state of heightened consciousness often called "Transport" and associated with the word "Circumference," when the poet feels directly in communion with nature and in a state of "identity"—another frequent term—with it. Nature is then surrounded by the circumference of human consciousness, and such a world is Paradise, the Biblical Eden, a nature with a human shape and meaning, a garden for man. "Home is the definition of God," and home is what is inside the circumference of one's being. In this state the mind feels immortal: "To include, is to be touchless, for Ourself cannot cease." It also enters into a condition of unity or oneness which is partly what the word identity means. "*One* is a dainty sum! One bird, one cage, one flight; one song in those far woods, as yet suspected by faith only!" Similarly the poet can speak, without any violation of grammar, of a "Myriad Daisy" (compare Wordsworth's "tree, of many, one" [1]), and, with Emerson, of the single Man who is all men:

> What News will do when every Man
> Shall comprehend as one
> And not in all the Universe
> A thing to tell remain?

Such an experience is based, not on the compelling argument, but on the infinitely suggestive image, or "emblem" as she calls it. "Emblem is immeasurable," she says, and speaks of human beings as the "trembling Emblems" of love. The language of emblems is as rational as the language of doctrine, but its logic is the poetic logic of metaphor, not the abstract logic of syllogism.

Circumference in its turn is the "Bride of Awe," and "Awe" is her most frequent name for the God that is reached by this experience. The human circumference is surrounded by a greater consciousness, to which the poet is related as bride to bridegroom, as sea to moon, as daisy to sun, as brook to ocean—all recurring images. Sometimes the poet uses the word "penin-

1. See Wordsworth, "Ode: Intimations of Immorality from Recollections of Early Childhood," 1.52.

sula" to describe an individual consciousness projecting into experience and attached to an invisible mainland—invisible because "No man saw awe," any more than we can see our own backbones. Awe is a lover, incarnate in the bee who loves the rose and the harebell, and a divine lover for whom a feminine poet may make the response of a bacchante or of a vestal virgin with equal appropriateness. Thus Emily Dickinson may say both:

> Circumference thou Bride of Awe
> Possessing thou shalt be
> Possessed by every hallowed Knight
> That dares to covet thee

and (where "their" means the world of her bodily impulses):

> To their apartment deep
> No ribaldry may creep
> Untumbled this abode
> By any man but God—

Awe is not a dogmatic God, and is tolerant enough to satisfy not only the poet's Christian longings but the paganism that makes her feel that there ought to be a god for every mood of the soul and every department of nature:

> If "All is possible with" him
> As he besides concedes
> He will refund us finally
> Our confiscated Gods—

In fact he may even be female, a sheltering mother. "I always ran Home to Awe when a child . . . He was an awful Mother, but I liked him better than none."

In Christian terms, this divine Awe, as she well understood, is the third person of the Trinity, the Holy Spirit, symbolized in the Bible by two of her favorite images, the bird and the wind, the giver of life to nature and of inspiration to humanity, the creative force that makes the poet's verses "breathe," and the "Conscious Ear" that imagination hears with. The conventional Biblical image for the Holy Spirit is the dove, and the poet, picturing herself as Noah sailing the flood of experience, associates the dove who brought him news of land with the fact that the name of another well-known navigator, Christopher Columbus, also means dove:

> Thrice to the floating casement
> The Patriarch's bird returned,
> Courage! My brave Columba!
> There may yet be *Land!*

To this person of God, Emily Dickinson continually turned when other things in Christianity puzzled her imagination or were rejected by her reason. She seems to associate him with the power which "stands in the Bible between the Kingdom and the Glory, because it is wilder than either of them." In the detached comment on the Atonement which she superimposes on the famous proverb, "God tempers the wind to the shorn lamb," the "Wind" is the power that escapes from the breakdown of doctrinal machinery:

> How ruthless are the gentle—
> How cruel are the kind—
> God broke his contract to his Lamb
> To qualify the Wind—

In a congratulatory message on the occasion of a wedding, the divine power of making one flesh out of two bodies is associated, not with the Father or the Son, but with the wind that bloweth where it listeth:

> The Clock strikes one that just struck two—
> Some schism in the Sum—
> A Vagabond from Genesis
> Has wrecked the Pendulum—

The confusion with a female principle, as when she says that "the Little Boy in the Trinity had no Grandmama, only a Holy

Ghost," is at least as old as the apocryphal Gospels, where Jesus speaks of the Holy Spirit as his mother. When she says, "The Bible dealt with the Centre, not with the Circumference," she means apparently that the Bible considers man in his ordinary state of isolation, separated from God by a gulf that only God can cross. Such a God is thought of as coming from the outside; but while God is known "By his intrusion," his movement in the human soul is to be compared rather to the tides moving in the sea. "They say that God is everywhere, and yet we always think of Him as somewhat of a recluse." If so, it takes a recluse to find him, and to discover him as the inmost secret of consciousness.

The first fact of Emily Dickinson's experience, then, was that whatever the Bible may mean by Paradise or Eden, the world of lost innocence and happiness symbolized by the unfallen Adam and Eve, it is something that is already given in experience. It is attainable; the poet has attained it; it is not, therefore, a "super-human site," nor could it survive the extinction of the human mind. Earth is heaven, whether heaven is heaven or not: the supernatural is only the natural disclosed: the charms of the heaven in the bush are superseded by the heaven in the hand— to paraphrase almost at random. To her the essence of the Gospel was the proclamation of the Paradisal vision in such passages as "consider the lilies." But the Bible also speaks of regaining this Paradise and living in it eternally after death. If so, then the experience of Paradise in life is identical with the experience of eternity.

The people we ordinarily call mystics are the people for whom this is true. Eternity to them is not endless time, but a real present, a "now" which absorbs all possible hereafters. Emily Dickinson also often speaks with the mystics of death as a rejoining of heaven, of "Forever" as "composed of Nows," of an eternal state of consciousness symbolized by a continuous summer and noon, of a coming "Aurora," a dawn that will have no night. But in her background there were two powerful anti-mystical tendencies at work. One was the rationalism of her generation; the other was the Puritanism in which she had been reared, with its insistence that the divine will was inscrutable, that it made sense only to itself, not to man, and that no human experience could transcend the limits of fallen humanity. For Emily Dickinson, therefore, the identity between the experience of circumference she had had and the postmortal eternity taught in the Bible remained a matter of "inference." It could be held by faith or hope but not by direct knowledge. This "inference" became the central issue in her struggle with her faith, a fact which she expresses most poignantly when she says: "Consciousness is the only home of which we *now* know. That sunny adverb had been enough, were it not foreclosed."

Paradoxically, the experience of unity with God and nature also produces a sense of division, or "bisection" as the poet often calls it, in the mind. Part of oneself is certainly mortal; part may not be, though even it must also go through death. In a poem beginning "Conscious am I in my Chamber" she speaks of the indwelling Spirit as the immortal part of herself; sometimes the distinction is between the poet herself and her soul; sometimes, and more commonly, it is between the soul and the mind or consciousness. "We know that the mind of the Heart must live," she says, and a letter to her seems like immortality because "it is the mind alone without corporeal friend." She also speaks of the body as a "trinket" which is worn but not owned, and in one striking poem the soul is attended by a "single Hound" which is its own identity. But she never seemed to accept the Platonic view that the soul is immortal by nature. If the first fact of her experience is a vision of earth as heaven, the second fact is that this vision is "evanescent," comes and goes unpredictably, and, so far as experience itself goes, ceases entirely at death. It is significant, therefore, that Emily Dickinson should so often symbolize her vision as a temporary and abnormal state of drunkenness:

> Inebriate of Air—am I—
> And Debauchee of Dew—
> Reeling—thro endless summer days—
> From inns of Molten Blue—

The liquor responsible for this state is usually called rum, or some synonym like "Domingo," "Manzanilla," or "Jamaica." When it is the more traditional wine, the word "sacrament," as in the poem "Exhiliration—is within," is seldom far away, for such imaginative drunkenness is a genuine communion. Still, it can lead to hangovers, "With a to-morrow knocking," and, whatever it is or means, it goes and is replaced by ordinary experience.

Ordinary experience is the sacramental or ecstatic experience turned inside out. Here the mind is not a circumference at all, but a center, and the only circumference is an indifferent and unresponsive Nature—"Nature—in Her monstrous House." We may still realize that such "Vastness—is but the Shadow of the Brain which casts it," but in this state the brain cannot cast any other shadow. Where the mind is a center and nature the circumference, there is no place for any divinity: that has vanished somewhere beyond the sky or beyond life. This is the state of "Those Evenings of the Brain," in which the body, so far from being a circumference incorporating its experience, is a "magic Prison," sealed against all intimations of immortality:

> The Rumor's Gate was shut so tight
> Before my Mind was sown,
> Not even a Prognostic's Push
> Could make a Dent thereon—

Like Blake, with whom she has been compared ever since Higginson's preface to the 1890 volume, Emily Dickinson shows us two contrary states of the human soul, a vision of innocence and a vision of "experience," or ordinary life. One is a vision of "Presence," the other of "Place"; in one the primary fact of life is partnership, in the other it is parting. Thus she may say, depending on the context, both "Were Departure Separation, there would be neither Nature nor Art, for there would be no World" and

> Parting is all we know of heaven,
> And all we need of hell.

But she has nothing of Blake's social vision, and the state that he associates with child labor, Negro slavery, prostitution, and war she associates only with loneliness.

Her two states are often associated with summer and winter, or, less frequently, with day and night. Often, especially in poems addressed to Sue, she speaks of a "Summer—Sister—Seraph!" who inhabits the paradisal world, in contrast to herself as a "dark sister," a "Druid" spirit of winter, frost and the north, waiting for the birds to come back, like Noah's dove, to tell her of a sunnier world beyond. Hence the times of year that have the greatest significance for her are the equinoxes, the March when the birds return and the white dress of winter breaks into color, and the moment in late summer when the invisible presence of autumn enters the year and makes "a Druidic Difference" in nature. The association of this latter period with the moment at which human life faces death makes it particularly the point at which the two lines of her imagination converge:

> God made a little Gentian—
> It tried—to be a Rose—
> And failed—and all the Summer laughed—
> But just before the Snows
>
> There rose a Purple Creature—
> That ravished all the Hill—
> And Summer hid her Forehead—
> And Mockery—was still—
>
> The Frosts were her condition—
> The Tyrian would not come

> Until the North—invoke it—
> Creator—Shall I—bloom?

Emily Dickinson is an impressionist in the sense that she tends to organize her visual experience by color rather than outline, and purple, the color of mourning and of triumph, is the central symbol for her of the junction between life and death. Various synonyms of it such as "Iodine," "Amethyst" and the "Tyrian" above run through her writings.

At times the poet speaks of the paradisal vision as being, not only a "stimulant" given in cases of despair or stupor, but a light by which all the rest of life can be lived, as providing a final answer to the question raised by its passing:

> Why Bliss so scantily disburse—
> Why Paradise defer—
> Why Floods be served to Us—in Bowls—
> I speculate no more—

At other times, in such poems as those beginning "Why—do they shut Me out of Heaven?" and "If I'm lost—now," she laments over a lost vision that hints at a still greater loss. Such sudden changes of mood would be inconsistent if she were arguing a thesis, but, being a poet, what she is doing is expressing a variety of possible imaginative reactions to a central unsolved riddle. The fact that her vision is transient sharpens the intensity of her relation to it, for

> In Insecurity to lie
> Is Joy's insuring quality.

Two recurring words in her poems are "suspense" and "expanse." The former refers to the shadow that falls between an experience and the realization that it has happened, the shadow that adumbrates death; the latter to the possession of the spiritual body which, for us, brings vision but not peace. "These sudden intimacies with Immortality, are expanse—not Peace—as Lightning at our feet, instills a foreign Landscape."

She deals mainly with the virtues of faith, hope, and love, but her life had shown her that love, which normally tends to union, may incorporate a great deal of its opposite, which is renunciation. Similarly with faith and hope: "Faith is *Doubt*," she says, and hope is the thinnest crust of ice over despair:

> Could Hope inspect her Basis
> Her Craft were done—
> Has a fictitious Charter
> Or it has none—

Like the Puritans before her, who refused to believe that their own righteousness would necessarily impress God into recognizing them, Emily Dickinson refused to believe that her own vision of Paradise guaranteed the existence of Paradise, even though she had nothing else to go on. And—Puritan to the last— she even faced the possibility that the Spirit of life within her might turn out to be Death; hence the ambiguous tone of such poems as "Doubt Me! My Dim Companion!" and "Struck, was I, nor yet by Lightning." She told Sue that if Jesus did not recognize her at the last day, "there is a darker spirit will not disown it's child." She means death, not the devil, though her pose recalls the demonic figures in Hawthorne. There are many poems about the physical experience of dying, some tranquil, some agonizing, some dealing with death by execution, by warfare, by drowning—in at least two poems the poet is an Andromeda swallowed by a sea monster. The region of death to be entered, or traversed, is usually a sea, sometimes a forest, or a "Maelstrom—in the Sky," or simply "a wild Night and a new Road," and in "I never told the buried gold," it is an underworld guarded by a dragon.

The world of death is not one that we have to die to explore: it is there all the time, the end and final cause of the vision of the center, just as Awe is the end and final cause of the vision of circumference. "I suppose there are depths in every Consciousness," she says, "from which we cannot rescue ourselves—

to which none can go with us—which represent to us Mortally—
the Adventure of Death." Some of her psychological poems take
us into this buried jungle of the mind. There are a few about
ghosts, where the two aspects of the self are treated in the vein
of Henry James's *The Jolly Corner*. But Emily Dickinson's sharp
inquiring mind has little in common with the ectoplasmic, and
these poems impress us as made rather than born. A more
genuine fear comes out at the end of this:

> Remembrance has a Rear and Front—
> 'Tis something like a House—
> It has a Garret also
> For Refuse and the Mouse.
>
> Besides the deepest Cellar
> That ever Mason laid—
> Look to it by it's Fathoms
> Ourselves be not pursued—

This is as near to hell as she ever brings us, as the original
version of the last two lines indicates:

> Leave me not ever there alone
> Oh thou Almighty God!

Yet even such a hell as this has a place and a function. Its
presence is in an odd way the basis of vision itself, for "the
unknown is the largest need of the intellect," and "could we
see all we hope—there would be madness near." Emily Dickinson has a poem about Enoch and Elijah, the two Biblical
prophets who were taken directly to heaven, but the figure
she identifies herself with is Moses, standing on the mountain
top with the wilderness of death on one side and the Promised
Land on the other, able to see his Paradise if not to enter it:

> Such are the inlets of the mind—
> His outlets—would you see
> Ascend with me the Table Land
> Of immortality—

Many, perhaps most, of Emily Dickinson's readers will simply take their favorite poems from her and leave the rest, with little curiosity about the larger structure of her imagination. For many, too, the whole bent of her mind will seem irresponsible or morbid. It is perhaps as well that this should be so. "It is essential to the sanity of mankind," the poet remarks, "that each one should think the other crazy." There are more serious reasons: a certain perversity, an instinct for looking in the opposite direction from the rest of society, is frequent among creative minds. When the United States was beginning to develop an entrepreneur capitalism on a scale unprecedented in history, Thoreau retired to Walden to discover the meaning of the word "property," and found that it meant only what was proper or essential to unfettered human life. When the Civil War was beginning to force on America the troubled vision of its revolutionary destiny, Emily Dickinson retired to her garden to remain, like Wordsworth's skylark, within the kindred points of heaven and home. She will always have readers who will know what she means when she says: "Each of us gives or takes heaven in corporeal person, for each of us has the skill of life." More restless minds will not relax from taking thought for the morrow to spend much time with her. But even some of them may still admire the energy and humor with which she fought her angel until she had forced out of him the crippling blessing of genius.

E. A. Robinson
and the Integration of Self

H. R. WOLF

I

The poetry of Edwin Arlington Robinson insists on an integrity
of self, on the possibility of the mind's knowing itself fully and
arranging itself coherently. The effort and inability of Robinson's characters to achieve this integrity result in his predomi-
nant tones and attitudes: low-keyed psychic tragedies and
elegies for undiscovered and unintegrated selves. The quest "For
songs undreamed of and unknown" puts him in the tradition of
romance and Romantic literature, a tradition that he uses quite
self-consciously; but, as it was for Freud, the grail is located
in the mind, and we must think of his genre finally as psychological romance and his poignancy as lying between the lines of
idealism and realism. When we consider that he was writing
of this quest at a time of idealistic uncertainty and relative
psychological unknowingness, at the crossroads of late Victorian
positivism and psychoanalytic origins (Freud's first important
papers on hysteria were published coevally with Robinson's
first poems, *The Children of the Night*), the arduousness of his
imaginative task becomes clear. Without a viable god and a
fully developed psychology, his craft and characters must
undergo severe tension. In "Ben Jonson Entertains a Man from
Stratford," they are seen haunted by an existential void: " 'No
Ben,' he mused; 'it's Nothing. It's all Nothing. / We come, we
go; and when we're done, we're done.' " Against this void in
"Rembrandt to Rembrandt," Robinson rests his message in
drawing relief from a field of matter that is at times indistinguishable from the human form: "The same god planned and

40

made you, beef and human; / And one, but for His whim, might
be the other." His human portraits accept this death of a divine
human image and, in their concerns for the difficulties of
identity, prefigure T. S. Eliot's "The Love Song of J. Alfred
Prufrock" and Ezra Pound's *Hugh Selwyn Mauberley* and,
later, the monologues of Robert Lowell's *Life Studies.*

This tenacious quest for identity in a union of hidden and
visible selves which Robinson paints runs counter to at least
four tendencies current in American culture, and, if we are to
see him in his proper psychological and philosophical setting,
we must, for a moment, look at them. Moreover, if we are
to rescue Robinson from the "periodization" of such a setting,
we must see how—despite its turn-of-the-century coloring (one
thinks of Thomas Eakins' portraits and Henry James's gaslight
heroes and heroines)—his concept of character does relate to us.
Robinson wrote when an image of man, recognizable, depict-
able, however unique the self, allowed people to set Shakespeare's characters, Rembrandt's portraits, Izaak Walton's *Life
of Donne,* James Boswell's *The Life of Samuel Johnson,* John
Keats's *Letters,* Edmund Gosse's *Father and Son,* and James
Joyce's *A Portrait of the Artist as a Young Man* into a common
tradition. This tradition is not open to us, though it is only in
the post–World War II period and in the psychedelic sixties
that the loss becomes an explicit cultural issue. The definitive
history of this "end of humanism" has yet to be written, but its
currents are clear. Leading among these currents in literature
and philosophy (often inseparable) is a tendency of self to
give way to self-consciousness, to self-reflexive cognition. Man
seeing himself seeing himself seeing himself ad infinitum has replaced introspective knowledge of the self and discovery of self
through action in the world.

From the writings of Luigi Pirandello through Jean-Paul
Sartre to Jorge Luís Borges, Alain Robbe-Grillet, and John
Barth, the mind progressively has reflected itself in its own
vanishing mirror. Epistemological angst replaced Cartesian

subjectivity, and Wallace Stevens superseded Robinson. In these reflections and the difficult perspectives of modern physics and perceptual psychology, matter dissolves. In *The Dehumanization of Art,* Ortega y Gasset describes the process as prophetically and clearly as any modern commentator:

The relation between our mind and things consists in that we think the things, that we form ideas about them. We possess of reality, strictly speaking, nothing but the ideas we have succeeded in forming about it. These ideas are like a belvedere from which we behold the world. Each new idea, as Goethe put it, is like a newly developed organ. By means of ideas we see the world, but in a natural attitude of the mind we do not see the ideas—the same as the eye in seeing does not see itself. In other words, thinking is the endeavor to capture reality by means of ideas; the spontaneous moment of the mind goes from concepts to the world. . . .

If we now invert the natural direction of this process; if, turning our back on alleged reality, we take the ideas for what they are—mere subjective patterns—and make them live as such, lean and angular, but pure and transparent; in short, if we deliberately propose to "realize" our ideas—then we have dehumanized and, as it were, derealized them. For ideas are really unreal. To regard them as reality is an idealization, a candid falsification. On the other hand, making them live in their very unreality is—let us express it this way —realizing the unreal as such. In this way we do not move from the mind to the world. On the contrary, we give three-dimensional being to mere patterns, we objectify the subjective, we "worldify" the immanent.[1]

The dissolution of the world requires that it must be reconstituted in the mind, and one thinks of Cubism, Paul Cézanne, and Georges Braque. The world becomes a special kind of meditation; the modern artist and intellectual are left to work in "fictions"; and if, for a moment, they mythologize them or forget that they are subjective, they have, from a certain philosophical point of view, surrendered their clerical position.[2] What follows from Ortega y Gasset's statement is that the mind can no more claim reality for itself than it can for the world.

The mind seeing itself must also subscribe to fictions. Both world knowledge and self-knowledge must take on the status of "constructs" or "models." This mode of awareness has led many recent artists to dramatize their craft by making the act of seeing it their subject. This occurs in action painting, in Stevens' poetry, and in Barth's recent fiction. To enter its kind of self-consciousness, one struggles in language or metalanguage while the posited world remains distant. Indeed, the world is too far off, and the literature resolves in "anagrams and crossword puzzles."

At the end of one story in *Lost in the Funhouse,* Barth has his narrator lament: "Oh God comma I abhor self-consciousness. I despise what we have come to; I loathe our loathsome loathing, our place our time our situation, our loathsome art, this ditto necessary story." As Jack Richardson comments of the character in a review of the book for the *New Republic:*

When a writer begins watching himself watch himself, when his last word winks a comment on its predecessor, when stories are tuned into meta-language games, when art observed is the subject of art—when this happens, literature degenerates into cute epistemology and the writer turns into something like a hysterical Bishop Berkeley. Such a method invariably leads to linguistic excesses—noxious puns, gimmicky neologisms, snobbish parodies. It is fashionably designed about current critical problems, which, in fiction, may be transcended or ignored, but not explicited. It gives the reader little life, an agonized art, and a strained sense of intimacy. And even if readable, it remains odd-duck literature, something for those who think life best manifests itself in anagrams and crossword puzzles.[3]

When "art observed is the subject of art" and the mind seeing itself see is the subject of art, and when both these attitudes hold—given that this self-reflexive activity is seen as infinitely regressive—our humanness takes on object status. The continuity of self and individual history, to say nothing of culture, becomes another fiction. Pushed to the extreme of Samuel Beckett, this psychological and aesthetic point of view assumes the elegance and vacuity of a logical proposition or geometric proof. If we pity Krapp, "the most disconsolate chimera in the modern theatre," we are, in some sense, acting irrationally, falsifying the play's vision by our humanity, the concreteness and reality of our emotions. As Denis Donoghue insists: "Each of Krapp's former selves is treated as a mere object, a temporary possession, capable only of arousing the contempt or the deathly desire of his present 'self'—such as it is. And logically the play ends with Krapp's present self staring motionlessly and saying absolutely nothing. The end of monologue is anaesthetized silence; nothing is fulfilled." [4]

This self-conscious or reflected self has, in turn, been opposed by a second set of thinkers. Norman O. Brown, R. D. Laing, and Alan Watts are disturbed, and validly, by an alienation from the body and from a body sense of the world that results and argue, in different ways, for a nondifferentiated sense of self and world. Their arguments may entail the sacrament of drugs, the polymorphous perversity of infantile sexuality, or the sanctity of madness, but they always lead to the annihilation of the self. This annihilation is poeticized into the possibility of a return to an oceanic world view, the blessed fusion of self and world that through the body of the mother preserves man in the earliest stages of life, but will destroy him as he develops if he does not achieve identity and the powers of cognition. This statement—perhaps wish—from Watts is typical:

Timothy Leary was not so wide of the mark when he said that we must go out of our minds (abstract values) to come to our senses (concrete values). For coming to our senses must, above all, be the experience of our own existence as living organisms rather than "personalities," like characters in a play or a novel—acting out some artificial plot in which the persons are simply masks for a conflict of abstract ideas or principles. Man as an organism is to the world outside like a whirlpool is to a river: Man and the world are a single natural process, but we are behaving as if we were invaders and plunderers in foreign territory. For when the individual is defined and felt as the separate personality or ego, he remains unaware that his actual body is a dancing pattern of energy that simply does not happen by itself. It happens only in concert with myriads of other patterns—called animals, plants, insects, bacteria, minerals, liquids and gases. The definition of a person and the normal feeling of "I" do not effectively include these relationships. You say, "I came into this world." You didn't; you came *out* of it, as a branch from a tree.[5]

In a world without "personalities," dramatic poetry cannot occur. Certainly, we cannot have Robinson's kind of poetry. We are more likely to have a poetry of the "concrete," a psychedelic, surface-oriented poetry, a poetry that will meet the retinal quality of underground films and the minimal canvases of Frank Stella.

These tendencies that oppose a viable image of man are complemented by two other tendencies: the "mediazation" of life in its real and banal form as TV—the confusion of art and life so that we now have the Vietnam War on tape with dinner —and in its provocative form as McLuhanism opposes the individual self and points to a neo-Medievalism of collective identity; and the new aestheticism of Susan Sontag, whose *Against Interpretation* forbids a coherent creation of a work of art as it denies the value of an individual restructuring of the experience of art:

The new sensibility understands art as the extension of life—this being understood as the representation of (new) modes of vivacity. There is no necessary denial of the role or moral evaluation here. Only the scale has changed; it has become less gross, and what it sacrifices in discursive explicitness it gains in accuracy and subliminal power. For we are what we are able to see (hear, taste, smell, feel) even more powerfully and profoundly than we are what furniture of ideas we have stocked in our heads. Of course, the proponents of the "two cultures" crisis continue to observe a desperate contrast between unintelligible, morally neutral science and technology, on the one hand, and morally committed, human-scale art on the other. But matters are not that simple, and never were.[6]

If Miss Sontag's vision were merely "corrective," it would be one thing, but she seems to offer the "furniture of ideas" as a concession. She says, for example, of Jean-Luc Godard: "That point is that Godard cannot envisage anything but arbitrary solutions to his problem. While each shot is autonomous, no amount of thinking can make it necessary. Since film for Godard is pre-eminently an open structure, the distinction between what's essential and inessential in any given film becomes senseless." [7] It is against this sense of the "arbitrary" that we turn to Robinson's shorter poems of character, to see them for what they are: agonizing struggles with contingency and the shape of self; to see in them a limit to the quest and an understanding, from where we stand, of the ideology of the arbitrary and the floating ego.

II

If one were to suggest a contemporary American artist to illustrate the poems of Robinson, it would be David Levine, the brilliant caricaturist of the *New York Review of Books,* the Daumier of the Left. We can imagine Levine dispatching Richard Cory, Aaron Stark, Cliff Klingenhagen, Reuben Bright, and Flammonde, to name only a few characters, with easily rendered, hard-edged lines. He could, because Robinson's characters, especially those of the short poems, display a rigidity that is, in a sense, a parody of authentic identity. They have, to use Wilhelm Reich's phrase, seemingly impenetrable "character armor." In fact, when their "armor" is broken, often in violent and self-destructive ways, as in "Richard Cory" and "Reuben Bright," a first impulse is to laugh. The sudden imposition of the human upon the mechanical, to use Henri Bergson's formula for comedy, provokes a momentary exhilaration. These characters seem always to overthrow their rigid, defensive selves—the selves that are machinelike in their repetition-compulsions. In their efforts, what underlying forces are trying to come into being are not always clear. Little or no dialogue occurs between the contending impulses, and when the self is so divided as to have unconscious materials completely cut off from consciousness, the break-through takes on hysterical qualities. Even in a psychoanalytic reading, we must be cautious in interpreting them. In a poem like "Aaron Stark," only limited insight is given into the underlying forces that assert themselves with a kind of inexplicable suddenness: "And then (and only then) did Aaron laugh." To understand the workings of these impositions, we would do better to start with a poem like "Mr. Flood's Party," where there is greater communication between the divided self that is striving toward integration. We may be able then to see beneath the surface of Robinson's "valiant armor."

Like many of Robinson's characters, Eben Flood is alone, an exile from himself—the self that is rooted at home in the past. Only through an imaginary reconciliation can he endure the present and the future and the past's real loss. Only by playing a friend to himself in Tilbury Town can he be welcomed home. But, as Robinson does not specify a state of mind for Eben in terms of characteristically concrete past events, we are tempted to read the poem first in generic terms as another variation of the *ubi sunt* theme. Upon further examination, a more specific sense of loss occurs, though the poem is not deuniversalized. It occurs because Robinson allows us always, within limits, to project our own experience onto his sketched-in portraits. Given the subjects of the poem as the fusion of the divided self and the separation of the self from the world, it is entirely appropriate that alcohol should be the medium of reconciliation. The medium is very much the message since excessive drinking (a common theme of Robinson) points to an infantile need. It alleviates the anxiety of separation by momentarily recreating

the infant's attachment to the mother and rehearses, as if it
had never been fully established, a basis of trust and mutuality.
That Eben has little trust in the world is made clear:

> There was not much that was ahead of him
> And there was nothing in the town below—
> Where strangers would have shut the many doors
> That many friends had opened long ago.

The intent of the poem seems to be to re-establish for Eben
a basis of trust, and we can see in Eben's relationship with the
jug an attempt, through role playing, to "master" the anxiety
of separation. He plays mother to himself and *objectifies*, or
depersonalizes, the child so as to defend against the painful
recognition that trust and love must be re-experienced:

> Then, as a mother lays her sleeping child
> Down tenderly, fearing it may awake,
> He set the jug down slowly at his feet
> With trembling care, knowing that most things break;
> And only when assured that on firm earth
> It stood, as the uncertain lives of men
> Assuredly did not, he paced away,
> And with his hand extended paused again . . .

In this context, to see the "two moons listening" later in the
poem as a breast image is not farfetched, however comic the
effect may be. It is not just his double vision that makes him
secure; it is his sense of mutuality, of the listening moons and
the harmonious landscape. His uplifted voice is the uplifted
face of the child in the archetypal relationship of the infant to
the good mother, a naturalized Madonna and Child:

> "Only a very little, Mr. Flood—
> For auld lang syne. No more, sir; that will do."
> So, for the time, apparently it did,
> And Eben evidently thought so too;
> For soon amid the silver loneliness
> Of night he lifted up his voice and sang,

> Secure, with only two moons listening,
> Until the whole harmonious landscape rang—.

This particular reading of "Mr. Flood's Party" may help explain the response to loss in "The Book of Annandale." Where Robinson is usually possessed by the "singular idea of loneliness" and has "nothing more to say" when "they are all gone away," he manages in the poem to deal with loss without falling prey to melancholia. Given Annandale's love for Miriam—"His love had been so much the life of her, / And hers had been so much the life of him"—we would expect extensive mourning, even melancholia. Where the ego has depended on the other for identity and well-being, the loss of the other predictably leads to extended grief. But Annandale is far from mournful; he feels, in fact, a partial sense of renewed life, an ambivalent reprieve:

> He knew the loss—therefore it puzzled him
> That he should sit so long there as he did,
> And bring the whole thing back—the love, the trust,
> The pallor, the poor face, and the faint way
> She last had looked at him—and yet not weep,
> Or even choose to look about the room
> To see how sad it was; and once or twice
> He winked and pinched his eyes against the flame
> And hoped there might be tears. But hope was all,
> And all to him was nothing: he was lost.
> And yet he was not lost: he was astray—
> Out of his life and in another life.

In "Mourning and Melancholia," Freud makes some relevant, parallel observations to Annandale's state:

The distinguishing mental features of melancholia are profoundly painful dejection, abrogation of interest in the outside world, loss of the capacity to love, inhibition of all activity, and a lowering of the self-regarding feelings to a degree that finds utterance in self-reproaches and self-revilings, and culminates in a delusional expectation of punishment. This picture becomes a little more intelligible when we consider that, with one exception, the same traits are met with in grief; but otherwise the features are the same. Profound mourning, the reaction to the loss of a loved person, contains the same feeling of pain, loss of interest in the outside world—in so far as it does not recall the dead one—loss of capacity to adopt any new object of love, which would mean a replacing of the one mourned, the same turning from every active effort that is not connected with thoughts of the dead. It is easy to see that this inhibition and circumscription in the ego is the expression of an exclusive devotion to its mourning, which leaves nothing over for other purposes or other interests.[8]

But there is a sense, too, in which a reader might insist that Annandale never gave himself to Miriam, that imbedded in her is an imago which reappears at her death and has intervened at least once during the marriage. Released, this imago brings to consciousness the latent fantasy figure that she embodied:

> Did everything but ache? And was a day
> To come some time when feeling should return
> Forever to drive off that other face—
> The lineless, indistinguishable face—
> That once had thrilled itself between his own
> And hers there on the pillow,—and again
> Between him and the coffin-lid had flashed
> Like fate before it closed,—and at the last
> Had come, as it should seem, to stay with him,
> Bidden or not?

Annandale puts the situation aptly and movingly in "Annandale Again": "My darkness had a smothered sun / Behind it, trying to shine through," and, although he regards it as a prevision of his second wife Damaris—"And there are times her eyes are wet / With wonder that I should foresee / So much of her before we met"—we can argue more convincingly that Annandale has found a second embodiment of this imago. If Annandale does not mourn Miriam's death, it is that she has been an embodiment of an imago that persists after her death. That this imago may be fraught with guilt feelings for him, that there is an "expectation of punishment," is suggested by Annandale's sudden death in "Annandale Again":

> There was a sick crash in the street,
> And after that there was no doubt
> Of what there was; and I was there
> To watch while Annandale went out.

Miriam and, later, Damaris are to Annandale what the vision of the "two moons" is to Eben Flood—embodiments of the mother-imago. Although we say that Annandale can deal with the death of Miriam because the mother-imago endures, Miriam *does* die and Annandale *is killed* after he has reinvested this mother-imago in Damaris. He is saved from isolation because he can merge his identity with the imbedded mother-imago, but this merger, at a deeper level, must be denied. The union with the mother must be defended against, but her imaginative presence can sustain a "literal" loss. This is a difficult psychic balance to sustain and not one that Robinson sustains easily. Of all his shorter narrative poems, "Annandale" and "Annandale Again" manage it best. In these poems he comes closest to probing the underpinnings of the sense of loss and aloneness, though ironically he does so by denying the sense. When we read "How Annandale Went Out," we have some idea how haunted Robinson may have been by the theme:

> "They called it Annandale—and I was there
> To flourish, to find words, and to attend:
> Liar, physician, hypocrite, and friend,
> I watched him; and the sight was not so fair
> As one or two that I have seen elsewhere:
> An apparatus not for me to mend—
> A wreck, with hell between him and the end,
> Remained of Annandale; and I was there."

The theme of reunion which is apparent in these few poems dominates much of Robinson's poetry either as reunion with

the landscape of childhood or as reunion with the familial figures
who inhere in that landscape. Home, especially Tilbury Town,
is his particular arcadia. In this respect, he partakes of a general
nineteenth-century mythos and Romantic predisposition to
make childhood into a paradisical experience. "Tintern Abbey"
is one paradigm of this modality. In this modality, the failure
of the family to provide love before the end of childhood
becomes the "fall into time." One thinks of Charlotte Brontë's
Jane Eyre and James's *What Masie Knew* as typal examples
of such falls. Although Freud contributes to this cult of childhood and to the quest for origins that so haunt the century,
he also dispels the myth of childhood as a recreated paradise.
Infantile sexuality and aggression become Satanic forces in the
garden of childhood. For Freud, life is conflict from the outset;
it and loss are synonymous. Expelled from the womb, forced
to give up the breast, imagining castration, leaving home,
man thrives through renunciation.

Robinson points explicitly to the pastoral quality of childhood
in "Aunt Imogen" and suggests the hidden conflicts only slightly.
At first, the poem may seem to deal only with the pastoral
dimension of childhood, of going home:

> They went together into the old room
> That looked across the fields; and Imogen
> Gazed out with a girl's gladness in her eyes,
> Happy to know that she was back once more
> Where there were those who knew her, and at last
> Had gloriously got away again
> From cabs and clattered asphalt for a while.

Young George, whom she embraces at the poem's end as a
redemptive act of love and compensation for the "penance of
a dream," sees the world as a place "Where everybody might
have everything / To do, and almost everything to eat." Robinson would have us believe that the aunt "was born to be Aunt
Imogen," that her destiny was to be a bountiful, surrogate mother

one month a year. But we ask most if the poem explains at all why Imogen must live with "that passionate ache for something of her own," why she must accept "that there was no love / Save borrowed love: there was no might have been." Perhaps we can say that her ability to find fulfillment in loving a child contains the explanation of her inability to satisfy her "passionate ache." Perhaps the pull toward home reflects the difficulty of meeting the present. Although loss can only be reconstituted in the present, there is, in all of us, a tendency to search for wholeness in the irrecoverable past. When she takes young George into her arms, we might be as justified in seeing a boy's wish for closeness with his mother as we are in seeing her attempt to reconstitute her sense of loss through association with infantile love:

> Now it was hers to dance the folly down,
> And all the murmuring; now it was hers
> To be Aunt Imogen.—So, when Young George
> Woke up and blinked at her with his big eyes,
> And smiled to see the way she blinked at him,
> 'T was only in old concord with the stars
> That she took hold of him and held him close,
> Close to herself, and crushed him till he laughed.

In effect, Aunt Imogen loves George for the same reasons that Eben Flood holds the jug and Annandale sees the "lineless, indistinguishable love," as a reconstitution of a child-mother relationship.

Although "The Gift of God" does not allude in any literal way to the birth of Christ, the mother in the poem regards the birth and imagined destiny of her son with a beatific trust that recalls the wonder of the virgin birth: "But she, with innocence unwrung, / Would read his name around the earth." What is significant is the way in which the child's well-being, whatever form his destiny may actually take, rests in the mind of the mother. The child's future is secure against the vagaries of fame because he cannot outrun his mother's blessed conception of him at birth:

> She crowns him with her gratefulness,
> And says again that life is good;
> And should the gift of God be less
> In him than in her motherhood,
> His fame, though vague, will not be small,
> As upward through her dreams he fares,
> Half clouded with a crimson fall
> Of roses thrown on marble stairs.

This closeness of mother and child in "The Gift of God" is the other side of the loneliness in "Mr. Flood's Party." The intensity of the union in one poem accounts for the pain of separation in the other. Union and estrangement reflect upon each other. Where the relationship between mother and child is a dependent one, as it is in "The Gift of God," the future can only offer the urge toward reunion and the pain, perhaps necessity, of isolation. For the child who must take his identity from his mother, there can be no autonomy without a sense of loss and no security without the loss of identity.

In these shorter poems, Robinson creates an implied polarity between separateness and oneness that may be looked at in terms not unlike the polarity Laing describes in *The Divided Self:*

If the individual does not feel himself to be autonomous this means that he can experience neither his separateness from, nor his relatedness to, the other in the usual way. A lack of sense of autonomy implies that one feels one's being to be bound up in the other, or that the other is bound up in oneself, in a sense that transgresses the actual possibilities within the structure of human relatedness. It means that a feeling that one is in a position of ontological dependency on the other (i.e. dependent on the other for one's very being), is substituted for a sense of relatedness and attachment to him based on genuine mutuality. Utter detachment and isolation are regarded as the only alternative to a clam- or vampire-like attachment in which the other person's life-blood is necessary for one's own survival. Therefore, the polarity is between complete isolation or complete merging of identity rather than between separateness and relatedness. The individual oscillates perpetually, between the two extremes, each unequally unfeasible.[9]

This polarity of isolation and merging can be seen touching, and opposed to, one another in "The Flying Dutchman" and "Luke Havergal." Both poems refer to a birthing world without a sun. In "Luke Havergal," "there is not a dawn in eastern skies," and in "The Flying Dutchman," "There is a dawning, though there be no sun." Though alone and priding himself on his aloneness, the flying Dutchman steers toward the haunting "old ghost of what has been before." Rather than be engulfed, he abandons "one fog-walled island more," and, in so doing, avoids the possibility of finding the "Vanished Land" he seeks. Death and consummation are opposed to life and estrangement. There can be no resolution, only "oscillation."

Where "The Flying Dutchman" moves toward the dawning, toward the irrecoverable beginning of life, Luke Havergal is called to the western gate, to death, where there is the promise of fulfillment. At the western gate he will find the "crimson leaves," as the child in "The Gift of God" will find a "crimson fall of roses" in his mother's dreams. It is, significantly, "trust" that Havergal must feel if he is to be called at the western gate by the mysterious "she" of the poem. We cannot know in any verifiable way who the "she" and the "I" of the poem are, though both are associated with death and both promise to relieve Havergal of his despair: "The dark will end the dark, if anything." Salvation is seen as the union with the female principle in death. To the extent that the poem is an invocation to death, suicide (another common theme of Robinson) may be thought of as an implied act and reluctance as Havergal's implied stance. Consummation means loss of self, death, and, in Laing's terms, represents one polarity of the "dependent" personality, as "The Flying Dutchman" represents the other.

Both are incomplete positions and contain within them the wish for the opposite polarity. Stasis and ambivalence mediate between emotional antitheses. Although Laing's formulation is useful, it fails to see the way in which symbolic death, the renunciation of the self, can serve to defend against impulses that are threatening to the ego at an unconscious level. Because the mother archetype pervades Robinson's poetry, merger presents difficulties at both a pre-oedipal and an oedipal level, ontologically and psychosexually. Consummation in death expresses a wish and defends against that wish at the same time.

III

From these perspectives, it is now possible to return with greater clarity to a few of the short character poems whose breaks in "character armor" turn on themselves. A close reading of the first stanza of "Aaron Stark" discloses—with an uncommon degree of clinical precision—an anal preoccupation, a miser syndrome. The ungiving, withholding Stark signals what he defends against—his "unkept" and "gnarled" impulses—at every turn. To fix this poem at an anal stage of development is not as important as relating the issues that surround anality to Stark. The issue is, I think, mastery control and autonomy. The struggle for autonomy, in Eriksonian terms, explains his anxious responses to the "sound of alien pity." The giving response seems to contradict the direction of emotion in the first stanza. Caught off guard by pity, he is in the position of having a tender feeling imposed upon him. Momentarily, he does not control the world. The poem benefits from the ambiguity surrounding the source of the sound. If the voice is his, an opposition of self and world takes on an intrapsychic dimension. He lives in a conflicted state which expresses itself in symptoms and compromise formations, not as the *awareness* of conflict.

At first reading, the tearing down of the "slaughter-house" at the end of "Reuben Bright" seems disproportionate to the experience of the poem, but there are, finally, justifying elements of unconscious content. There is the suggestion, through denial, that Reuben has aggressive impulses, if his butcher's trade had not already created an unavoidable nuance. There is also the suggestion that his relationship with his wife has an infantile component: "and cried like a baby half that night." We can only explain the self-punishing aspect of his mourning by inferring an unconscious aggressive feeling toward his wife that is incompatible with his unconscious love of her. Further, the extreme sense of loss and self-punishment must reawaken archaic feelings of loss and anger. Even if Reuben did not cry like a baby, we would supply an infantile element in his experience, a hidden attachment to the mother. We either understand the poem intuitively or supply a meaning that makes appeals to an extraliterary hypothesis. Unless we feel or supply an underlying, child-mother attachment, the poem must remain closed and unaccountably affective.

The underlying presence of a mother-son attachment in "Reuben Bright" could be amplified by locating certain romance materials in "Miniver Cheevy" and "Flammonde," and relating these materials to Freud's essay on the "Family Romance" and Otto Rank's *The Myth of the Birth of the Hero* (linking the theme of the exiled prince to the structure of the oedipus complex), but this exploration would take us more deeply into the Freudian literature and would not appropriately render the mood of Robinson's poems. The point is, after all, that Robinson's poems *do not* contain an *open* relationship between conscious and unconscious materials. The poems dramatize conflicted selves who are *almost* out of touch with themselves, or with whom the reader is almost out of touch, except at an intuitive level. These selves suffer from *telic* disorganization: one part of them is cut off from another part. At best they meet at a symbolic interface whose defensive armor we must penetrate.

In his *Disease, Pain, and Sacrifice: Toward a Psychology of Suffering*, David Bakan addresses himself to a psychic discontinuity applicable to them: "Clearly, the way to overcome the injuriousness of a mechanism is to change that which is ego-alien to something which is not ego-alien, to recognize that that which may have the sense of being 'other' (as the word 'id' strongly suggests) is really the person himself, to overcome the automaticity of the functioning of such mechanisms that have only the *appearance of defense* so that indeed the person may be really defended instead of injured by them." [10]

There are intrapsychic discontinuities, and there are interpersonal discontinuities. The married couple in "Firelight" live in mutual solitude:

> Wiser for silence, they were not so glad
> Were she to read the graven tales of lines
> On the wan face of one somewhere alone;
> Nor were they more content could he have had
> Her thoughts a moment since of one who shines
> Apart, and would be hers if he had known.

Both discontinuities can occur together. In "Mortmain," Avenel's unexplored erotic and romantic possibilities are buried with her brother. She is cut off from her present and future as she stands aloof from Seneca's love. Because she cannot break the bonds that tie her to her dead brother—a forbidden and concealed entanglement—she cannot meet Seneca. In severing her present from her past, she destroys the possibility of egosyntonic love. There, then, is neither an arbitrary nor a free-floating self in Robinson's poetry. His characters strive for *telic* unity and discover the defensive armor that "protects" the hidden self and the "negative" aspects of eros and aggression. In their low-keyed psychic tragedies it is possible that Robinson, like Brown, Laing, and Watts, may be suggesting that the cult of nonego is the final defense against the difficulties of self-knowledge. If Robinson's poetry must be approached, as I think it must be, from a view of ego structure, and if at the same time readers are disposed to dismiss it because of the ego boundaries inherent in it, perhaps the dilemma can be resolved partially by turning to those humanistic psychologists who like A. H. Maslow are trying to enlarge the sphere of self by replacing the ego with more encompassing notions of the self.[11]

NOTES

1. *The Dehumanization of Art* (Anchor Books, 1956), pp. 34–35.

2. See Frank Kermode, *The Sense of an Ending* (New York, 1967).

3. "Amusement and Revelation," *New Republic*, CLIX (November 23, 1968), 30–33.

4. "The Human Image in Modern Drama," *Lugano Review*, Nos. 3–4 (1965), p. 163.

5. "Wealth vs. Money," *Playboy*, XV (December, 1968), 235.

6. *Against Interpretation* (Delta Books, 1966), p. 300.

7. "Godard," *Partisan Review*, XXXV (Spring, 1968), 303.

8. *Collected Papers*, trans. Joan Riviere (New York, 1959), IV, 153.

9. *The Divided Self* (Penguin Books, 1966), pp. 52–53.

10. *Disease, Pain, and Sacrifice: Toward a Psychology of Suffering* (Chicago, 1968), p. 30.

11. A. H. Maslow, "Some Educational Implications of the Humanistic Psychologies," *Harvard Educational Review*, XXXVIII (Fall, 1968).

Robert Frost's Circle of Enchantment

JAN B. GORDON

'You read your Emily Dickinson
and I, my Robert Frost.'
—Simon and Garfunkel

By defining the very poetic act as a "temporary stay against confusion,"[1] Robert Frost was effectively guaranteeing that the work of the imagination, like the New England winter, was a necessary, though impermanent, assault upon reality. If "outside" weather is the stuff against which poetry must survive, Frost is as much concerned with reconciling the entangling climate to an "inside" condition of linguistic reverie. Because the same route of pilgrimage must serve as the medium for exploring both weathers, Frost's metaphysical journey is beset by difficulties at its onset. One of the difficulties stems from the defensive nature of the aesthetic "boy's will," promoting a distorted dualism: "Every poem is an epitome of the great predicament; a figure of the will braving alien entanglements."[2] To explore the shape of that figure is to comprehend the topology of both landscapes.

As early as "A Dream of Julius Caesar," written in 1891 for the Lawrence High School *Bulletin,* this poetic identity is both threatened and sustained by the objects of perception:

> All nature seems to weave a circle of
> Enchantment round the mind, and give full sway
> To fleeting thoughts and dreams of bygone years.[3]

In this apprentice poem the mind and nature are partners in alienation. Although striving to establish its sovereignty over the natural scene, there is a perverse solipsism at work here, for it is only with the aid of an apparently "hostile" nature that the mind gains a distinct sense of "self." Only an encounter with the nature that destroys the "self" can bring about self-knowledge. This companion problem to the establishment of identity has, to be sure, been central to American poetics, ever since Emerson gave our national conscience a schizoid hue by his polarization of the Party into those parties of hope and memory. Not unlike the exploring American tourist who combines the zeal of initiating discovery with painful attention to the establishment (and propagation) of his identity, Frost's transient ego is the victim of contrary demands. In his essay "On Emerson" Frost criticized (and one suspects misunderstood) his regional ancestor's Manichaean disposal of evil. Although his favorite Western poem contained the line, "Unit and universe are round," Frost was well aware that in nature "the circle becomes oval." The effort to locate "self" and "other" in their distinct contexts is always distorted by our motive for metaphor that prompts the interchangeability of center and circumference.[4]

The verse with which Frost prefaced his *Complete Poems* (1949) suggests the tortuous nature of this pilgrimage to self-discovery; the pasture spring must be cleaned in order to bring about the Edenic paradise. Yet, even in the act of preparation for the rebirth the poet must "fetch the little calf / That's standing by the mother." Nature's humanization is the expense of achieving prelapsarian grace. Throughout Frost's poetry the reader senses a struggle between the natural and human realms that is demarcated by a host of familiar emblems—walls, brooks, bridges, ice—which simultaneously separate and link the combatants. The oft-noticed conservatism of Frost's statements— the refusal to tread either out far or in deep, or the fact that the swinging birches never swing out too far but always return to a middle range—is in fact a kind of phenomenological "trimming." For the problem of defining a poetic "self," with all its attendant vocational questions, while simultaneously exploring the contours of the self-in-the-world, provides the charm for so much of Frost's personal and artistic reminiscence, while simultaneously giving his poetry a unique spatial configuration.

Characteristically, Frost's first volume, A Boy's Will (1913), is colored with the somber shades of autumn: "Sorrow" is moistened by the dark strokes of November rain; a lingering brown leaf disturbs "A Late Walk"; and the southwester blows about the fragments of a world that is wintering. Not unlike Yeats's early volumes, similarly influenced by the flickering rhythms and participial phrases of the *fin de siècle*, Frost's nature is part of a general, misty flux against which the will asserts itself. Initially, the poetic voice attempts to define itself by a defensive gesture, by locating its own metaphoric space as a mode of self-preservation against the vagaries of autumn weather:

> We make ourselves a place apart
>   Behind light words that tease and flout,
> But oh, the agitated heart
>   Till someone really find us out.
>
> 'Tis pity if the case require
>   (Or so we say) that in the end
> We speak the literal to inspire
>   The understanding of a friend.
>
> ("Revelation")

In "Now Close the Windows," the narrator secures a sense of selfhood by creating an illusory suspension of nature's decay, whereas "In Neglect" is populated by the speaker and an imaginary companion (presumably the reader) who occupy a "wayside nook" in an effort of induced solitude.

This predisposition to locate a space of one's own in A Boy's Will gives the poems in the volume a characteristic structure. Typically, the speaker initially seeks to refuge himself from a refracted, phenomenalized nature within the confines of a real or imaginary sanctuary. Yet for any number of reasons the refuge is impermanent. The ravages of New England weather, for example, always usurp the sacred space of the imagination in spite of the architectonics of defense. The winds

> Burst into my narrow stall;
> Swing the picture on the wall;
> Run the rattling pages o'er;
> Scatter poems on the floor;
> Turn the poet out of door.
>
> ("To the Thawing Wind")

Of paramount interest here is the way in which the same nature that presumably served as the object of the picture and the poem turns its destructive fury on its own representation as art. This points to the first difficulty faced by Frost's poetic voice. For those "light words" through which the poet had sought self-definition not only are imperfect defenses against nature but are betrayed by nature for a second reason: the "outer" weather creates a competing music that in the act of destruction absorbs the poet's "inner" art. In "A Dream Pang" the "song / Was swallowed up in leaves that blew away," adding further insult to a speaker who has withdrawn into his forest bower. Through such invasions the distinction between "inside" and "outside," so crucial to the voice under the illusion that it has found itself a place apart, is violated. For, in addition to the surrender of the privacy of artistic utterance, the self discovers that, contrary to having a room of its own, self and world share the same metaphoric space. In "Storm Fear" the Emersonian blizzard, anthropomorphized as a dog, pursues the family protected behind a chamber window. Although they initially appear mutually alien ("I count our strength"), the gradual blurring of landscape distinctions in the piled drifts creates a subdued mood that equalizes the combatants. The reference to the "comforts of the barn" shifts the drama from the literal to the allegorical; clearly the distinction between "self" and "other" is theologically melioristic as the hound of heaven pursues the hart in hiding. There is a higher refuge that both share, belying the speaker's decision to isolate his progeny. Although a measure of union has been achieved, the reader comes to feel himself the victim of poetic trickery.

The realization that the poetic identity and the objects of perception share similar attitudes brings about a radical shift in Frost's circle of enchantment. Abandoning his epistemological fortress, the speaker attempts to locate "correspondences"— structures in nature that sympathize with the geometry of the mental act—in an effort to transcend both. In this way the speaker hopes to bridge the mutual isolation and undeclared warfare of self and other. Such a decision takes Frost, as it did Emerson, into a Jungian realm of origins where both natural world and self exist in an undifferentiated unity. In the poem "In a Vale," the narrator locates the defensive structure in a "misty fen" that, possessing its own source of music, is a kind of total-environment artistic pleasure dome:

> The fen had every kind of bloom,
>   And for every kind there was a face,
> And a voice that has sounded in my room
> Across the sill from the outer gloom
>   Each came singly unto her place. . . .

Here, what the poetic mind had defined as the "other," as one of those alien entanglements, is seen to possess more than human attributes. The landscape is primordial, a spot

> Where the bird was before it flew,
> Where the flower was before it grew,
>   Where bird and flower were one and the same.

An elementary notion of archetype is the result of Frost's attempt to find a correspondence between the interior circle and a grotesque landscape. Often this struggle to reduce the differences takes on the aspect of a religious ceremony, as in "Rose Pogonias," where a "saturated meadow" becomes a setting for

A circle scarcely wider
  Than the trees were tall;
Where winds were quite excluded,
  And the air was stifling sweet. . . .

Although the poem commences as an "objective" description
of a natural scene, the attempt to arrive at a unity is suggested
by the intrusion of the first person plural pronoun which
draws the reader into the poem at the same time as it suggests
companionship between the speaker and nature:

We raised a simple prayer
  Before we left the spot,
That in the general mowing
  That place might be forgot;
Or if not all so favored,
  Obtained such grace of hours,
That none should mow the grass there
  While so confused with flowers.

This "temple" represents a teleological suspension both spatially
and temporally. Yet its imaginary existence is indicated by the
very encroachment of ordinary existence—"the general mowing"—that is less likely to suspend disbelief. In one sense, the
poem itself is a part of the temporary stay against confusion,
and its abrupt conclusion effectively ends both the "grace of
hours" and the grace of space. The attempt to define a synonymous structure in nature is no more rewarding than the construction of some mental fortress. In one case, nature always
invades the sacred space of the mind; and in the other, the trials
of human existence threaten to break down the tenuous correspondence that the mind has found in nature.

Almost at the same time, the speaker becomes aware of
another difficulty. Such a mode of bridging epistemological
alienation may bring about a unity less desirable than anticipated, reflected in the fear of "a sameness of the wood." Dis-

solved into a specular "we" in which the self and the objects of
its perception lose this individuation, that common world
shared by the two decays into a drab uniformity:

> The same leaves over and over again!
> They fall from giving shade above
> To make one texture of faded brown
> And fit the earth like a leather glove.
>
> . . . . . .
>
> They must be pierced by flowers and put
> Beneath the feet of dancing flowers.
> However it is in some other world
> I know that this is the way in ours.
>
> ("In Hardwood Groves")

The "groves," another example of the secluded spot in nature,
are of course not so secluded, and the title of the poem is enough
to suggest the extent of the betrayal. Hardwood groves are,
after all, pretty soft, as is identity, and both are merged as
plural companion(s) in the soft, suffused lights of a poetic
autumnal. This motif, later repeated in a host of other poems,
including "Nothing Gold Can Stay," indicates a fear that the
location of some objective correlative in nature only results
in the repetition of the human problem of cyclic aging and
renewal. So many of Frost's pilgrimages into the "outer" world
conclude not only with the disappearance of the object of the
quest, but more importantly, within a third obscure realm that
belongs to neither the totally objective nor the subjective:

> One of my wishes is that those dark trees,
> So old and firm they scarcely show the breeze,
> Were not, as 'twere, the merest mask of gloom,
> But stretched away into the edge of doom.
>
> ("Into My Own")

The desire to pierce through nature's mask as nature pierces
through the poet's various masks—ghost houses, private rooms,
circles of cut grass—results in a humanization of nature that is

of cosmic importance, insofar as it leads to a Fall just as significant as the seasonal fall. In spite of all his philosophical
manipulation of the New England landscape, Frost is essentially
in the same time and place as he was in the beginning: the
possessor of a poetic will that, having found itself confronting
alien entanglements, suddenly discovers that a boy's will is
indeed the wind's will and that the two are part of a flickering
autumnal mood that reduces all externality to the same fluid
tone. A metaphysic based upon some conviction of "correspondence" is correlated satisfactorily, but neither the "quest"
nor a phenomenological defensiveness can ever transform. The
poetic self has a choice of either a self-induced siege at the
hands of nature which strengthens, temporarily, a sense of
selfhood, or a nonproductive contingency which dissolves all
identity in such mature poems as "Two Look at Two."

As if this were not sufficient cause for doubts, Frost is left
with a third alternative: the fear that each natural object has
its own "circle of enchantment": and that the barrier man has
constructed for himself is not the exclusive domain of human
will. In at least one poem in *A Boy's Will*, this suspicion exists
as part of the poet's fantasy complex:

> I dream upon the opposing lights of the hour
> Preventing shadow until the moon prevail;
> I dream upon the nighthawks peopling heaven,
> Each circling each with vague unearthly cry . . .
>   ("Waiting")

Although the bat at dusk seems to have "made out [the
speaker's] secret place," the animal loses it when he pirouettes.
The "other" (those "opposing lights of the hour") loses an
interest in usurping man's privacy upon the realization that
they, too, fashion their own architecture. The horror of this
alternative is self-evident; not only is man separated from
nature, but each natural entity makes its own circle that
separates it from all else. Even the very condition of alienation,

which had previously been the particular province of man's quest for self-identity, is seen to be the one given feature of nonhuman existence. In the very act of doing its thing, the nighthawk isolates itself from all else, and insofar as it accomplishes this, the birds can be said ironically to "people heaven"—a frightful example of our earthbound tendency to anthropomorphize. Toward the conclusion of his first volume Frost's poetic universe is becoming acclimatized to the approaching winter. In the last poem, "Reluctance," the pilgrimage has ended, and the voyager whose sense of self was revealed in the "I" of the first stanza has returned from his wandering. Each natural object is isolated from its companions in a hibernation through which a self-enclosed sufficiency becomes the one universal condition:

> Ah, when to the heart of man
> Was it ever less than a treason
> To go with the drift of things,
> To yield with a grace to reason,
> And bow to accept the end
> Of a love or a season?
>
> ("Reluctance")

The season as well as nature has conspired against the poet's wishes to "bridge" his own identity with that of the cosmos. The approach of winter snows, combined with the discovery that all nature is the victim of mutual enclaves, coincides with the poem that makes *A Boy's Will* itself an enclave. To move from this nadir to "Mending Wall," the first contribution to *North of Boston* (1914), is to encounter a radical shift in Frost's sensibility; the intimation of mutual alienation is now an a priori condition of both humanity and nature—and, somewhat sadly, the first permanent experience they share while maintaining, now, an enforced identity.

The initial poem in this volume, in spite of its relevance to Frost's evolution as a poet, has long been misinterpreted by those who choose to reduce "Mending Wall" either to New England folk wisdom or to a more international political wisdom. In discoursing upon the gaps that find their way into this barrier each spring, the narrator questions the relevance of walls in an area where apple trees will never cross to devour pine cones. There is a natural segregation in nature, and her human occupants have heightened this segregation to a social ritual, even while the speaker in the poem attempts to instruct his neighbor in the uselessness of the ritual. As in so many rituals, the pragmatic reply "Good fences make good neighbors" is repeated. The poem's proverbial tone ironically stems from the proverb at the center which the speaker rebukes. The very fact that the speaker regards his neighbor as one who "moves in darkness" undercuts his own wisdom; in effect, a verbal wall would exist whether the stone fence did or did not.

"Mending Wall" indicates that Frost's concerns have widened to include a language which is no longer merely the agent for reflecting a regional landscape but part of that landscape. The repeated phrase is as significant as repeated space: both enclose identity in a metaphoric capsule. Of even greater importance is the extent to which Frost adopts a relativistic technique that hinges on point of view in order to compensate for his metaphoric monadology. The poem "The Vantage Point" in *A Boy's Will* first exhibits this tendency:

> If tired of trees I seek again mankind,
>   Well I know where to hie me—in the dawn,
>   To a slope where the cattle keep the lawn.

The poetic voice has retreated behind its barriers, and its ability to create a panorama is a function of his disappearance —"Myself unseen, I see in white defined." In the second stanza of the poem, the perspective is altered, as the poet discovers that vision is always a function of an envisioning self.

> And if by noon I have too much of these,
>   I have but to turn on my arm, and lo,

> The sun-burned hillside sets my face aglow,
> My breathing shakes the bluet like a breeze,
> I smell the earth, I smell the bruised plant,
> I look into the crater of the ant.
>
> ("The Vantage Point")

High noon becomes the occasion of an acute shift, through which the narrator assumes a "character" in the drama of his own creation. He is able to experience the world in all its preconscious contingency only by transforming himself into a self-conscious role. It is as if there were a third participant in the Frostian confrontation; the voyager has become a voyeur who reinforces identity by creating, in effect, a double identity. A kinetic narrator has now become part of the object of his own imagination, and the result is a combination New England folk poem and an objectivist poem. Whereas in the first stanza the narrator participated in "seeking" or "saw" only insofar as objects were made apparent to the mind, the second stanza is characterized by a Whiteheadian "prehension" rather than apprehension. The hillside sets his face aglow in much the same way that he had set dwellings aglow in the highly pictorial first stanza. Not only what one sees but how one participates in the vision is dependent on vantage point.

As could be expected, Frost alters the form of his art as a complement to these changing thematic interests. One such innovation in the second volume is the development of the dramatic monologue, the verbal counterpart to an increasingly relativistic landscape: "I've just found out what makes a piece of writing good (my latest opinion of anything): it is making the sentences talk to each other as two or more speakers do in drama." [5] The "truth" of any encounter is no longer a function of one's probing intellect primarily because the object of the "mental thrust" returns the quest. And this dialectic creates the earthly drama, the "strange apparition":

> Eyes seeking the response of eyes
> Bring out the stars, bring out the flowers,

> Thus concentrating earth and skies
> So none need be afraid of size
> All revelation has been ours.
>
> ("All Revelation")

The poetic vision overlaps another one, and they function together as a matter of principle upon the same visible world. Something visible to the poetic eye is becoming a viewer. Explorations no longer stop at barriers. Everything rather comes to rest upon an insurpassable richness, a miraculous multiplication of perceptible being which gives the same things that had previously given testimony to their remoteness a power to be things for more than one perceiver. Human and animal bodies have not the hidden faces enclosed within a private circle of enchantment, but a Husserlian "other side," a perceiving side whose significance is based on what is perceptible to me. Everything depends upon the fact that the deer in the woods over which the poetic eye glances is redeemed from its "space of consciousness" and intrudes equally well into the circuit of other bodies. The metaphoric world depends upon the fact that our glances are not "acts of consciousness," each of which claims an invariable priority, but openings of our flesh which are immediately filled by the universal flesh of the world:

A dramatic necessity goes deep into the *nature* of the sentence. Sentences are not different enough to hold the attention unless they are dramatic. No ingenuity of varying structure will do. All that can save them is the speaking tone of voice somehow entangled in the words and fastened to the page for the ear of the imagination. That is all that can save poetry from sing-song, all that can save prose from itself.[6]

Frost seems to be implying that unless we have recourse to the saving ruse of speech, putting a common domain of thoughts between us as a third party, the encounter of self and other is intolerable. There is nothing left to look at but a look, as seer and seen are mutually interchangeable. In "Two Look at Two" the glances of the two lovers are immobilized on each other. Nothing can distract them or distinguish them from each other, since identity is abolished. Each circle of enchantment bears contingency with nothing except its duplicate:

> A doe from round a spruce stood looking at them
> Across the wall, as near the wall as they.
> She saw them in their field, they her in hers.
> The difficulty of seeing what stood still,
> Like some up-ended boulder split in two,
> Was in her clouded eyes:

In terms of reflection, all we have here is two "points of view" with nothing in common—two "I thinks," each of which believes itself the winner of the trial that typifies Frost's pilgrimages. Vision produces what reflection will never understand: a combat which at times has no victor and a thought for which there is no titular incumbent. Some of the most familiar of Frost's dramatic monologues seem to follow a set pattern of response: I look at him. He sees that I look at him. I see that he sees it. He sees that I see that he sees it. Even though in principle reflections upon reflections go on ad infinitum, vision is such that the obscure results of two glances adjust to each other, and there are no longer two consciousnesses with their own teleology, but two mutually enfolding glances, alone in the world. In one sense, vision traces what is accomplished by desire when it pushes two "thoughts" out toward a line of fire between them.

It is this ability of Frost to make of language a means or a code for thought and hence to break it that characterizes a poem like "Home Burial." The wife takes refuge behind the assurance that the speaker's failure of vision will be mirrored by a failure of language:

> She let him look, sure that he wouldn't see,
> Blind creature; and awhile he didn't see.

> But at last he murmured, 'Oh,' and again, 'Oh'
> 'What is it—what?' she said
>
>   'Just what I see.'

The husband, so intent upon sharing his wife's grief for the death of their child, realizes that "Words are nearly always an offense," that he must be taught how to speak of anything that would please his wife. Yet, in the very act of learning this new speech, he is forced to suffer a loss of identity, and with it comes a new sympathetic identification with the other figure in the poem that has lost its identity, the deceased child:

> A man must partly give up being a man
> With women-folk. We could have some arrangement
> By which I'd bind myself to keep hands off
> Anything special you're a-mind to name.

When we make language a code, as we most often do in times of bereavement, we prohibit ourselves from understanding that we have a passion for speaking and must, sometimes compulsively, speak to ourselves. If language duplicated externally a thought which in its solitude legislated for every other possible thought, it would not be, in Freud's terms, a total reinvestment of our own life. Frost in his dramatic monologues comes very close to one of the tenets of contemporary phenomenology; notably, that the very idea of a complete statement is inconsistent. We do not comprehend a sentence because it is complete in itself; we say that it is complete or sufficient because we have understood. Thought and speech anticipate each other and continually take each other's place. The weakness of every parallelism or every attempt to locate a "correspondence" is that it provides itself with correspondences between the two orders while concealing the operations which produced these analogies by an anterior encroachment.

Throughout Frost's experiments with the dramatic monologue, he shows us that things are said and are thought by a

Speech and by a Thought which we do not have, but which has us. Although the earlier volumes had located the existence of a wall between us and others, his later experiments with form demonstrate that it is a wall we build together, each putting his boulder in the niche left by the other. Expression becomes a matter of reorganizing things said and bending them to a certain enhancement of meaning. There are two types of expression in Frost's dramatic monologues: that which is of itself comprehensible and sayable, usually formulaic folk wisdom, and, second, that which is no more than a precise uneasiness in the world of things said. Expression is a matter of acting in such a way that the two gather each other in or cross each other. The thought of Frost's natives never advances until the horizon of meaning it opens up becomes, through speech, what in theatrical language is a *real décor*. No more than space is made of simultaneous points in themselves, is the communicative world a bundle of parallel consciousness. Our traces mix and intermingle in the process making a single wake of "public durations." The field of existence is identical with the field of language and eventually, one suspects, with the field of history.

This convergence is precisely what makes "West Running Brook" such a crucial poem in Frost's poetic development. The exercise is a logical extension of the problems confronted earlier in "Vantage Point." Although the poem commences with a wife asking her husband a simple question as to direction, the dialogue quickly becomes a lesson in epistemology:

> 'Fred, where is north?'
> 'North? North is there, my love.
> The brook runs west.'
> 'West-running Brook then call it.'
> (West-running Brook men call it to this day.).

Every conversation, particularly those centering about the problems of perspective, always involves history. There is the assumption that although the name of the brook would seem to imply its function as a range finder within the larger context of history, the confession of its having been misnamed indicates that even geological history is itself the victim of human perspective—as much as husband and wife are. Frost's landscapes, which had earlier provided the setting for a drama of alien entanglements, have now become a participant in a strange numbers game—a victim of the multiplication of perceptible being:

> 'We must be something.
> We've said we two. Let's change that to we three.
> As you and I are married to each other,
> We'll both be married to the brook. . . .'

And, in waving to the human pair, it becomes the specular image of their own imaginative ability to transform the scene. There are indications from Frost's early letters that this mirroring is a first step along the road to redemption and, just as significantly, a different road from that on which he commenced the journey. As with everything else in Frost's native land, he no sooner arrives at a terminus, at some end of the journey, than such an ontological gesture becomes an illusion. Even in early correspondence a proliferation of roads or selves is the only solution to egoistic nominalism. In one of these letters, Frost describes meeting a stranger at an intersection of two lonely crossroads:

I felt as if I was going to meet my own image in a slanting mirror. Or say I felt as we slowly converged on the same point with the same noiseless yet laborious strides as if we were two images about to float together with the uncrossing of someone's eyes. I verily expected to take up or absorb this other self and feel the stronger by the addition for the three-mile journey home. But I didn't go forward to the touch. I stood still and let him pass by.[7]

Frost has come to realize that the success of his pilgrimage, which would presumably be terminated when geographic "place" and personal "place" are identities, may be brought about only by a paradoxical refusal to proceed on the trial by existence. The direction is rather backward, to an undifferentiated unity.

> It has this throwing backward on itself
> So that the fall of most of it is always
> Raising a little, sending up a little.

The first symptom of this reconstituted "world" is a displacement of pronouns, a kind of poetic Stengelese, that blurs all distinctions between natural and human:

> It is from this backward motion toward the source
> Against the stream, that most we see ourselves in,
> The tribute of the current to the source.
> It is from this in nature we are from.
> It is most us.

As if to cross "it" and "us" even more completely, the poet discovers that his own name may be equally applied to the natural scene where its glaze reflects hidden meanings, rather than continuing to discovery: "the lurking frost that steals forth at sunset." It is this sudden reversal of the questing ego that characterizes the poems of *West Running Brook,* where the dissolution of identity is accompanied by a dissolution of the sense of place. Whereas the poems of the early volumes were blatantly geographic, as is reflected in the titles, these locations become but metaphors in Frost's more mature work. New Hampshire is transformed from a place with human products to a set of human attitudes. One of the implications of the title poem is precisely that language and perspective are a priori conditions of geographic identity—that a misplaced attitude led to the misnaming of a brook. This reversal, which amounts to no less than a renunciation of self, a violation of what Frost calls the "native simile," is the only way to shift the "pairing" from self and other to self and its reflection:

In going from room to room in the dark,
I reached out blindly to save my face,
But neglected, however lightly, to lace
My fingers and close my arms in an arc.
A slim door got in past my guard,
And hit me a blow in the head so hard
I had my native simile jarred.
So people and things don't pair any more
With what they used to pair with before.
                    ("The Door in the Dark")

The notion of a Fall that links the seasonal threat of the earth with man's own test of faith is also slightly transposed during the course of Frost's poetic development. For as long as an imagination quests for Paradise, the primal scene remains just out of reach. Man has failed to locate Eden either indoors, defensively, or outdoors by an analogical correspondence. Only the realization that his very search is but part of a drama, and hence necessitates role playing, can ever bring man near to Eden. This self-consciousness alone is sufficient to bring about a redemption and, paradoxically, insure the failure of winter assaults. The problem, of course, is that it is as difficult to keep the drama going as it had been to keep the quest going; such nobility requires a constant shift of roles, as Frost's Masques reveal. A different concept of identity, with a corollary attenuation of New England "sincerity," is one of the consequences. Nature can employ many various masks; in order to avoid the reduction to silence, Frost is forced to change stances. Perhaps his remark after watching an All-Star Game in Washington, D.C., is most revelant: "One of the hardest things to accept as just is a called third strike." His own landscape is filled both with those who have been caught looking at one down the pipe and those like Johnny Temple who grow old fouling them off a choked bat in that "little gem of a field," Griffith Park:

Here come real stars to fill the skies,
And here on earth come emulating flies,

That though they never equal stars in size,
(And they were never really stars at heart)
Achieve at times a very star-like start.
Only, of course, they can't sustain the part.
                        ("Fireflies in the Garden")

Although Robert Frost makes substantial use of the myth of
the Fall, incorporating, as we have seen, temples, chalices, and
serpents as part of the equipment of Paradise, the reader must
be wary of ascribing the traditional associations of the pastoral
mode. Unlike the familiar pattern, most of Frost's participants
know from the outset that the Fall will be fortunate in a double
sense: that renewal always accompanies spring and, second,
that the particular delimiting environment widens out so that
this vast multiplication of perceptible being is accompanied by
an infinitely wider range of choices. Insofar as the characters are
cognizant of both infinite repetition and infinite choice, they
assume mythological roles rather than live mythologically. The
difficulty with regarding Frost's poetic figures as variants on the
old tradition of the American Adam is that they more nearly
belong to the context of Books XI and XII of *Paradise Lost*
than Book V. Not unlike the Adam who, once having been instructed in history by the angel, is capable of adapting his
behavior to an ontology that will guarantee salvation, Frost's
"figures" must "learn" the history of New England in order to
shape their future. The expulsion from regional paradise is completed with the paradoxical notion of learned futurity. It is in
this light that the notion of rebirth and initiation that R. W. B.
Lewis, among others, has found so central to the American
"experience" may warrant some redefinition. Without discussing in detail Frost's adaptation of the pastoral, the reader discerns that his application of the mode often substitutes arcane
formulations for metaphysics, so that we are exposed not so
much to the wise natural man, but to the carnival clairvoyant
spouting cracker-box philosophy. The attendant high degree of
self-consciousness often precludes the required innocence of
Adamic man who, in one sense, created the world as he named

it. The subtle shift in perspective is as significant as the movement from *Moby Dick* to *The Confidence Man;* the concentration on self-reflection means that Frost now pretends to be exploring, when in effect he is justifying. Sadly, many of the critics who admire Frost do so because they envision his "pastoral" drama as part of the universality of the human dilemma, rather than the particular transformations wrought by an imagination that uses familiar symbols in a bizarre game that is often contingent rather than universal.

More often than not, Frost's rural settings are psychological projections. Every detail is accountable point for point to a psychic conflict in a poem like "A Servant to Servants." The result of this psychologizing of space is that the persona's role conflicts with either the real or assumed autonomy of the pastoral. One of the most common features of the mode is the expectation of interruption by love, regained identity, or some external force. Since this landscape is in one sense the victim of an a priori interruption, we are never exposed to Eden, but only the illusion of exposure. This point could be accentuated by noting the relative lack of urban centers in Frost's landscapes. Unlike the pastorals of Blake with its Golgonooza or Auden's "Centers of collective consciousness," Frost's would appear to have lost its constitutive center, and with it a certain *telos.* Consequently, closer scrutiny reveals that many of the so-called "deep questions" in Frost's poetry are nonquestions simply because the poetic voice has become a metaphor, as Frost himself realized, moving through the clichés of an American poetic tradition.

"Directive," a poem included in *Steeple Bush* (1947), is a perfect example of Frost's use of the trappings of the pastoral mode, so often swallowed as genuine by his readers. The overriding theme of the poem is the necessity for loss, directed by a speaker who summons his reader to regress

> Back in a time made simple by the loss
> Of detail, burned, dissolved, and broken off
> Like graveyard marble sculpture in the weather . . .

The speaker warns us that the locale of this retreat has lost all identity, except insofar as it has relevance to the needs of the pilgrims. Yet, a further reading of the poem reveals that the "loss" is a function not so much of the effects of time, but of space, and hence the particular perspective of the viewer:

> The height of the adventure is the height
> Of country where two village cultures faded
> Into each other. Both of them are lost.

On all such interior journeys we are tempted, as was the Frost of the early volumes, to regard our experience as exclusive—to "put a sign up CLOSED to all but me," while making our circle of enchantment and defending our sense of selfhood. But the discussion of the "children's house of make believe," which occupies such a substantial part of the poem, makes the speaker's sincerity, artificially reinforced by a "confessional" tone, quite false. For the children's abode was, to them at least, not a playhouse, but a real house, just as this village, now a plaything of the poetic imagination, was once "a house in earnest." This trip, which had as its purpose the discovery of "a time made simple," nevertheless reaches the height of its adventure at the point of the blending of identities. The loss and purification which had been an object of the quest are possible only by a transposition to art:

> Make yourself up a cheering song of how
> Someone's road home from work this once was,
> Who may be just ahead of your foot.

Even the waters of ablution reside in but another plaything, a child's toy made into a chalice. The poem is precisely such a work of art, a strange plaything whose high adventure depends upon loss and subsequent translation, but not discovery. The very directive "Drink and be whole again beyond confusion" is impossible if the adventure or the "song" is to continue. In the largest sense the poem itself is a justification for the construction of playthings upon playthings which is the sole "answer" to the directive. As long as the poetic voice can utter the phrase "I like to think I am in everything," as Frost does in "The White-Tailed Hornet," there can never be a genuine redemption, but only a redemption from cliché.

One suspects that this characteristic of Frost's art accounts for its unique charm and appeal to a particularly exclusive, though vociferous, audience. The stylistic traits are remarkably similar to those exhibited in the visual art of Andrew Wyeth. The comparison is noteworthy insofar as both artists are remarkably national in their appeal. The late President Kennedy, in his attempts to imbue American life with a sense of its own artistic consciousness, doubtlessly realized the similarity of styles when he invited both men to grace the same White House functions. And there is evidence, in Wyeth's assertion that "Robert Frost strikes people the same way [as my own art]," [8] that both men were well aware of certain shared qualities. Like Wyeth, Frost concentrates on tone rather than hue, leading to a constant mutedness of aesthetic statement. Yet, in spite of the subtlety of tone, Wyeth's lines are edged—an innovation that sets up a remarkable paradox for the viewer. The "magically real" sensation that we receive upon viewing the best of Wyeth, like his 1963 tempera *Adam,* is largely attributable to a dry quality that stems from reduction. To borrow the categories of Wölfflin, both Frost and Wyeth are linear rather than painterly. And in the art of both men there is a kind of airlessness that redeems the art on one hand and the poetry on the other, by just deflecting them from illustration. It is this strange quality that keeps Wyeth's art from degenerating into something resembling the work of, say, a Norman Rockwell. The painting *Distant Thunder,* which depicts a young person and a dog on a gently sloping hillock, approaches the condition of a quaint illustration for a children's book. The dog's response to the thunder which interrupts the sunlit landscape, the cloudless sky, the uniformly brown tone, and youthful sleep creates a false sense of identification between the viewer and the only human figure, both of whom are excluded from audioinitiation. The too pleasant prospect that both viewer and character share—a monotonous, uniform scene created by the painter—will be interrupted, for the monotony of a sunny day contains its own potential for violence. Paradoxically, it is this very sense of false identification that keeps Wyeth above a false sentimentality.

One might usefully compare Frost's "Stopping by Woods on a Snowy Evening" to note a similar approach to a theme that bores by its conventionality. A sense of identification between the reader and the traveler is maintained throughout the poem, since both participate in a common tone, a whiteness that lulls the pace. Not unlike the dog in *Distant Thunder*, Frost's horse is aware of an inclemency unknown to the human protagonist. Just as Wyeth's edged lines create the illusion of spectator participation, so the repetition in the famous lines "And miles to go before I sleep, / And miles to go before I sleep" serve to shift the antecedent of "I" from the narrator of the poem to its reader, who similarly concludes his reading of the poem at the same time that the narrator is lulled into silence. The poem commences with a statement of assumed possession that is a function of identity: "Whose woods these are I think I know" only to reach doubts that necessitate repeated lines. And, if Wyeth's charm stems from his departure from the caricature of a Rockwell, the fascination that Frost's "Stopping by Woods on a Snowy Evening" holds for us derives in part from what he has done to a typically Currier and Ives scene.

And the similarities do not cease with either medium or message. A look at *Christina's World*, perhaps Wyeth's most popular canvas, reveals a mowed "circle of enchantment" near the center of the prospect, from which Christina has been exiled. The path of the broken-down wagon, once the sole escape from the bit of American Gothic in the background, is now overgrown with weeds, cutting off the ruts which link inside and outside. This **structural** organization is heightened, of course, by the arthritic Christina Olson, whose contorted limbs give her a strange participation in a landscape that approaches allegory as a limit. One is reminded of the numerous emotionally maimed or physically disabled figures who populate Frost's "world"—hired hands, boys who lose their hands to modernity, or witches of Cöos. Often the characters of Frost's first five volumes, like Wyeth's figures who turn their backs to us, are faceless inhabitants of chambered nautili which they alone construct.

Strangely, Frost's favorite among Wyeth's paintings, *Wind from the Sea*, which, with its eerie lift of curtains into a decrepit room, could almost have been an illustration for "To the Thawing Wind," seems to have been abandoned in the later Wyeth for the thematics of *Her Room* (1963). On the doorknob of the entrance to the chamber there is a dimly reflected self-portrait of the painter. Like the later volumes of Robert Frost, Andrew Wyeth of late seems to be working with the notion that vantage point, and hence reflection, is always at issue in every initiation.

In many respects, the poem "The Lockless Door," which Frost placed near the end of *New Hampshire* (1923), begins to suggest the new freedom. The door behind which the poetic voice has sought refuge is without a lock:

> Back over the sill
> I bade a 'Come in'
> To whatever the knock
> At the door may have been.
> So at a knock
> I emptied my cage
> To hide in the world
> And alter with age.

Rather than defending himself against the variability of nature, as he had done earlier, Frost in effect widens the "circle of enchantment" so as to almost extinguish its boundaries, or at least transform its privacy into public "zones." Although the poems often commence with the typically Frostian architectonics featured by "inside" and "outside," the imagination always attempts to remove itself, initially by a recognition of pluralism:

> We sit indoors and talk of the cold outside
> And every gust that gathers strength and heaves
> Is a threat to the house.
>
> ("There Are Roughly Zones")

A closer reading of the poem reveals that the very vulnerability of humans and human institutions stems from man's desire to obliterate his own self-imposed limitations. In this particular poem, man escapes his own "circle" only by settling ever nearer to another "circle:" "You would say his ambition was to extend the reach / Clear to the Arctic of every living kind."

His realization of the proliferation of circles of enchantment, while it would seem to reduce alienation, actually increases the awareness of it. For the imagination is introduced to an additional uncertainty. In its heightened self-consciousness, the imagination reflects upon its prereflective consciousness of something else. The self (or ego) of which I become conscious is not the subject performing this act of reflection, but its intentional object which has emerged in retrospect from the prereflective consciousness that it reflects upon. The intentional relationship of consciousness to its object cannot be relaxed in favor of self-consciousness or reversed by reflection's "turning back" and converted into the "centripetal" relationship to a subject:

> He thought he kept the universe alone;
> For all the voice in answer he could wake
> Was but the mocking echo of his own
> From some tree-hidden cliff across the lake.
>
> ("The Most of It")

The search for "counter-love" or "original response" is doomed to failure because self-consciousness is attempting to obscure the merely derivative status of the self by a fraudulent search. One can be exposed only to an "embodiment." Neither the centrifugal movement toward "zones" nor the centripetal relationship to a subject, that would place Frost in an idealistic camp, suffices: "We dance round in a ring and suppose, / But the Secret sits in the middle and knows" ("The Secret Sits").

The final volume, *In the Clearing* (1962), is the logical extension of the poetic geometry that we have been exploring in the present essay. To understand its place in Robert Frost's poetic development is to understand some of the reasons for the keen disappointment felt by his admirers upon its publication. Frost had begun his poetry, it is recalled, with a pictorial gesture traditional to nineteenth-century American water-colorists. He had beckoned the reader to come along on a voyage to clean the pasture spring just as men like Ralph Earle had stood in the foreground of their landscapes, pointing to the tarn in the somewhat darker background as an invitation to a hesitant reader. We had commenced the journey with attempting to define *A Boy's Will*, which led us into *A Further Range* (1936) only to find that our "new Jerusalem" was but a "clearing." In his last volume, the poetic self has moved into the periphery, where legend has it that fairies and elves dance about in a ring. If the frontispiece of the volume begins with a celebration of God's descent into flesh, the "charge . . . Of the soul's ethereal / Into the material," it concludes with the poetic self having become ethereal:

> So the picture's caught
> Almost next to naught
> But the force of thought.

In "A Cabin in the Clearing" Frost reduplicates the geography of the entire volume in the dialogue of "Mist" and "Smoke":

> Mist
> I don't believe the sleepers in this house
> Know where they are.
>
> Smoke
> They've been here long enough

To push the woods back from around the house
And part them in the middle with a path.

Mist
And still I doubt if they know where they are.
And I begin to fear they never will
All they maintain the path for is the comfort
Of visiting with the equally bewildered.
Nearer in plight their neighbors are than distance.

Like the inhabitants of this last volume, Frost's "self" has lost its
way in the clearing of its own creation. The bewilderment of
which Frost's readers are so painfully aware is now part of the
self-conscious decorum of his characters. The "debate" between
the "guardian wraith of starlit smoke" and the "damper counterpart of smoke" is a matter of vantage point and perspective,
an enlargement of a technique that Frost had used to advantage
in *A Further Range*. There, he had entitled a group of poems
"Taken Doubly" and had given each poem a double title, as if
to accentuate the mode of approaching allegory as a limit. Typically, one title was used to describe the central figure in each
poem, and the second title a mixture of folk wisdom that seeks
to interpret the doings of that figure: for example "The Gold
Hesperides" is doubly titled "or How to Take a Loss." Structurally, these poems would seem to imply that every either/or
situation is a victim of language, and insofar as this language is
made universal, individual identity is prey to a diffuseness. This
theme is taken up again in "A Cabin in the Clearing," where, in
spite of their knowledge of "the native tongue," which would
presumably insure both identity and, simultaneously, sense of
place, the figures are among the lost:

Smoke
If the day ever comes when they know who
They are, they may know better where they are.
But who they are is too much to believe—
Either for them or the onlooking world.
They are too sudden to be credible.

Although geography continues to be dependent upon identity in Frost's egoistic nominalism, the lack of both reinforces the diffuseness. The return to this pattern is reminiscent of the *fin-de-siècle* mood of *A Boy's Will*. In moving to the circumference of his circle of enchantment, Frost is no nearer to either identity or discovery. As if to accentuate this somewhat painful conclusion to his pilgrimage, Frost's metaphysic is decisively circular. Even America herself, which has been, at least loosely, the subject of much of Frost's poetry, seems to exemplify the difficulty.

> America is hard to see.
> Less partial witnesses than he
> In book on book have testified
> They could not see it from outside—
> Or inside either for that matter.
> We know the literary chatter.
> ("America Is Hard To See")

And, strangely enough, Frost's last volume tends to replace the dialogue of inner and outer with a type of "literary chatter." It is almost as if Frost were using a folk logorrhea to ward off the confusion of alien entanglements. In the poem written for John F. Kennedy on his inauguration, "Gift Outright of 'The Gift Outright,'" Frost had advocated "Less criticism of the field and court / And more preoccupation with the sport." This tending to "sport," to play the part of an antidivine jokester, is Frost's assumed metaphorical stance while *In the Clearing*. Specifically, in a poem like "Auspex" Frost returns to his childhood in the California Sierra for an event that should have had dire consequences: the attack upon his person by "a great eagle bird in all its terror." His Protestant parents attempted to read into the event divine rejection, presumably to quiet the boy's fears. In effect, they allegorized a common natural event to prove the virtues of submission to Jove's mastery. The result, the narrator seems to imply, is a reduction, a limitation of being:

> I have remained resentful to this day
> When any but myself presumed to say
> That there was anything I couldn't be.

The words could just as well have been addressed to Frost's "darker" readers who presume to limit his being by imposing some external, tightly allegorical readings on natural occurrence. A willful expansion or contraction of selfhood means that allegorical boundaries, like so many of Frost's other boundaries, are continually violated.

> It is right in there
> Betwixt and between
> The orchard bare
> And the orchard green,
>
> When the orchard's right
> In a flowery burst
> Of all that's white,
> That we fear the worst.
>
> For there's not a clime
> But at any cost
> Will take that time
> For a night of frost.
>   ("Peril of Hope")

This diaphanous notion of selfhood is, of course, a divine imposition of sorts. In establishing himself as the eternal questioner, Frost resorts to the ever-present disguises of the riddle maker who, if he does not utter "I am that I am," comes very close in his last volume to a manner resembling that of Ogden Nash. Often the target of these utterances is Frost's earlier verse, as in "The Draft Horse," so strangely reminiscent of "Stopping by Woods on a Snowy Evening." Here, the speaker moves "Behind too heavy a horse / Through a pitch-dark limitless grove." But the beast, rather than recognizing the "other" with a shake of his head, is killed, leaving the rider and his "double" to their own devices. No longer is the Frostian landscape one in which reader and speaker move in and out; it is rather a universe of infinite regress where every object has its shadow and hierarchy is meaningless:

> We assumed that the man himself
> Or someone he had to obey
> Wanted us to get down
> And walk the rest of the way.

It is absolutely necessary that these lines strike us as they do: the somewhat artificial coda to a poem. For just as the universe is tautologous, so the poetic universe, its reflection, is a riddle. Frost's last volume raises the whole question of parody as an essential element of his accomplishment. Even within the same volume, poems like "Auspex" and "Reflex" appear as mutually parodic, making a mockery of the "sincerity" that is the thematic concern of both. If the inhabitants of this landscape still construct defensive fortresses, they parody those of *A Boy's Will* with walls of mirrored glass rather than stone:

> The winter owl banked just in time to pass
> And save herself from breaking window glass
> And her wings straining suddenly aspread
> Caught color from the last of evening red
> In a display of underdown and quill
> To glassed-in children at the window sill.
> ("Questioning Faces")

All that we can ever be saved from is our own reflection. Just as the oracular riddle repeats itself, Frost's universe has come full circle:

> The Universe is but the thing of things,
> The things but balls all going round in rings,
> Some of them mighty huge, some mighty tiny,
> All of them radiant and mighty shiny.
> ("Accidentally on Purpose")

All of this, of course, raises the incessant question of

Frost's modernity. The failure to communicate except by means of the reflexive riddle and the multiplication of "selves" to combat a Nature that divides "within her inmost self" ("From Iron") make Frost a poet nearer to Wallace Stevens than to Robert Lowell. Although "in and outdoor schooling" is still necessary to comprehend Frost's fooling, one has the suspicion that the joke was his way of being in both places simultaneously:

I have written to keep the over curious out of the secret places of my mind both in my verse and in my letters to such as you. A subject has to be held clear outside of me with struts and as it were set up for an object. A subject must be an object. There's no use in laboring this further years [sic].[9]

Frost's statement that he wrote to clear up some confusion in his mind, as "a way out of something," would suggest that the poetic act was inextricably involved in the whole question of solipsism. The entire problem that had occupied Robert Frost from his earliest volume, as we have seen, was the relationship between identity and geographic place. And Frost's solution from the imprisonment of either is a metaphoric circle of art where, now, even words are part of the arc:

I like to say, guardedly, that I could define poetry this way: It is that which is lost out of both prose and verse in translation. That means something in the way the words are curved.[10]

All that is worth writing about, when subject and object have been made interchangeable, is that process by which maker and made have mutually reinforcing roles. The very fact that so many commentators commence their discussion of Frost with the poetry and conclude with a discussion of the man is a remarkable index to the extent to which Frost has become a participant in his art.

The favorable response of the same young readers who enjoy Allen Ginsberg and Charles Olson to a poem like "Design" would suggest either the enormous poetic powers of Frost or the likelihood that he is being misread. And one suspects that Frost's charm derives from a unique mixture of both; after all, the distance separating the circularity of the poetic riddle which concludes with an ellipsis from the intentionality of projective verse is not great. In that "global village" where the only hope for humanization is man's effort to extend the self beyond its temporal and spatial barriers, perhaps all poetic utterance will be identical with human utterance, complete with those interstices that fill our everyday thoughts. If so, the whiteness that characterizes our margins as well as our marginal types becomes part of the ontology of poetic discourse. Preserving our mental Edens becomes a question of two alternatives: the circular tautology or the rapture of silence. On that January 20, 1961, when an aged Frost appeared at the Presidential inauguration of a true New Englander, the bright Washington sunshine burst through a cold day, much as the light glistens through the thawing verse of *In the Clearing*. The result was "a temporary blindness," as Frost lost his way while reading "The Gift Outright." Now in his life, as previously in his art, an embarrassing silence greeted the commencement of a New Frontier; at last, the poetic self had become a participant in the Dangling Conversation that was to be a memorial to the performance of both.

NOTES

Unless otherwise noted, all citations from the poetry of Robert Frost are taken from *The Collected Poems of Robert Frost* (New York, 1949), published by Holt, Rinehart and Winston, or *In the Clearing* (New York, 1962), also published by Holt, Rinehart and Winston. I wish to acknowledge with thanks suggestions offered by my colleagues, Martin Pops and Murray Schwartz, who read portions of the present essay in manuscript.

1. *Selected Prose of Robert Frost*, ed. H. Cox and C. Lathem (New York, 1966), p. 18.

2. *Ibid.*, p. 25.

3. Cited by Lawrance Thompson in *Robert Frost: The Early Years* (New York, 1966), p. 102.

4. See Frost's "On Emerson" in Cox and Lathem: "Another poem could be made from that, to the effect that ideally in thought only is a

circle round. In practice, in nature, the circle becomes an oval" (p. 118). Although space considerations did not allow an explanation of this distortion, Frost's last two volumes seem to be preoccupied with the circumscription of two geographic centers, good and evil, so that the metaphoric circle does indeed elongate into the oval.

5. *Selected Letters of Robert Frost,* ed. Lawrance Thompson (New York, 1966), p. 427.

6. Cox and Lathem, pp. 13–14.

7. *Selected Letters,* p. 45.

8. See the interview by E. P. Richardson, "Andrew Wyeth," in *Atlantic,* CCXIII (June 1964), 68.

9. *Selected Letters,* p. 385.

10. *Interviews with Robert Frost,* ed. Connery Lathem (New York, 1966), p. 203.

Wallace Stevens' Poetry of Being

BY J. HILLIS MILLER

We were as Danes in Denmark all day long
And knew each other well, hale-hearted landsmen,
For whom the outlandish was another day

Of the week, queerer than Sunday. We thought alike
And that made brothers of us in a home
In which we fed on being brothers, fed

And fattened as on a decorous honeycomb.*

There was once a time when man lived in harmony with his
fellows and his surroundings. This harmony was a unified culture, a single view of the world. All men thought alike and
understood each other perfectly, like the most intimate of
brothers. Since they all shared an interpretation of the world,
they did not think of it as one perspective among many possible
ones. Any other interpretation was queer, outlandish, something
wild, ignorant, barbarian. Each man felt at home. He was a
Dane in Denmark, not a Dane in Greece or Patagonia. Just as
he possessed his fellows in the brotherhood of a single culture,
so he possessed nature through their collective interpretation of
it. He was a landsman, an inlander, someone dwelling close
to the earth. Since man, society, and environment made one
inextricable unity, as of Danes in Denmark, no one was aware
of himself as a separate mind. Each man was like the bee in the
honeycomb, the dwelling place which he has exuded from his
own body and which now forms his food. All self-consciousness

* *The Collected Poems of Wallace Stevens* (New York, 1954), p. 419.
This volume will hereafter be cited as CP. Other abbreviated sources in
this essay: Wallace Stevens, *Opus Posthumous* (New York, 1957),
cited as OP, and *The Necessary Angel: Essays on Reality and the
Imagination* (New York, 1951), cited as NA.

was lost in this reflexive feeding and fattening, and man "lay sticky with sleep" (CP, 419).

So enduring and beneficent did this order seem that it was impossible to believe that man himself could have made it. Surely, we thought, our happy world must be the gift of some supernatural beings, and these gods must guarantee its rightness and permanence. They seemed outside of or beyond our world, "speechless, invisible" (CP, 262). They ruled us and sustained us "by / Our merest apprehension of their will" (CP, 262). Our culture was revelation of the invisible and speech of the speechless gods.

Suddenly something catastrophic happened, and all our happy order was destroyed:

> A tempest cracked on the theatre. Quickly,
> The wind beat in the roof and half the walls.
> The ruin stood still in an external world.
>
> . . . . .
>
> It had been real. It was not now. The rip
> Of the wind and the glittering were real now,
> In the spectacle of a new reality. (CP, 306)

Once the theater is destroyed it can never be rebuilt. The fact that it can be destroyed proves that even when it existed it was not what it seemed. It seemed a divine gift, something as solid as the earth itself. Now man discovers that all along it was a painted scene. The true reality has always been the wind and the indifferent glittering of an external world—a world in which man can never feel at home.

When the tempest cracks on the theater the whole thing disintegrates: "Exit the whole / Shebang" (CP, 37). Men are no longer brothers, but strange to one another. The land withdraws to a distance and comes to be seen as no longer included in man's interpretations of it. When nature becomes outlandish, the gods disappear. They do not withdraw for a time to an unattainable distance, as they did for De Quincey or Matthew

Arnold. They vanish altogether, leaving nothing behind. They reveal themselves to be fictions, aesthetic projections of man's gratuitous values. Having seen the gods of one culture disappear, man can never again believe in any god: "The death of one god is the death of all" (CP, 381; see also OP, 165).

This evaporation of the gods, leaving a barren man in a barren land, is the basis of all Stevens' thought and poetry. The death of the gods coincides with a radical transformation in the way man sees the world. What had been a warm home takes on a look of hardness and emptiness, like the walls, floors, and banisters of a vacant house. Instead of being intimately possessed by man, things appear to close themselves within themselves. They become mute, static presences:

To see the gods dispelled in mid-air and dissolve like clouds is one of the great human experiences. It is not as if they had gone over the horizon to disappear for a time; nor as if they had been overcome by other gods of greater power and profounder knowledge. It is simply that they came to nothing. Since we have always shared all things with them and have always had a part of their strength and, certainly, all of their knowledge, we shared likewise this experience of annihilation. It was their annihilation, not ours, and yet it left us feeling that in a measure, we, too, had been annihilated. It left us feeling dispossessed and alone in a solitude, like children without parents, in a home that seemed deserted, in which the amical rooms and halls had taken on a look of hardness and emptiness. What was most extraordinary is that they left no mementoes behind, no thrones, no mystic rings, no texts either of the soil or of the soul. It was as if they had never inhabited the earth. There was no crying out for their return.   (OP, 206, 207)

There was no crying out for their return because we knew they would never come back. They would never come back because they had never been there at all.

In this impoverishing of the world when the gods disappear, man discovers himself, orphaned and dispossessed, a solitary consciousness. Then are we truly "natives of poverty, children of malheur" (CP, 322). The moment of self-awareness in Stevens coincides with the moment of the death of the gods. God is dead, therefore I am. But I am nothing. I am nothing because I have nothing, nothing but awareness of the barrenness within and without. When the gods dissolve like clouds, they "come to nothing." When the gods come to nothing, man is "nothing himself," and, since this is so, he "beholds / Nothing that is not there and the nothing that is" (CP, 10).

After the death of the gods and the discovery of nothingness, Stevens is left in a world made of two elements: subject and object, mind and matter, imagination and reality. Imagination is the inner nothingness, while reality is the barren external world with which imagination carries on its endless intercourse. Stevens' problem is to reconcile the two. But such a reconciliation turns out to be impossible. This way and that vibrates his thought, seeking to absorb imagination by reality, to engulf reality in imagination, or to marry them in metaphor. Nothing will suffice, and Stevens is driven to search on tirelessly for some escape from conflict. This endless seeking is the motive and life of his poetry. The human self, for him, is divided against itself. One part is committed to the brute substance of earth, things as they are, and the other just as tenaciously holds to its need for imaginative grandeur. Self-division, contradiction, perpetual oscillation of thought—these are the constants in Stevens' work. Is it possible, as some critics have thought, that he is just confused? Is it from mere absence of mind that he affirms on one page of his "Adagia" that reality is the only genius (OP, 177), only to reverse himself two pages later and declare just as categorically that imagination is the only genius (OP, 179)?

The critic can develop radically different notions of Stevens' aims as a poet, and for each of these it is easy to find apposite passages from the text. It can be shown that Stevens believes poetry is metaphor, and that he believes all metaphors are factitious. At times he is unequivocally committed to bare reality. At other times he repudiates reality and sings the praises of imagination. Nor is it just a question of contradictions in the logical statements of the prose which are reconciled in the poetry. For each position and for its antithesis there are fully elaborated poems or parts of poems. It is impossible to find a single one-dimensional theory of poetry and life in Stevens. His poetry defines a realm in which everything "is not what it is" (OP, 178). Such poetry is not dialectical, if that means a series of stages which build on one another, each transcending the last and moving on to a higher stage, in some version of the Hegelian sequence of thesis, antithesis, synthesis. At the beginning Stevens is already as far as he ever goes. After the disappearance of the gods, the poet finds himself in a place where opposites are simultaneously true. It seems that this situation can be dealt with in poetry only by a succession of wild swings to one extreme or another, giving first one limit of the truth, then the other. To escape such oscillation Stevens must find a way to write poetry that will possess simultaneously both extremes.

The elaboration of such a mode of poetry is Stevens' chief contribution to literature. In the meditative poems of his later years he takes possession of a new domain. The finished unity of his early poems, which makes many of them seem like elaborately wrought pieces of jewelry, is gradually replaced by poems which are open-ended improvisations. Such poems are not a neat enclosure of words forming a complex organic unity. They begin in the middle of a thought, and their ending is arbitrary. "The Man with the Blue Guitar" has a special place in Stevens' canon. It marks his turning to the new style. The reader has the feeling that the poem has been going on for some time when he hears the first words, and the last verses are not really an ending. The twanging of the strings continues interminably. Such a poem could be endless, and indeed three more "Stanzas for 'The Man with the Blue Guitar'" are given in *Opus Posthumous* (72, 73). The man with the guitar is described in "An Ordinary Evening in New Haven" as a permanent presence, someone always there in the mind's eye, watching the poet, and reminding him of his obligation to a faithful thinking of things as they are (CP, 483).

Life, for Stevens, is a series of states of consciousness with neither start nor finish. If the poem is to be true to life it must be a constant flowing of images which come as they come and are not distorted by the logical mind in its eagerness for order. "One's grand flights," says Stevens, "one's Sunday baths, / One's tootings at the weddings of the soul/ Occur as they occur" (CP, 222). Just as "The Man with the Blue Guitar" refuses to round itself off formally with beginning, middle, and end, so the parts which are given do not organize themselves into a whole, or even into part of a whole. There is no coherent pattern of symbols and metaphors, each one referring to all the others. One metaphor or symbol is introduced, developed for a while, then dropped. Another motif appears, is developed in its turn, disappears, is replaced by another which has no connection with the other two, and so on. "The Man with the Blue Guitar" proceeds in a series of disconnected short flights, each persisting for only a brief span of time. Each short flight, while it lasts, is like a "half-arc hanging in mid-air / Composed, appropriate to the incomplete" (CP, 309).

The same thing is true of Stevens' other long poems, "Esthétique du Mal," or "Notes toward a Supreme Fiction," or "An Ordinary Evening in New Haven." These poems keep close to the quality of life as it is. Such poems, like life, proceed in a series of momentary crystallizations or globulations of thought, followed by dissolution, and then reconglomeration in another form. "Thought," says Stevens, "tends to collect in pools" (OP, 170). A man's mental energy tends to organize itself momentarily in a certain shape, but life flows on, and a new pattern is called for. The mind has a powerful resistance to doing the same thing twice, and "originality is an escape from repetition" (OP, 177). "As a man becomes familiar with his own poetry," says Stevens, "it becomes as obsolete for himself as for anyone else. From this it follows that one of the motives in writing is renewal" (OP, 220). Stevens always emphasizes the evanescence of poetry. Poetry is like a snowflake fluttering through the air and dissolving in the sea. It is radically bound to a time experienced as a sequence of present moments, each real and valid only so long as it is present. "Poetry," says Stevens, "is a finikin thing of air / That lives uncertainly and not for long" (CP, 155). In the "Adagia," "Poetry is a pheasant disappearing in the brush" (OP, 173). Most succinctly: "A poem is a meteor" (OP, 158).

This fragmentary quality is evident in Stevens' titles, both those for individual poems and those for books. Each poem by itself, like the whole mass of them together, is a hesitant and uncertain movement toward a goal which is never reached. He calls a poem "Prelude to Objects," or "Asides on the Oboe," or "Extracts from Addresses to the Academy of Fine Ideas," or "Debris of Life and Mind," or "Notes toward a Supreme Fiction," or "Prologues to What is Possible," in each case emphasizing the broken, partial nature of the poem, the way it is a piece of something larger, or is only an indirect and incomplete movement toward its object, something preliminary and unfinished. The titles of his books of poetry suggest the same qualities. The harmonium is a small keyboard organ used in the home. The book of poems called *Harmonium* seems to be a series of improvisations on this amateur's instrument. But Stevens wanted to call his first book "The Grand Poem: Preliminary Minutiae."[1] This title would have been a perfect expression of the nature of all his poems. "Harmonium" too suggests something of this notion of tentative fragments. Stevens may have been remembering this, as well as trying to affirm the unity of his work, when he wanted to call his collected poems *The Whole of Harmonium* (OP, xiv). The titles of his other books are just as tentative: *Ideas of Order, Parts of a World, Transport to*

[1] *Poems by Wallace Stevens*, selected, and with an Introduction by Samuel French Morse. (Vintage Books, 1961), p. viii.

Summer (in which one side of the pun gives the idea of motion in the direction of summer), and *The Auroras of Autumn* (an apt phrase to describe poems which are a flickering continuum of light). Only *The Rock* suggests something final and stable, but that title was affixed after Stevens had attained the ultimate immobility of death. All his poems taken together form a single poem. This poem is a long series of provisional pools of imagery, each drawn toward a goal which can never be named directly or embodied in any poem. Man can never live again in a unified homeland. "We live in a constellation / Of patches and of pitches, / Not in a single world," and we are therefore always "Thinkers without final thoughts / In an always incipient cosmos" (OP, 114, 115).

Within the "endlessly elaborating poem" (CP, 486) which is life, the same sequence of events is constantly happening over and over again. First something happens which "decreates," which destroys an earlier imagination of the world. Then man is left face to face with the bare rock of reality. This happens every year in autumn. When the leaves have all fallen, "we return / To a plain sense of things," and "it is as if / We had come to an end of the imagination" (CP, 502). This clearing away is experienced not as a loss but as a gain. What is removed was a fictive covering of the rock, and what is exposed is the real in all its clarity:

> The barrenness that appears is an exposing.
> It is not part of what is absent, a halt
> For farewells, a sad hanging on for remembrances.
>
> It is a coming on and a coming forth.
> The pines that were fans and fragrances emerge,
> Staked solidly in a gusty grappling with rocks.   (CP, 487)

The autumnal experience of decreation, as of leaves turning brown and falling, gives man a sense of "cold and earliness and bright origin" (CP, 481). It is as if the poet were like the first man facing an "uncreated" world, with everything still to be imagined.

This experience of coldness and earliness is only the start. The poet is not satisfied to confront a bare and unimagined world. He wants to possess it, and it can be possessed only by being imagined well. Man is inhabited by a "will to change" (CP, 397) which is just as unappeasable as his will to see the rock of reality exposed in all its bareness. The experience of decreation is followed by the reconstruction of a new imagination of the world. Spring follows winter, the rock is covered with leaves which are the icon of the poem, and what had been the simplicity of beginning becomes the ornate complexity of the end. The poet moves from "naked Alpha," "the infant A standing on infant legs," to "hierophant Omega," "twisted, stooping, polymathic Z" (CP, 469). If the beginning is bare and simple, the end is multiple and encrusted with color, like an illuminated manuscript, or like a splendid robe of state, "adorned with cryptic stones and sliding shines, . . . / With the whole spirit sparkling in its cloth, / Generations of the imagination piled / In the manner of its stitchings, of its thread" (CP, 434).

No sooner has the mind created a new fictive world than this "recent imagining of reality" (CP, 465) becomes obsolete in its turn and must be rejected. This rejection is the act of decreation and returns man once more to unadorned reality. The cycle then begins again: imagining followed by decreation followed by imagining and so on for as long as life lasts. In this rhythmic alternation lies our only hope to possess reality. Each moment is born in newness and freedom, with no connections to the past. Man must match the ever-renewed freedom of time with an equally radical freedom on his own part, a willed disencumbering of himself of all the corpses of the past. This is the sense in which "all men are murderers" (OP, 168), for "Freedom is like a man who kills himself / Each night, an incessant butcher, whose knife / Grows sharp in blood" (CP, 292), and "All things destroy themselves or are destroyed" (OP, 46). So Stevens cries: "what good were yesterday's devotions?" (CP, 264). This refusal of the past gives him a possession of the present moment in all its instantaneous vitality: "I affirm and then at midnight the great cat / Leaps quickly from the fireside and is gone" (CP, 264).

The present is the great cat who leaps from the fireside and is gone. It can never be seized or held, and it lasts only for the blink of an eye. But if life is a series of such moments, how is it possible to justify even the cycle of decreation followed by a reimagining of reality? This cycle seems to move with a slow and stately turning, like the sequence of the seasons which is so often its image. If the poet pauses long enough to write the poem of winter, it will already be part of the dead past long before he has finished it, and so for the poems of the other seasons. It seems that the poet will make sterile vibrations back and forth between one spiritual season and the other, always a little behind the perpetual flowing of reality.

There is one way to escape this impasse, and the discovery of this way gives its special character to all Stevens' later poetry. He can move so fast from one season to another that all the extreme postures of the spirit are present in a single moment. If he can do this he will never pause long enough at any extreme for it to freeze into dead fixity, and he will appease at last his longing to have both imagination and reality at once. An oscillation rapid enough becomes a blur in which opposites are touched simultaneously, as alternating current produces a steady beam of light; and the cycle of decreation and imagining, hopelessly false if the poet goes through it at leisure, becomes true at last to things as they are if he moves through it fast enough. Each tick of the clock is "the starting point of the human and end" (CP, 528). In "this present" there is a "dazzle-dazzle of being new / And of becoming," "an air of freshness, clearness, greenness, blueness, / That which is always beginning because it is part / Of that which is always beginning, over and over" (CP, 530). The present is always beginning over and over, because it has no sooner begun than it has gone all the way to the end and has moved so rapidly that "this end and this beginning are one" (CP, 506). All the possible elements of experience are always present in every instant of time and in every season or weather of the mind: consciousness in its emptiness detached from reality and seeking it in bare impoverishment, the imagination covering the rock with leaves, flowers, and fruit, the drying and falling of the leaves in autumn.

Stevens' *Collected Poems* moves in a stately round through the whole cycle of the seasons, from the gaudy, springlike poems of *Harmonium,* like new buds on the rock, through *Transport to Summer* and *The Auroras of Autumn,* and then back again to winter's bareness with *The Rock.* Every authentic image, from one end of his poetry to the other, recapitulates this sequence in a breath. In "Notes toward a Supreme Fiction" Stevens says that a true poem allows the reader to share, for a moment, the "first idea." This means having a vision of things in the radiance of their presence, without any intervening film between man and the pure sensation of things as they are. To do this, Stevens says, is to see things in "living changingness" (CP, 380), to go in a moment from the white candor of the beginning in its original freshness to the white candor of the end in its multiplicity of imaginative enhancements. "We move between these points: / From that ever-early candor to its late plural" (CP, 382).

In "The Owl in the Sarcophagus" (CP, 431–436) Stevens gives his fullest dramatization of the way time moves from beginning to end in a moment. The poem is about "the forms of thought," that is, about the universal limits between which human thought moves, and in terms of which man lives, for "we live in the mind." If man lives in the mind, he dies there, too:

It is a child that sings itself to sleep,
The mind, among the creatures that it makes,
The people, those by which it lives and dies. (CP, 436)

Man dies in the mind because the mind, too, is bound by time. This means that it is defined by the fact that it will one day die. Life dwells within death, is constantly coming from and returning to death, as its origin, home, and end. The owl, Minerva, the mind, lives in a sarcophagus, and the poem describes "the mythology of modern death" (CP, 435). It embodies the forces which determine the mind's activity, "the creatures that it makes." These forces are "death's own supremest images, / The purest perfections of parental space, / The children of a desire that is the will, / Even of death, the beings of the mind / In the light-bound space of the mind, the floreate flare . . ." (CP, 436).

Since the figures of the poem live in the perpetual present of mental space, they live "in an element not the heaviness of time" (CP, 432), that is, in "a time / That of itself [stands] still, perennial" (CP, 432). The moment is "less time than place" (CP, 433) because it is outside of time, though it is the only living part of time.

The figures of the mythology of modern death are three: sleep, peace, and "she that says / Good-by in the darkness" (CP, 431). Sleep is the beginning, the radiant candor of pure mind without any content, mind as it is when it faces a bare unimagined reality, or mind as it is when it has completed the work of decreation and is ready "in an ever-changing, calmest unity" (CP, 433) to begin imagining again: "Sleep realized / Was the whiteness that is the ultimate intellect, / A diamond jubilance beyond the fire" (CP, 433).

If sleep is the beginning, peace is the end, "the brother of sleep," "the prince of shither-shade and tinsel lights" (CP, 434). "Peace after death" is the end in the sense that it represents a fulfillment of imagination. Sleep is prior to life, since ultimate intellect cannot even be called consciousness, or is consciousness with no content. Peace is the death at the end of life, the death of a consummation of the imagination. Peace, like sleep, is that death man touches in every moment as he moves all the way from the immaculate beginning to its late plural. Peace is "that figure stationed at our end, / Always in brilliance, fatal, final, formed / Out of our lives to keep us in our death" (CP, 434).

What of the third figure, "she that says good-by"; who is she? She broods over the moment of life, the infinitesimally brief flash between start and finish which is living reality, surrounded on all sides by death. She dwells in what Stevens calls in another poem "the mobile and immobile flickering / In the area between is and was" (CP, 474). This moment, evanescent as it is, is the only reality, and it is only in the moment, a moment which changes and evaporates with the utmost rapidity, that man can glimpse things as they are. Things exist only in the time they are moving from is to was, and the third figure is the embodiment of this presence of the present, a presence which is like that of a glow in molten iron, such a glow as fades even as we watch it.

How is it possible to write poetry which will match the mobility of the moment? It would seem that any image or form of words would be too fixed to move with a time which changes so instantaneously. A poem of any length would be far too long to be a meteor. It would transform the living flow of reality into a clumsy machine wholly unable to keep up with time. Such a poem would be a dead relic of the past long before the reader had reached the last line.

Stevens gradually develops, as his poetry progresses, a way of matching the fluidity of time. He comes to write a poetry of flickering mobility, a poetry in which each phrase moves so rapidly it has beginning and ending at once. Instead of being fixed and unyielding, a solid piece of language interacting with other words, each image recapitulates within itself the coming into being of the moment and its disappearance. The fluctuation between beginning and ending has become so rapid that it takes place in a single phrase, or in a "syllable between life / And death" (CP, 432). Each image in a poem of such phrases is a meteor. "An Ordinary Evening in New Haven," for example, constantly generates itself out of its own annihilation, ending and beginning again indefatigably. It expresses, in its "flickings from finikin to fine finikin," "the edgings and inchings of final form, / The swarming activities of the formulae / Of statement, directly and indirectly getting at" (CP, 488).

At first, after the dissolution of the gods, it seemed that Stevens was left, like post-Cartesian man in general, in a world riven in two, split irreparably into subject and object, imagination and reality. All his work seems based on this dualism. Any attempt to escape it by affirming the priority of one or the other power leads to falsehood. But as his work progresses, Stevens comes more and more to discover that there is after all only one realm, always and everywhere the realm of some new conjunction of imagination and reality. Imagination is still present in the most absolute commitment of the mind to reality, and reality is still there in the wildest imaginary fiction. The later Stevens is beyond metaphysical dualism and beyond representational thinking. In his late poems it is no longer a question of some reality which already exists out there in the world, and of which the poet then makes an image. The image is inextricably part of the thing, and the most extreme imaginative "distortion" is still based on reality. There is only one ever-present existence: consciousness *of* some reality. Imagination is reality, or, as Stevens says: "poetry and reality are one" (NA, 81). In another formulation: "the structure of poetry and the structure of reality are one" (NA, 81). If this is the case, there is no real thing which is transformed into various imaginary aspects. The real thing is already imagined, and "imaginative transcripts" are as much a part of reality as anything else is. "What our eyes behold," says Stevens, "may well be the text of life but one's meditations on the text and the disclosures of these meditations are no less a part of the structure of reality" (NA, 76). As he puts it in the title of a very late poem: "Reality is an activity of the most august imagination" (OP, 110).

This discovery of the identity of all the elements of life means a redefinition of poetry. Words are not pictures of reality. They are part of the thing, tangled inextricably with the event they describe. "The poem is the cry of its occasion, / Part of the res itself and not about it" (CP, 473), and therefore "description is revelation" (CP, 344). Words are the vortex of the whirlpool where imagination and reality merge, for "words of the world are the life of the world" (CP, 474).

This seems to be Stevens' ultimate position: a resolution of imagination and reality in a theory of the identity of poetry and life, and the development of a poetry of flickering mobility to sustain this identity. But there is one more aspect of his thought, and this is the most difficult to see or to say.

It begins with an increasing movement toward nothingness in Stevens' later poetry. Along with the phrases expressing the swarming plenitude of the moment, there is something different. At the same time as its tensions are resolved, Stevens' poetry gets more and more disembodied, more and more a matter of "the spirit's alchemicana," and less and less a matter of the solid and tangible, the pears on their dish, the round peaches with their fuzz and juice. It seems as if the poetry becomes more and more intangible as the oscillations between imagination and reality get more and more rapid, until, at the limit, the poem evaporates altogether. At the extreme of speed all solidity disappears. It is as if the same speed which allows beginning and ending to merge also releases something else: a glimpse of the nothingness which underlies all existence.

The word or the idea of nothingness comes back more and more often. Nothingness appears as early as *Harmonium*, but there it is associated with the bareness of winter. Only the snow man, the man who is "nothing himself," is free of imagination's fictions and can behold "nothing that is not there and the nothing that is." Stevens' later poetry is continuous with this early intuition of nothing, but the theme of nothingness gradually becomes more dominant. In the later poetry nothingness appears to be the source and end of everything and to underlie everything as its present reality. Imagination is nothing. Reality is nothing. The mind is nothing. Words are nothing. God is nothing. Perhaps it is the fact that all these things are equivalent to nothing which makes them all equivalents of one another. All things come together in the nothing. Stevens speaks of "the priest of nothingness who intones" on the rock of reality (OP, 88). In another poem the wind "intones its single emptiness" (CP, 294). He tells of a room "emptier than nothingness" (CP, 286), or of a moon which is "a lustred nothingness" (CP, 320). He asks for a "god in the house" who will be so insubstantial that he will be "a coolness, / A vermilioned nothingness" (CP, 328), and speaks of metaphysical presences which are like "beasts that one never sees, / Moving so that the foot-falls are slight and almost nothing" (CP, 337). Again and again he says that all things, "seen and unseen," are "created from nothingness" (CP, 486; OP, 100), or "forced up from nothing" (CP, 363). The growth of leaves on the rock of reality comes from nothing, "as if," says Stevens, "nothingness contained a métier" (CP, 526). In another poem, the first breath of spring "creates a fresh universe out of nothingness" (CP, 517).

The rock of reality seems not to be a substantial reality, material and present before the poet's eyes. It seems to have come from nothingness. If it has come from nothingness, its source still defines it, and all things dwell in the "stale grandeur of annihilation" (CP, 505). As Stevens says in a striking phrase: "Reality is a vacuum" (OP, 168).

A number of his poems attempt to express the way reality is a vacuum. In such poems "we breathe / An odor evoking nothing, absolute" (CP, 394, 395). "A Clear Day and No Memories" (OP, 113) describes a weather in which "the air is clear of everything," "has no knowledge except of nothingness,"

and "flows over us without meanings" in an "invisible activity."
"Chocorua to Its Neighbor" (CP, 296–302) is an extraordinarily
disembodied poem, the subject of which is a strange shadow,
"an eminence, / But of nothing" (CP, 300). In "The Auroras of
Autumn" a serpent is present everywhere in the landscape, and
yet present as form disappearing into formlessness:

> This is where the serpent lives, the bodiless.
> His head is air. . . .
>
>   ❋   ❋   ❋   ❋   ❋
>
> This is where the serpent lives. This is his nest,
> These fields, these hills, these tinted distances,
> And the pines above and along and beside the sea.
>
> This is form gulping after formlessnesss,
> Skin flashing to wished-for disappearances
> And the serpent body flashing without the skin. (CP, 411)

Such poems accomplish a hollowing out or subtilizing of
reality. They give the reader the feeling of what it is like to see
reality not as a solid substance, but as something less tangible
than the finest mist. They attempt to make visible something
which is "always too heavy for the sense / To seize, the
obscurest as, the distant was" (CP, 441). They are based on the
presupposition that the center of reality is a nothingness which
is "a nakedness, a point, / Beyond which fact could not progress
as fact / . . . Beyond which thought could not progress as
thought" (CP, 402, 403). If it is true that the underlying substance of reality is a vacuum, "the dominant blank, the unapproachable" (CP, 477), we must give up the idea that reality is
a solid rock and see it as a nameless, evanescent flowing, something hovering on the edge of oblivion. "It is not in the premise
that reality / Is a solid," says Stevens in the last words of "An
Ordinary Evening in New Haven." "It may be a shade that
traverses / A dust, a force that traverses a shade" (CP, 489).

If reality is a vacuum, imagination is no less empty. It is the
"nothing" of "Imago" (CP, 439), which lifts all things. Man in

a world where reality is nonentity "has his poverty and nothing more" (CP, 427). Such a man is defined as "desire" and is "always in emptiness that would be filled" (CP, 467).

It seemed that Stevens was moving closer and closer to a full possession of the plenitude of things, but as the tension between imagination and reality diminishes there is an unperceived emptying out of both, until, at the moment they touch, in the brevity of a poem which includes beginning and ending in a breath, the poet finds himself face to face with a universal nothing.

Nevertheless, this apparent defeat is the supreme victory, for the nothing is not nothing. It is. It is being. Being is the universal power, visible nowhere in itself, and yet visible everywhere in all things. It is what all things share through the fact that they are. Being is not a thing like other things, and therefore can appear to man only as nothing; yet it is what all things participate in if they are to exist at all. All Stevens' later poetry has as its goal the releasing of the evanescent glimpse of being which is as close as man can come to a possession of the ground of things. The paradoxical appearance to man of being in the form of nothing is the true cause of the ambiguity of his poetry. Man's inability to see being as being causes the poet to say of it: "It is and it / Is not and, therefore, is" (CP, 440), and yet in the supreme moments of insight he can speak directly of it in lines which are a cry of ecstatic discovery:

> It is like a thing of ether that exists
> Almost as predicate. But it exists,
> It exists, it is visible, it is, it is. (CP, 418)

The nothing is, but it is not merely the nothingness of consciousness. Human nature participates in being, but so do all other existences. Wherever the poet thinks to catch it, it disappears, melting into the landscape and leaving just the pines and rock and water which are there, or being absorbed into the mind and taking the mind's own shape: "If in the mind, he vanished, taking there / The mind's own limits, like a tragic thing / Without existence, existing everywhere" (CP, 298). Being is released in the flash of time from is to was, just as it is released in the expansion of perception to occupy space. Being is the presentness of things present, the radiance of things as they are, and is therefore "physical if the eye is quick enough" (CP, 301).

In two late poems, "Metaphor as Degeneration" (CP, 444) and "The River of Rivers in Connecticut" (CP, 533), Stevens sees being as a river, hidden behind all the appearances that tell of it, and yet flowing everywhere, through all space and time and through all the contents of space and time. In these two poems he gives his most succinct expression of his apprehension of being:

> It is certain that the river
>
> Is not Swatara. The swarthy water
> That flows round the earth and through the skies,
> Twisting among the universal spaces,
>
> Is not Swatara. It is being. (CP, 444)
>
> It is not to be seen beneath the appearances
> That tell of it. The steeple at Farmington
> Stands glistening and Haddam shines and sways.
>
> It is the third commonness with light and air,
> A curriculum, a vigor, a local abstraction . . .
> Call it, once more, a river, an unnamed flowing,
>
> Space-filled, reflecting the seasons, the folk-lore
> Of each of the senses; call it, again and again,
> The river that flows nowhere, like a sea. (CP, 533)

At the heart of Stevens' poetry there is a precise metaphysical experience. Or, rather, this experience is beyond metaphysics, since the tradition of metaphysics is based on a dualism putting ultimate being in some transcendent realm, above and beyond what man can see. Being, for Stevens, is within things as they are, here and now, revealed in the glistening of the steeple at Farmington, in the flowing of time, in the presentness of things present, in the interior fons of man.

Stevens' experience of being is "a difficult apperception," "disposed and re-disposed / By such slight genii in such pale air" (CP, 440). To speak directly of this apperception, to analyze it, is almost inevitably to falsify it, to fix it in some abstraction, and therefore to kill it. Though man participates in being, he does not confront it directly. It is the center of which each man is an eccentric particle, for he is always "helpless at the edge" (CP, 430). When he tries to grasp it, it disappears. Man can never possess "the bouquet of being" (OP, 109), that fugitive aroma. The best we can do is "to realize / That the sense of being changes as we talk" (OP, 109) and go on talking in the hope that if we are careful to see that "nothing [is] fixed by a single word" (OP, 114), nothing will be, in another sense, fixed momentarily in a word, and we shall have another evanescent insight into being.

The only passage in Stevens' prose which speaks directly of his perception of being, "that nobility which is our spiritual height and depth" (NA, 33, 34), is curiously evasive. It is evasive because its subject is evasive. There is *something* there, Stevens says, but it can only be described negatively, for to define it is to fix it, and it must not be fixed:

I mean that nobility which is our spiritual height and depth; and which I know how difficult it is to express it, nevertheless I am bound to give a sense of it. Nothing could be more evasive and inaccessible. Nothing distorts itself and seeks disguise more quickly. There is a shame of disclosing it and in its definite presentations a horror of it. But there it is. The fact that it is there is what makes it possible to invite to the reading and writing of poetry men of intelligence and desire for life. I am not thinking of the ethical or the sonorous or at all of the manner of it. The manner of it is, in fact, its difficulty, which each man must feel each day differently, for himself. I am not thinking of the solemn, the portentous or demoded.

On the other hand, I am evading a definition. If it is defined, it will be fixed and it must not be fixed. And in the case of an external thing, nobility resolves itself into an enormous number of vibrations, movements, changes. To fix it is to put an end to it. (NA, 33, 34).

To fix it is to put an end to it, but in poetry it can be caught unfixed. The mobile, flickering poetry of Stevens' later style, poetry which fears stillness beyond anything, is more than a revelation of the impossibility of escaping the war of the mind and sky. It is a revelation of being. The poem names being, the humanlike figure which the mind is always confronting at every extreme, but which it is never able to catch and immobilize in words. The nothing which makes it impossible ever to rest, which makes nonsense of any attempt to express things rationally, and which always drives the poet on to another effort to seize the nothing by marrying imagination and reality—this nothing turns out to be being. The poetry of flittering metamorphosis is the only poetry which is simultaneously true to both imagination and reality, and it is the only poetry which will catch being. Being is "the dominant blank, the unapproachable," but it is nevertheless the source of everything, all man sees and all he is. The ultimate tragedy is that being is transformed instantaneously into nothing, and therefore though the poet has it, he has it as an absence. Only a poetry of iridescent frettings will remain in touch with it, for "life / Itself is like a poverty in the space of life, / So that the flapping of the wind . . . / Is something in tatters that [man] cannot hold" (CP, 298, 299). Being is inherent in human nature, but it is inherent as a center which can never be embraced. In the process of going in a moment through the whole cycle from A to Z something is released, glimpsed, and annihilated, like those atomic particles which live only a millionth of a second. This something is being. As soon as it is named, it disappears, takes the limits of the mind, or melts into the limited existence of the object. But for a moment it is seen. "It is and it / Is not and, therefore, is."

The motive for rapid motion in Stevens' poetry is not only

that speed reconciles imagination and reality. Speed also makes possible a vision of being—in the moment of its disappearance. After reading one of Stevens' poems the reader has the feeling that, after all, nothing has happened, no change of the world such as science or technology can perform: "And yet nothing has been changed except what is / Unreal, as if nothing had been changed at all" (OP, 117). At the end it *was* there. It is already part of the past. Poetry is a pheasant disappearing in the brush. So Santayana, in "To an Old Philosopher in Rome," lives "on the threshold of heaven" and sees things double, things and the presence of being in things, "The extreme of the known in the presence of the extreme / Of the unknown" (CP, 508). To see things transfigured in this way is still to see them just as they are, in all their barrenness and poverty. This world and the other are "two alike in the make of the mind" (CP, 508), and the old philosopher's ultimate insight, like Stevens' own, is not at all a vision of things beyond this world:

> It is a kind of total grandeur at the end,
> With every visible thing enlarged and yet
> No more than a bed, a chair and moving nuns,
> The immensest theatre, the pillared porch,
> The book and candle in your ambered room . . . (CP, 510)

But merely to see being in things is not enough. Being must be spoken. The speaking of poetry liberates being in the presence of things. Through words man participates in being, for words of the world are the life of the world, and "the word is the making of the world, / The buzzing world and lisping firmament" (CP, 345). Poetry does not name something which has already been perceived, or put in words a pre-existent mental conception. The act of naming brings things together, gathers them into one, and makes present the things which are present. Speaking belongs to being, and in naming things in their presence poetry releases a glimpse of being.

From De Quincey through Arnold and Browning to Hopkins,

Yeats, and Stevens the absence of God is starting point and basis. Various poets, Browning or Yeats, for example, beginning in this situation are able to make a recovery of immanence. Perhaps it is Stevens' way, the movement from the dissolution of the gods to the difficult apperception of being, which represents the next step forward in the spiritual history of man. Stevens may be in the vanguard of a movement "toward the end of ontology," as Jean Wahl calls it.[2] Central in this movement is the idea that all our spiritual height and depth is available here and now or nowhere. The last stanza of "A Primitive like an Orb" is one of Stevens' most eloquent statements of his belief that all the words and all the experiences of man are part of being, eccentric particles of the giant "at the center of the horizon," the giant who can never be fully possessed or spoken in any words, but who is shared by all. If this is the case, the simplest phrase, in all its limitation, is indeed "the human end in the spirit's greatest reach" (CP, 508):

> That's it. The lover writes, the believer hears,
> The poet mumbles and the painter sees,
> Each one, his fated eccentricity,
> As a part, but part, but tenacious particle,
> Of the skeleton of the ether, the total
> Of letters, prophecies, perceptions, clods
> Of color, the giant of nothingness, each one
> And the giant ever changing, living in change. (CP, 443)

[2] See *Vers la fin de l'ontologie* (Paris, 1956).

Paterson: Listening to Landscape

SISTER BERNETTA QUINN, O.S.F.

Symbolic geography appealed to William Carlos Williams from boyhood. The first verses he ever composed, cited by Edith Heal in *I Wanted to Write a Poem*, vibrate with more than the primary level of their three images:

> A black, black cloud
> flew over the sun
> driven by fierce flying
> rain (IWWP, 4) *

His initial book, published in 1909 by Rutherford's Reid Howell at a quarter a copy, contains a landscape sonnet which, though typical of *juvenilia*, is not without interest in respect to *Paterson* (*Poems*, pp. 16–17). Inspired by the emotion which its author confessed drove him into becoming a poet and which today would be called the pain of estrangement, "The Loneliness of Life" presents the sea ("overwhelming tide," "torrent of mortality") as a barrier between him and the "high green land," a paradisiacal image. After mapping out the wide prospect visible from this height, with the intention of choosing his kingdom, Williams realizes that reality rules out sunlit realms and that he must be content to wander "in another

---

* The following texts of Williams' work have been used in this paper. Each is accompanied by the abbreviation which will hereafter be employed in citations. IWWP—*I Wanted to Write a Poem*, ed. Edith Heal (Boston, 1958); CLP—*The Collected Later Poems*, rev. ed. (New York, 1962); P—*Paterson* (New York, 1963); GAN—*The Great American Novel* in *American Short Novels*, ed. R. P. Blackmur (New York, 1960); SP—*Selected Poems*, ed, Randall Jarrell (New York, 1949); KH—*Kora in Hell: Improvisations* (San Francisco, 1957); SA—*Spring and All* (Dijon, 1923); BS—*The Broken Span* (New York, 1941); BU—*The Build-Up* (New York, 1952).

country," amidst strange fields, along banks, or among plains where a network of overhanging flowers cuts him off from a knowledge of either the birds or the citizens of this *paysage intérieur*, a landscape of melancholy common to adolescence. From so diffuse a lyric, his power of delineation grew until Norman Holmes Pearson in *The Literary Review* can rightly say of him that "perhaps only Frost among contemporaries can rival him in the creation of a landscape." [1]

Never very far from philosophic idealism, Williams anthropomorphizes Nature both in *Paterson* and in some of his shorter poems, as a correlative to its dependence on an intelligence which gives mountain and river, forest and sky, their places in the order of being. The Passaic, existing as itself but also as stream of consciousness, is obviously more than H_2O moving over limestone, no matter how "charged with the grandeur of God" or, in nontheistic terms, how irradiated by "the light that never was on land or sea" its material substance is. Among the brief lyrics, "The Mind Hesitant" treats this river and its surroundings in a manner which literary criticism might call personification, but which bears a more profound significance in the wake of American philosophy:

> Sometimes the river
> becomes a river in the mind
> or of the mind
> or in and of the mind
>
> Its banks snow
> the tide falling a dark
> rim lies between
> the water and the shore (CLP, 118)

These lines reveal Williams' preoccupation with epistemology in connection with the Passaic, even prior to *Paterson's* analyses.

Many a novel or poem, of course, has used a river and its banks as key metaphor. Dr. Williams loved the books by Mikhail Sholokhov on the Don, his wife obtaining them from

the Rutherford Free Public Library so that through her voice
and their exchanged comments he might enjoy them in the
last precious if difficult years. "O thou, our father, gentle Don!"
sings the old Cossack tune quoted in the Preface of *And Quietly
Flows the Don*—the father-son which had echoed throughout
his own *Paterson*. In the first chapter the Russian writer evokes
his river setting: "A pearly drift of mussel-shells, a grey-broken
edging of shingle, and then—the steely-blue, rippling surface of
the Don, seething before the wind." Like Williams, the biog-
rapher of the Don River returned in early manhood to the
village where in 1905 he had been born; as the impetus for
the rest of his career he chose the locale with which he was
most familiar.

The river as multiple image has become dominant in contemporary fiction and verse. A landscape facing a mirror is two
landscapes. A river which is both outside and inside a mind
is two rivers, until the imagination marries these into a third:
the poem. Hearing the double landscape of the Passaic Great
Falls does not necessarily mean listening to it; we often *hear*
persons speak without *listening to* them. While undiscrim-
inating speakers may interchange *listen* and *hear*, the first
term implies paying attention, giving heed to, being influenced
or persuaded by, whereas the second stresses primarily perception by means of the ear and can result from a completely
involuntary process rather than requiring the effort which
listening takes.

Williams' epic fashions a replica of the Great Falls landscape
synonymous with "the tale of the tribe" in an attempt to save
man from a Tower of Babel chaos. To appreciate what he does,
one must listen not only with the ears but with the eyes: the
brush preceded pen or typewriter in turning the Paterson area
into art. A history of nineteenth-century landscape in this country could well focus on the Passaic as recorded in paint, from
colonial days onward. Until recently, Paterson's cataract was
the most popular New Jersey subject (as well as an attraction

for nonresident landscapists) from the date of its first depiction by Labadist missionary Jasper Danckaerts. Thomas Sully by 1807 had produced three landscapes of the site. In the New Jersey Historical Society library at Newark, Passaic Falls "portraits" include the work of Charlotte Julie Bonaparte, Napoleon's niece; also that of the Hudson River painter Thomas Doughty. These and other canvases document the power of the river in its youth, which, now that it is "a diminished thing," might well be incredible without the testimony of art. Men like Asher B. Durand, long-time citizen of New Jersey and the engraver of the unfinished book *The American Landscape*, have preserved Passaic Great Falls scenery as it was in the days that are no more.

Every water color or oil of the falls since 1840 shows the iron bridge constructed 260 feet above it by Bernard Hartley. From among the available depictions Mrs. Williams chose Earl Horter's drawing for the cover of the paperback second printing of the 1963 New Directions edition of the epic. The print preserves a magnificent maelstrom of water, long since vanished, creating in readers a nostalgia for the fullness of American life which Williams, like Whitman before him, so marvelously celebrates.

When one begins to read about the Passaic, a river not at all famous like the Hudson, Ohio, Mississippi, or Rio Grande, its rightness as symbol becomes more and more apparent. The word "Passaic," from an Indian verb meaning "to split or divide," has an earlier form indistinguishable in pronunciation from Patch, the name of that old-time Jersey Patriot headlined in Book I as N. F. PATERSON! (P, 25). Because few have "listened," the Passaic's story is buried in yellowed pages and aging memories. When Alexander Hamilton contemplated the place which was to be "his" city, he beheld the river at the height of its strength, overwhelming even without the aid of the binoculars later "chained / to anchored stanchions along the east wall" of the escarpment (P, 71). Hamilton saw in the torrent merely a source of monetary wealth, whereas for the poet Williams its energy pouring over the cliff represents something immensely more valuable: the redemption of man from inarticulacy. With the disbanding of the Society of Useful Manufactures, Hamilton's scheme failed. The true essence of the falls, its permanent rather than transitory meaning for man as it hurls itself toward the rocks below, perpetually eludes the seeker.

The very difficulty of his task engaged Williams' total resources, as did the wrestling with the angel Jacob's, whose "ladder" links the falls and the city. He recognized, as did the Cubists whom he was among the first to applaud in their Manhattan exhibits, that by separating the components of an object or scene, an artist can expose hidden significance, adding a time dimension to space and achieving wholeness without a representationalism uncongenial to that artifice which is the nature of both painting and poetry. In *Paterson,* he tries to disentangle the white skeins of the plunging Passaic, to unravel into some sort of order the strands woven by the water.

The view from Garret Mountain bridges Paterson and New York:

On a clear day New York is plainly visible with every tower and spire showing on the horizon. The Palisades stretch out until the mountain to the north of Tappan Zee comes upon the scene. In the opposite direction one can catch a faint glimpse of the Statue of Liberty, while further westward the hills of Staten Island may be seen.[2]

They are like sister cities, despite the fact that Manhattan, now truly a giant, has eclipsed Paterson. If New York has had its laureates (Lorca, Whitman, Crane), so has Paterson, with its surrounding landscape. Longfellow and Irving have been among them, the second writing his only poem about the falls, souvenir of his many youthful walks along the riverbank. Looked at closely enough, Passaic is as worthy of song as any world capital:

Wherein is Moscow's dignity
more than Passaic's dignity?
A few men have added color better
to the canvas, that's all.[3]

Including all four directions in its progress, the Passaic River loops around the state, its most profound curve near Horse Neck, named after its shape—a circumstance which to Yeats might have suggested the artist as horseman. Uniquely suited to Williams' symbolic purpose is the way his river "rides" right up to New York City, intimately a part of his life from intern days on.

Even the illnesses of poet and city find analogy in the history of Paterson. Book V's anecdote of the cholera plague illustrates how. After describing sunset behind Garret Mountain, its pine-green drowned by crimson which in turn washes away into blackness, Williams manages to have a single candlelight appear in the town below and a voice, as if reading aloud, begin: "There is the story of the cholera epidemic," recounting how a prominent Dutchman halted his team on the other side of the river from the market and trundled in his vegetables by wheelbarrow so as to spare his horses the danger of that infection, which was rampant among Paterson's citizens (P, 229).

Out of his Middle Atlantic region Williams made first of all a synecdoche of America, saving himself in so doing from the label of regionalist. As Randall Jarrell implies of him in his Introduction to Williams' *Selected Poems*, he himself is the vehicle of the figure: "He is the America of poets" (SP, xii). Like the hero of *The Great American Novel*, Williams says: "I do not want to call myself a United States, but what in— but what else am I?" (GAN, 316). But beyond this autobiographical slant, he worked up a "case history" of the particular as no other writer has done. "Anywhere is everywhere," *Paterson* V affirms (YALC). The names of the places through which the Passaic flows form a symbolic litany: New Providence, with its emigrating Dissenters' associations; Union County;

Roseland, suggesting the flower-rock-woman who is America; Morris County, Ryle Park, and Paterson itself, keeping alive the memory of famous New Jerseyites. Spanning the river at the title city of the poem, Lincoln Bridge heightens this nationalism. The very word "Paterson," derived from the Indian *Pasqueg* (Lockwood Memorial Library transcript), forms the center ring "in the American grain."

The Society for Useful Manufactures, locating its buildings on an island between Totowa Avenue and Little Falls Turnpike, paid too little attention to these place-name reminders of America's thirst for beauty and heroism, showing by its insular position its separation in ideals. Immersed in the river without sharing its spirit, the plant was a deaf "foreigner" in regard to the waters all around it and equally estranged from men except insofar as they were functions. The venture collapsed; the "giants" of the landscape survived.

Paterson establishes precisely the primary analogate for its symbolism. As accurate an observer as Durand, who labored over each individual leaf so that a botanist might have been satisfied with it, Williams developed his native gift through both his practices, medicine and art. All education consists, it has been said, in knowing the names of things. From habits of exactitude deepened by his scientific studies, he keeps in mind the geological formation behind the falls as he brings to an end Book I:

> And the myth
> that holds up the rock,
> that holds up the water thrives there—
> in that cavern, that profound cleft,
>   a flickering green
> inspiring terror, watching . .
>
> And standing, shrouded there, in that din,
> Earth, the chatterer, father of all
> speech . . . .
>
> (P, 52)

The stone contributing the color to this passage is greenstone, a species of "trap" abundant in New Jersey and its neighbor Connecticut. Introduced into the language from the Swedish *trappa* ("a stair"), the word "was originally applied to certain rocks whose beds, or strata, in consequence of the action of the weather on their edges, assumed the form of steps or stairs, and retreated in ascending." [4] Williams has already delineated as giants the city Paterson, the falls, Mount Garret,"—and Singac, the Backbone: buried in the ground whence / it shows, holding the Little Falls draped smoothly over it / cropping up there" (Lockwood Memorial Library, Buffalo). This new monstrous personage, the Earth, in its flickering green shroud, owes its poetic existence to the expansion of an area peculiarity that hundreds of people day after day stare at unthinkingly. Even the literal level of a symbol can remain invisible both to the "inner eye" and to ordinary conscious notice.

The first reach of Williams' landscape to be realized into symbolic form is that above the Passaic's origins—in fact, the whole expanse preceding the catastrophe at Paterson. Book I sketches in a wasteland hanging above the city like a threat:

> . . . from oozy fields
>   abandoned to grey beds of dead grass,
>   black sumac, withered weed-stalks,
>   mud and thickets cluttered with dead leaves—
> (P, 15)

The adjectives connote gloom and decomposition: *oozy, grey, dead, black, withered, cluttered.* Yet these are not antithetical to joy and "composition": "By the Road to the Contagious Hospital" has familiarized generations with the annual phenomenon of life taking hold after winter's negations. Since the time in *Paterson* I is Williams' favorite month, March, the intention may be an effect of necessary death preceding rebirth. Imagery brightens as

> the river comes pouring in above the city

> and crashes from the edge of the gorge
> in a recoil of spray and rainbow mists—
>
> (P, 15)

Here, internal relations of the physical elements in his "imitation" count for more than identifying countryside or time of year in the macrocosmic world. Each word impinges upon every other, the least (like a strand in a tapestry) crucial to the beauty of the whole, not to mention its strength. Juan Gris, about whom Williams wrote Charles Henri Ford, "That man was my perfect artist" (YALC, November 16, 1930), would have understood intuitively this sentence from *Kora in Hell:*

The features of a landscape take their position in the imagination and are related more to their own kind there than to the country and season which has held them hitherto as a basket holds vegetables mixed with fruit (KH, 22).

Place, in this view, chooses the imagination as its canvas. Ben Jonson and Charles Dickens knew the secret of constructing to scale a set of distortions of the real world capable of acting as complex metaphor. *Paterson* does the same thing, as effective in its own way as *Volpone* or *Oliver Twist.*

Though Williams does not totally avoid mythological reference, he strips it away as far as possible so as to relate details of setting in an absolutely fresh way. How different his economy here from historian Archdeacon's description of the rainbow over the falls: "Neptune, jealous of Flora's balmy gift, his trident seized and sent a shower of pearly drops which formed the variegated iris that encircles the chasm." [5] Even in his Preface, *Paterson's* author has alluded to this characteristic of the region with the motion and energy of Hopkins, in a sound pattern akin to but not onomatopoeia:

> Rolling in, top up,
> under, thrust and recoil, a great clatter:
> lifted as air, boated, multicolored, a
> wash of seas—
>
> (P, 13)

This rainbow, inseparable from its traditional use as a symbol for hope, accords with Williams' affirmative disposition. A defeatist epic would be alien to him, as is clear from his rejection of this tendency in the poetry of T. S. Eliot. The Passaic is his *Bridge*, here lifted on high and glittering in color as the wood duck's neck in sunlight, elsewhere gray as the steel of Crane's arch over the East River, in certain passages before "Atlantis" brings it to apocalyptic irradiation.

As a foreground for the fields of gray grass bordering the upper stream, for the uncultivated tracts of sumac, weeds, thickets, Williams as landscapist etches into his poem church spires and office towers as reminders of the disappearance of wildness. What Cooper feared for New York State and Faulkner for Mississippi, Williams lived to see happen to New Jersey. In "The Bear" Faulkner thought of the past as the untamed forest, a purity which the present was determined to kill. In *Paterson*, the Passaic River, like Yoknapatawpha, continues into the present, but is constantly being transformed by technology.

A nineteenth-century artist or traveler alert for "prospects" could have regarded as picturesque the frightening leap of the river into the canyon at Paterson. Despite the close resemblance of the plunge to Africa's Victoria Falls, the scene as pictured in the Horter jacket design is unmistakably American in the architecture of its six or seven houses with their wide-spreading trees shown above the chasm. The illustration is apt for a poet who, when he described a tree as a feature of a view, did so in such a way as to make the landscape indelibly American. When he renders a flowering locust in *Paterson*, using the imagistic technique of "The Red Wheelbarrow," Williams gives the impression that he is looking out of his second-floor study window at 9 Ridge Road and contemplating his own back yard:

> the shelving green
>   locust
> whose bright small leaves
>   in June

                    lean among flowers
                    sweet and white at
                        heavy cost
                                        (P, 117)

Even among nineteenth-century American artists Horter's work is not major, like Demuth's exquisite flora and Sheeler's Pennsylvania buildings; yet were Williams alive to be asked, he would very likely have approved his wife's preference for this honest landscape with its invitation to look at and listen to the falls as they roar through the poem.

The sweet locust, Sam Patch's pine, and the sycamore near the drop-off, in fact all *Paterson's* trees right down to the "frosty elm" of Book VI, spring from a determination to turn his corner of America into symbol. Perhaps the only masterpiece of letters in the twenties by a "patriate," *In the American Grain* consists of his evaluation of the Nuevo Mundo in its entirety from Leif Ericson until Lincoln. So tenaciously did the book penetrate the imagination of his contemporaries that Alfred Stieglitz took from it the name for his Madison Avenue gallery, An American Place, where Marin, Demuth, O'Keeffe, and other exciting modernists exhibited and which afforded Williams a welcome setting for good talk on his trips to Manhattan—not exactly a refuge, but at least a renewal.

From this prose macrocosm, he narrowed the span until, like a camera lens, his eye focused on just enough of America for a sequel, this time a replica of his own roots near Paterson, New Jersey, reaching out from that great heart the falls, with its *clatter, thunder, tumult, roar, din, reverberation* in expectancy of being translated into the "love, that stares death / in the eye" (P, 130).

In the unpublished tract on education "The Embodiment of Knowledge" (YALC transcript, p. 22), Williams declares that an artist must paint a tree as its shape and color impress themselves upon his sensual being—body, mind, memory, place: in short, himself. And an artist in New Jersey cannot help seeing the Americanism of its trees. "Render that in pigment," Williams writes, "and he asserts his own existence and that of men about him—he becomes prophet and seer—in so far as he is worthy to be so."

Long before *Paterson,* Williams had used the running silver of this metaphor so thoroughly American, the Passaic, to interrelate lives of fictional characters in his 1938 collection of short stories. What Winesburg is to Anderson the river is to *Life along the Passaic River:* a center to hold together the separate yet entwined lives of Williams' people, with the doctor figure (explicitly as persona or implicitly as author) paralleling George Willard as unifying factor. This anthology, especially in its title story, goes some distance toward establishing the sense of place essential to *Paterson:* the new Third Street Bridge located between the towns of Passaic and Wallington, Morris Canal with its freighters, the Country Bridge downstream, its rotting timber undergoing repair—these all anticipate later documentation of the locale even if, since most of the action takes place indoors, it scarcely begins to exploit the riverscape.

To qualify for his task, Williams was more fortunate than Twain the cub pilot, learning the Mississippi foot by rippling foot, in that the Passaic is only eighty-five miles long from its source in the Great Swamp, near Mendham in Morris County, to its outlet in Newark Bay. In linking the river to his city-man, Williams has it roll up out of chaos, "a nine months' wonder" (P, 12). The mystery of its origin corresponds to that of the Great Swamp, once the ancient Passaic Lake, with forgotten glaciers behind that and even possible volcanoes. Its upper wanderings match the alternation of vigor and lassitude, light and perplexity, peace and turmoil, which makes up the pied patterning of any human life. Even a single day of canoeing downstream will bring one from the sight of trim, cultivated farms into unforeseen tangles of marsh grass, and then out again into easier channels. Descending in a southeasterly direction, the river wends its way from the swamp until it enters the valley proper at Millington near the "giant" Singac.

Today, the time and change lamented by Whittier in "Snow-bound" prevent pilgrims to northern New Jersey from seeing in Williams' river a symbol of fortune in mortal affairs (individual or corporate), let alone the year's quarters according to which he first worked out the organization of his poem when Book IV was intended as a stopping point. As early as his own boyhood much of the pristine glory had passed away. To take readers back to an era when wilderness and civilization lay side by side, he had to devise some means of recalling the past. This he does by borrowing from his library research. Ringwood Manor's landscape in Book I is a flashback of the Pompton-Ramapo Valley as it was in the days when Washington sought haven there from military concerns:

> In the hills, where the brown trout slithered among the shallow stones, Ringwood—where the old Ryerson farm had been—among its velvet lawns, was ringed with forest trees, the butternut, and the elm, the white oak, the chestnut and the beech, the birches, the tupelo, the sweet-gum, the wild cherry and the hackleberry with its red tumbling fruit (P, 21).

Williams deserves the credit for these inserted but not invented prose sections, which proliferate throughout the epic, just as truly as Gris does for a newspaper clipping used in one of his collages.

Ordinary objects achieve a freed status through entering into a previously nonexistent arrangement. Though Williams never met Gris, he felt the liveliest response to the aesthetic of the Spanish painter in his bold enterprise of untangling the skeins of life (life for which the river is an immemorial emblem) so as to separate out dead strands from the imagination. *Spring and All* devotes over forty lines to the Gris method (SA, 30–32). Section VII of its lyrical meditations describes Gris's "sunlight in a / yellow plaque upon the / varnished floor," which Williams regards as recognizable yet detached in a strange way, so that their power as "things" is released (SA, 32). He compliments a Gris landscape within a collage as "a picture of sea and mountains (particularly fine) which the onlooker is not for a moment permitted to witness as an 'illusion,'" since a shutter protrudes from under a cloud, while grapes and a guitar appear on the canvas: "the mountain and the sea are obviously not 'the mountain and the sea,' but a picture of the mountain and the sea" (SA, 32). Painting is reality, not realism. Williams' experiment bears out Gris's rejection of the classic in order to "make it new." The painter gave courage to the poet, particularly in his refusal to be typed as belonging to any school. Effortlessly Williams left Imagism behind as a label, without discarding its merits in image clarity. Like Emerson, he despised consistency; had he not, he would never have proceeded past *Paterson* IV.

When it has flowed along fifty-two miles past the Great Swamp, the river reaches Little Falls at Passaic. Its crescendo is then only five miles off. On a bright day, the view from the red-rock ledge near Passaic's Little Falls still remains superb. Approaching its drop, the water weaves so tight a fabric that gun-colored silk could not look smoother or more lustrous. In a brilliant sun it appears like solid light, a concept important in Pound's *Thrones*. But serene though it be, no canoe can go over that graceful bend into the seething, back-racing, "white" water below, frothier in recent years because of the detergents dumped in farther up the stream.

One record of *Paterson*'s tentative beginnings, a yellow sheet among the YALC Williams papers, demonstrates how the climax at the Federal City had been intended from the start to send out filaments of symbolic power into every corner of the poem: "It is the FALLS, continuously falling; use it as background to everything else, to heighten everything else and to stitch together every other thing." Williams has encircled this whole sentence, which appears on a page numbered 107, with heavy blue crayon, also marking it at the side in red crayon. The word "stitching" recalls the textile industry in what is called the Lyons or Manchester of America; from this frame of reference Williams takes his secondary metaphor, the art that goes into a fabric, brought to perfection in Book V's Unicorn Tapestries at the Cloisters in New York. In this fifth book water-fall allusions are not totally absent, though they are oblique, as might be warranted by the remoteness of the falls from the monastic garden bordering the Metropolitan Museum's relics of the Middle Ages. Poetry is not music. However, just as one can think of a symphony as a tapestry of sound, so can a "listener to landscape" enter into this oasis of quiet beside the Hudson and, text of *Paterson* in hand, find a music of symbol in the small woodland glade reminiscent of the "back country" of Book I.

Williams once said that a poem connects the past with the present so that we know we are alive, "for seeing particulars all about us, and being instructed by the poem that the past was no different, we get our sense of continuity and the world becomes real to us." [6] Not until these particulars are arranged, however, as in a landscape, will this resemblance of today to yesterday emerge: in his next sentence the poet warns us that we must recombine the particulars as men of imagination have always done. "No ideas but in things" seems a limited slogan until one considers it as counsel to brave men bent on embodying knowledge by translating the abstract into the concrete. The solidarity of man turns from theory to tangibility, for instance, when Paterson becomes "a second organism, more rational, permanent and decorative than the animal organism of flesh and bone: a work of natural yet moral art, where the soul sets up her trophies of action and instruments of pleasure." [7] Elsewhere Williams has spoken of this need to reconstruct setting through the imagination: "Art raises the dignity of man, it allows him to say, I am, in concrete terms. It defines his environment" (YALC, "The American Spirit in Art" transcript, p. 4).

In Book II the poet gives directions for enjoying from the rampart of Garret a panorama of Paterson, present tense:

> and look away north by east where the church
> spires still spend their wits against
> the sky .   to the ball-park
> in the hollow with its minute figures running
>
> (P, 71)

The adverb *still* joins past and present, both in its modern sense and in the Renaissance meaning of *always*. The ballplayers are like those six little boys jumping through mud puddles in Breughel's *Christ's Fall beneath the Cross*, which Williams loved to visit with the other Breughels hanging in Vienna. The Flemish genius painted the things and let the ideas take care of themselves. The children in the picture devoted to the *Via Crucis* pay no heed to the cone-shaped cliff off center right, its windmill perched on a protruding platform weirdly defying gravity. They are just as unmindful of the drama being enacted at the heart of the canvas, where seven men try to lift the Cross from the shoulder of the fallen Jesus. In the scene above from *Paterson,* neither river nor church spire intrudes into the game going on below, a world which the poet can see from his summit, a watchtower somewhat akin to Breughel's pinnacle. Unnoticed by "the great beast," Williams watches the subject of his "incarnated idea," much as Breughel centuries before leaned over the easel whereon his materials rested for the transfer from vision to visibility of *Landscape of the Fall of Icarus.* Only the poet, on this Sunday afternoon, is conscious of the foreground to the sport of players deaf to the Passaic's massive tones:

> —beyond the gap where the river
> plunges into the narrow gorge, unseen

> —and the imagination soars, as a voice
> beckons, a thundrous voice, endless
> —as sleep: the voice
> that has ineluctably called them—
>   that unmoving roar!
>   (P, 71)

No one but him meditates on the irony of the next three lines:

> churches and factories
>   (at a price)
> together, summoned them from the pit   .

Earth, its glacial contours anciently carved out, keeps more of a region's youth intact than does water. The landscape southwest of the river is Paterson's mate, Garret Mountain. Climbing her symbolizes the conquest of love: *"A man's desire is to win his way to home hilltop"* (KH, 12). Williams' enthusiasm for mountains brims over in his appreciation of the Maine and other landscapes of his intimate friend Marsden Hartley, a man who would readily have understood the choice of Garret as representing Woman. To Hartley, painting a mountain meant wooing it to the point where it revealed to the artist its individuality, then seeing beyond even this to the mystery made "flesh." His mountains are triumphs wherein shine essential characteristics, quite as vital as those caught by his predecessors Copley, Stuart, and Eakins in their paint analyses of early Americans. Mme. M. Debrol praises this penetration: "That is what Marsden Hartley has been the first to show, and to give us—an exact portrait grown into a vision, of that formidable thing, so touching, immovable, tender, intangible, colossal, living—the mountain." [8] One of his most unusual works, an Arizona landscape in the Cézanne manner (the only pastel he ever executed), now hangs in the living room of Williams' Rutherford home.

As the reader looks at the "giants" Paterson, Garret, the falls, playing out their drama, sometimes the poem calls upon

him to listen to silence. Such a moment is that held-breath
expectant hush before storm, inner or outer, that deceptive
gentleness above the Passaic major falls when the only movement is the rustle of a water bird in a bush growing out of the
bank:

> the river, curling, full—as a bush shakes
> and a white crane will fly
> and settle later! White, in
> the shallows among the blue-flowered
> pickerel-weed, in summer, summer! if it should
> ever come, in the shallow water!
>
> (P, 30)

Here, with just a few strokes, Williams has created one of his
most attractive landscape vignettes, set to a lingering melody.
It would seem that the crane leaves its perch, coming to rest
in the not-distant underbrush. Four pages ahead, what is
probably the same bird descends among daisies:

> the bird alighting, that pushes
> its feet forward to take up the impetus
> and falls forward nevertheless
> among the twigs. The weak-necked daisy
> bending to the wind . . .

Williams counted among his most prized pictures an Audubon engraving of a heron, an old print which he discovered in
very poor condition and had carefully restored for the dining
room of his Rutherford home. In it the water bird and its mate
inhabit, like this white crane, a locale which is specific in its
detail. Always fond of Audubon, he sees symbolism even in the
artist's name, which he breaks apart in Book V into "Au-du-bon,"
or "the lost Dauphin," recounting how the naturalist left his
boat "below the falls of the Ohio at Louisville / to follow / a
trail through the woods," where he encountered buffalo and
"a horned beast among the trees / in the moonlight following
small birds" (P, 245–246). Williams and Audubon belong to

the category of those who, with Agassiz-like perseverance, attack the problem of interrelating a mass of facts "on a new ground, difficultly":

> an assonance, a homologue
> > triple piled
> pulling the disparate together to clarify
> and compress
>
> (P, 30)

Instead of pen and ink or tubes of oils the poet has beat, cadence, rhyme, echoes and re-echoes to help him, if the resources of sound involved in "listening to landscape" be stressed; beyond these, appeals to the other four senses, but especially sight, comprise his media.

While one might logically place the Great Falls with the myriad painted or scenic examples of the Salvator Rosa American Sublime popularized by the Hudson River school in the last century, more frequently the less sensational term "picturesque" is applied to the area. Captain Frederick Marryat, novelist who visited Paterson during an 1837–1838 tour of the United States, sees the falls as an Augustan topographical poet might or a French landscapist of the Poussin school:

A more beautiful wild spot can hardly be conceived; and to an European who has been accustomed to travel far in search of the picturesque, it appears singular that at so short a distance from a large city, he should at once find himself in the midst of such a strange combination of nature and art.[9]

Actually the torrent, even today at its fullest, exceeds the picturesque: it *is* sublime. Who can "revise" the falls? Down they rush with the kind of inevitability that drove Williams himself as he wrote out his experiences and frank convictions in the almost completely unrevised *Autobiography,* done so quickly that not even his most perceptive critic Florence Williams shared in its preparation. Unique among his work in its freedom from changes (usually poem or essay went through several drafts), the book is Williams' prose *Paterson*.

Marryat saw the exterior falls only. The mind's eye is sharper than the physical eye. Though the limestone bed of the Passaic be hidden, the protagonist reaches it as he sits deep in conversation with a woman, like himself one of the sleeping giant's thoughts: "I wish to be with you abed, we two / as if the bed were the bed of a stream" (P, 35). Through river imagery the man visualizes their union:

> . . . to
> go to bed with you, to pass beyond
> the moment of meeting, while the
> currents float still in mid-air, to
> fall—
> with you from the brink, before
> the crash—
>
> to seize the moment.
>
> We sit and talk, sensing a little
> the rushing impact of the giants'
> violent torrent rolling over us, a
> few moments. (P, 35)

The bed is emblematic, the crash a way of expressing sexual union. In one version of *Paterson* IV (YALC) Williams writes of how to some persons the towers of East Manhattan might stand for the American mind thrusting itself into the sky, whereas for him the proper symbol was a bed. Paterson's frustrations here are realms apart from the concord celebrated in a perfect little lyric appearing in Book III:

> the rock
> married to the river
> makes no sound
>
> and the river
> passes—
> (P, 131)

The lines recall Kenneth Rexroth's praise of a book by his friend as "a sheaf of stillness" in his poem, "A Letter to William Carlos Williams."

This theme of marital happiness receives its lengthiest treatment in the account of the tragic death of a young minister, drawn like thousands of other tourists to the Great Falls. Among those to climb the Hundred Steps were Mr. and Mrs. Cumming, whose story Williams is not the only poet to tell, though none other has braided into a design the actual newspaper clipping included in Book I (P, 23–24). The newlyweds came for "the wonderful prospect," for "a fine view of the sublime curiosities" of "the falls of the Passaic, and the surrounding beautiful, wild and romantic scenery." Their tragedy lay in the crashing of the "language" of the water against a stone ear, not the woman's, but rather the deaf ear of her pompous husband, whose last words to her were: "My dear, it is time for us to set our face homeward."

The New Jersey jumper Sam Patch incorporates sterility of another sort, different from that of the Rev. Mr. Cumming, but ever so similar in that it springs from a deafness and dumbness of the heart. Seldom do New Jersey antiquarians fail to elaborate on, among Passaic disasters, the marvels of Patch, who met his doom later in the Genesee waterfall of New York State. Whenever his exploits are prolonged in time through paint or narrative, one feature of the Paterson landscape stands out: a single pine at the rock's edge. The tree turns symbol, like Patch himself:

> On the embankment a short,
> compact cone (juniper)
> that trembles frantically
> in the indifferent gale: male—stands
> rooted there .
> (P, 30)

The adjective (or perhaps noun) "male" points up its Freudian relevance. Ironically, this pine overhanging the precipice seems

to live on sterility itself.[10] Had Patch remained at home, where
he had mastered the secret of survival despite odds, it might
have proved for him the sign of longevity that the pine through
the centuries has been for the Chinese. When he got away
from his roots, traveling around the country and finally moving
to the Genesee River area, he met death by water like Mrs.
Cumming, though her response to the falls was silence except
for a scream of fear, and his was words:

> Patch leaped but Mrs. Cumming shrieked
> and fell—unseen (though
> she had been standing there beside her husband half
> an hour or more twenty feet from the edge).
>
> :a body found next spring
> frozen in an ice-cake; or a body
> fished next day from the muddy swirl—
>
> both silent, uncommunicative
>
> (P, 31)

This pine tree is important among the means of identifying
the author of *Paterson* with "the Great Descender" Sam Patch.
Marianne Moore warmly commends Pound's designation of
Williams as "rooted" in his *Dial* article, "A Poet of the Quattrocento." [11] If one thinks of the epic as "woven," the fact that
Patch was a cotton spinner heightens the parallel: from 1794
on, cotton had been manufactured in the city of Hamilton.
Textiles as resembling the river in symbolism, though less ex-
tensively used, suggest a third equivalent: mathematics, as
exemplified in the abbreviation for the organization that
financed the cotton looms, the S.U.M. Williams has played on
this last idea in the Preface:

> To make a start
> out of particulars
> and make them general, rolling
> up the sum, by defective means—
> (P, 11)

and again, "Renews himself / thereby, in addition and subtrac-
tion." (P, 12–13). Through the efforts of the "Father of the
Silk Industry," John Ryle, Sam Patch's trade was so over-
shadowed that in 1869 Paterson adopted as its coat of arms a
man planting a mulberry bush, but cotton was never superseded. In 1923, Paterson's *Press Guardian* tells how, through
shipping, lines of communication from the city's cotton factories
touched every part of the world. Its pages furnish another link
with Hart Crane's "abstract" recreation of his country's nineteenth-century history: "The first cotton duck was woven in
Paterson, and for many years furnished sails for the American
clipper-built ships, which carried American products to the
remotest quarters of the globe." [12] In his poem *The Bridge*,
Crane expands this sailing-vessel symbol which tries through
a cinemagraphic epic catalogue of clipper names and appropriate sea images to achieve what Williams seeks to draw out of
the radiation of trade from his chosen American manufacturing
center.

A still clearer reduction of Williams himself to Patch emerges
in the fact that New Jersey genealogies list a Noah Williams,
who died in 1824 and whose son Ezra married Margaret
Faitout, from which union came a son also named Noah.[13] It
would be unlikely that Williams would fail to look up his own
surname in the references he devoured during the eight years
he worked on the original first four books. The biblical con-
queror of the flood, Noah, outwitting it through his ingenious
fidelity to the divine voice, stands as patron both of Patch
("N for Noah; F for Faitoute; P for short," P, 25) and the in-
novator who disregarded cries of "Folly" as he continued his
verse experiments in *Paterson* to show that some things can
be done as well as others.

Horter's picture shows the falls as a natural wonder, an
aspect illustrated again and again by historical examples in the
text of the poem. No painter, however, has attempted to
render the river as it goes beserk after an accumulation of

heavy rains: the setting of Book III, together with a prelude depicting the Great Fire. Williams hits upon a variation of synesthesia to make vivid the aftermath of the conflagration, still a third horror—"the cyclonic fury" (P, 138) of the 1903 tornado.

> Blow! So be it. Bring down! So be it. Consume
> and submerge! So be it. Cyclone, fire
> and flood. So be it. Hell, New Jersey, it said
> on the letter. Delivered without comment.
>   (P, 120)

Through a skillful verb, "pours," he likens the wind to the falls:

> It pours
> over the roofs of Paterson, ripping,
> twisting, tortuous :
>
> a wooden shingle driven half its length
> into an oak
>   (the wind must have steeled
> it, held it hard on both sides)
>
>   The church
> moved 8 inches through an arc, on its
> foundations—
>   Hum, hum!
>
>   —the wind
> where it poured its heavy plaits (the face
> unshowing) from the rock's edge—
>
>   where in the updraft,
> summer days, the red-shouldered hawks ride
> and play
>   (in the up-draft)
>
>   and the poor cotton-
> spinner, over the roofs, preparing to dive
>   . looks down
>   (P, 135–136)

Williams, like all who were in the vicinity, can never forget this disastrous windstorm which followed the fire, an event the omission of which would lead to an incomplete "profile" of the man-city. The "focus of narration" character in *The Great American Novel,* when faced with the objection that writing such a book would be like painting the wind, catches at the comparison, exclaiming "Ah, that would be something" (GAN, 327). Again and again, in devising his modern replica of the Passaic, Williams comes as close as he can to making readers see the invisible wind. Its auditory properties he manages with mastery.

Without a touch of didacticism, Book III begins the descent, the declining years of that symbolic lifetime "below the cataract / soon to be dry" (P, 118), where "the river whirls and eddys." The energy of summer past, Paterson continues to keep it in his thought, a cascade tumbling down, righting itself, refalling, "falling / and refalling with a roar" (P, 119). *Kora in Hell,* improvised before Williams had determined the form his central poem would take, likens this part of man's pilgrimage to the year's waning and also to a path leading down from a peak:

In middle life the mind passes to a variegated October. This is the time youth in its faulty aspirations has set for the achievement of great summits. But having attained the mountain top one is not snatched into a cloud but the descent proffers its blandishments quite as a matter of course (KH, 46).

Every man thinks in youth of its unavoidable successors—age and death. Thus as early as Book II, Williams had introduced this universal premonition through an interior landscape wherein memory is given the role of leading the mind to a new world, "a place formerly / unsuspected" (P, 96). Making use of twilight imagery, he arranges his lines like the steps of Jacob's ladder:

The descent
    made up of despairs
        and without accomplishment
realizes a new awakening   :
        which is a reversal
of despair.

    For what we cannot accomplish, what
is denied to love,
    what we have lost in the anticipation—
        a descent follows,
endless and indestructible.

(P, 97)

No matter how vigorously Williams repudiated Eliot's verse, *Paterson* occasionally includes passages like this one, which might very well have come from *Four Quartets*. The poet, when he has progressed as far as Book IV, creates an epic catalogue of synonyms for the lower river, almost apotheosizing it:

My serpent, my river! genius of the fields
Kra, my adored one, unspoiled by the mind,
observer of pigeons, rememberer of
cataracts, voluptuary of gulls! Knower
of tides, counter of hours, wanings and
waxings, enumerator of snowflakes, starer
through thin ice, whose corpuscles are
minnows, whose drink, sand   .

(P, 226)

He sounds like an elderly man reminiscing over his wife at the height of her charms. Most lives, fortunately, come to know this gentle sunset tranquillity.

Well below its "catastrophe" the river of Williams' poem continues calmly toward its conclusion. After leaving Rutherford behind, the Passaic brushes Lyndhurst, flows along beside North Arlington, Belleville, Harrison—all significant place names. It enters Newark (suggesting an American version of the Old Testament covenant's replacement), with its bay a short distance west of the spot where the Hackensack empties into the sea. Finally it has reached its terminus as a separate entity, where

> Above
> the darkness of a river upon
> winter's icy sky
> dreams the silhouette of the city.
>   (BS, 9)

Even when the ocean rests within the arms of land, it retains its power, as it did when Whitman, like Williams, lived in New Jersey, their lifetimes coinciding for nine years. In an essay for Milton Hindus' *Leaves of Grass One Hundred Years After*, Williams praises a portrait of the Camden poet "facing the breakers coming in on the beach," unable to understand their language: "But the waves on the Jersey shore still came tumbling in, quieting him as their secret escaped him, isolating him and leaving him lonesome—but possessed by the great mystery which won the world to his side." [14] Perhaps no one can decipher the meaning of the sea; perhaps, indeed, this incomprehensibility is its meaning.

Again and again, as Pound did in his early lyric, Williams has acknowledged Whitman to be his father and the father of what is most vital in American poetry. At one time he intended to blend into *Paterson* III:

> the greatest moment in the history
> of the American poem was when
> Walt Whitman stood looking to sea
> from the shelving sands
>   —and the waves
> called to him and
> he answered, drilling his voice to
> their advance
>   (YALC)

A good son trades with his patrimony. *The Collected Early Poems, The Collected Later Poems, Paterson,* and the posthumous volume represent the multiplied talents, or, as some translations have it, "dollars."

The treacherous sea is no more a final home for man than for the river. That historian of the Passaic, Harry Emerson Wildes, characterizes the Passaic's outlet thus:

Nothing in Nature is more deceptive than the Jersey coast. On balmy summer days, the smooth Atlantic breathes a welcome. The soft swell whispers to the sailor, luring him farther from the strand; the shimmering expanse of water, hospitable as home, promises peace and relaxation.[15]

But sand pits and sand bars, unpredicted tempests, other dangers, await, threats more to be feared in winter, which is here the symbolic import. Williams stresses these dread presentiments in the marine beauty of

> the blood dark sea!
> nicked by the light alone, diamonded
> by the light   .   from which the sun
> alone lifts undamped his wings
>   of fire!
>   (P, 236)

He has just rejected the sea as home, turning his thoughts back to the riverbank:

> The sea is not our home   .
>
> —though seeds float in with the scum
> and wrack,   .   among brown fronds
> and limp starfish   .
>   (P, 235)

Serpent with its tail in its mouth, the Passaic is back once more in the oozy, gray, withered marshes with which *Paterson* began.

New York now spreads before the poet like a rose, for which he finds himself unable to express his love. Though that city had always allured him, Williams had long ago rejected it as bride. He was right in this rejection, for Manhattan is a rose only from a distance. Actually, it is a great sprawling beast, its noise of human activity divorced from the imagination, as if the roar of the falls were to exist apart from its source in the swirling frothy river. An early book-by-book outline for the epic—the lyric "Paterson: the Falls"—turns this insight into poetry:

> Fourth,
> the modern town, a
>
> disembodied roar! the cataract and
> its clamor broken apart—and from
> all learning, the empty
> ear struck from within, roaring . . .
> (CLP, 11)

Only Hopkins can grieve as effectively over ruined Nature. The rotting wreck of a barge spoiling the Rutherford river front during Williams' life, and removed by the United States government in 1968 as part of Mrs. Lyndon Johnson's beautification project, might stand as analogue for the extremity of the Passaic, "flowing through refuse / the dried sticks of weeds" ("A Marriage Ritual, 1928," BS, 9–10). The autobiographical hero of Williams' novel *The Build-Up* voices a like lament for lost loveliness:

The first thing that had attracted Stecher to Riverdale was the river. When he was a young man, just over from Germany to escape military service, he used to come from the city out to the quiet stream to fish. There were still bass to be caught from its banks. But now the pollution from the Paterson factories had long since ended that (BU, 59).

Some truths we do not like to hear. Dr. Williams knew that readers were going to find the literal level of Book IV, Section I, unpleasant, perhaps even unacceptable. Fact and fiction, is and ought, vehicle and tenor, have ever been confused or at least have tended to take unfair advantage of one another. Yet his passion for honesty demanded that he say what he had to. Describing the first four units of his epic in a 1958 *Forum* article, "And Many and Many a Time," he writes: "What goes on with people isn't pretty. With the approach to the city, international character begins to enter the innocent river and pervert it; sexual perversions, such things that every metropolis when you get to know it houses." [16] Having completely shifted his technique, as the casting into roles in his pastoral "imitation" indicates, he fearlessly opens Book IV with an atmosphere of decadence, what he himself called in a work sheet "an effete calm" (YALC). He does not intend to please at the expense of integrity.

The river is no rainbow with a pot of gold at its end. Thus the aging Corydon tells Phyllis to

> Go
> look out of that window   .

> That is the East River. The sun rises there.
> And beyond, is Blackwell's Island. Welfare Island,
> City Island   .

> > (P, 180)

Here are kept New York's criminals, poor, elderly, insane. She reprimands her uninterested auditor, then goes on composing an oral eclogue:

> the three rocks tapering off into the water   .
> all that's left of the elemental, the primitive
> in this environment. I call them my sheep   .

This is the brave new world seen by shepherdess Corydon, whose name appears in the YALC manuscript drafts of *Paterson V* as a corruption of Miranda: Miramba. The view is a stark, wintry one, consonant with the originally planned season for the fourth book, though in the idyll as eventually used no time of year is specified. Somehow a coldness in the landscape edging Manhattan comes through by contrast with the symbolic journey to Anticosti, a "tour of Paradise" given to Phyllis as paid companion by her no-longer-young admirer, eager to exchange her apartment stocked with books in all languages for a yacht complete with the luxuries of champagne and salmon fishing in the sun. The action of the Corydon-Phyllis interlude takes place indoors, except for that visible below: the corpse-haunted picture framed by the apartment window. Not until the second division of Book IV, the Mme. Curie mosaic narrative, does Williams become definite: "Winter. Snow through the cracks" (P, 208).

Phyllis considers the ironic verses recited by her employer nonsense. She writes to her father: "Today she was telling me about some rocks in the river here she calls her sheep. If they're sheep I'm the Queen of England" (P, 181). When Corydon says that these rocks are all that remain of the elemental, the reader by remembering "The Delineaments of the Giants" becomes conscious of the hooped-serpent movement. Garret Mountain's flowers are replaced by gulls' excrement staining the rocks below that Passaic outlet. This desecration has earlier appeared as

> Half the river red, half steaming purple
> from the factory vents, spewed out hot,
> swirling, bubbling.
>
> (P, 48–49)

The dye works' pollution equates that of the language, a degradation illustrated by Phyllis' coarse replies to Corydon and by her crude letters, rather than by her conversations with Dr. Paterson. Corydon's speech is false, but not completely so: the poet's compassion prevents that.

As Paterson grows older, he sees more and more of the world's suffering, just as Williams the physician did. A fouling of the river water unknown to the peaceful, pure meanderings of the upper Passaic keeps pace with this awareness. Evil Bosch-like faces leer over the mirrored loveliness, blotting it out; just as, in this excerpt from "The Mind's Games," suffering blots out beauty when Williams remembers people systematically starved

> —for a purpose, at the mind's
> proposal. What good then the
> light winged fly, the flower or
> the river—too foul to drink of or
> even to bathe in?
>
> (CLP, 109)

Toward its finish the Passaic moves sluggishly through some of the ugliest industrialized landscapes in America, the valley-of-ashes kind which Nick Carroway as first-person observer describes in *The Great Gatsby*. This drabness is so depressing that the sea comes as a relief, though it is hardly the ocean of Tennyson's "Crossing the Bar." From the Goodell infanticide as a newspaper reports it to the end of Book IV, a "sea of blood" surges in crimson tide from New Jersey to the New York City sequences, what Williams once referred to in his notes of composition as a "transfusion" (YALC).

When *Paterson* was first published in 1951, both author and reviewers considered the poem complete. Book IV's last image is a rephrasing of the Preface's "For the beginning is assuredly / the end—" (P, 11); it puts in metaphorical form the circular motion natural to a river: "the final somersault / the end" (P, 238). Sucked up into the sky from the sea, the Passaic returns to the Great Swamp as rain. *The Build-Up* dramatizes through interior monologue this crucial paradox:

The spring, not ten feet from the kitchen door, must have determined the location of the house in the first place. It was the source for more than the mere water it gave. And though the farm had been abandoned long since for higher ground, the old house still stood. It attracted Gurlie with her sense of the primitive, the elemental. It was a source, a rebeginning. Water is the source of everything (BU, 268).

In his own springtime, Williams improvises, like Peter Quince, in *Kora in Hell: "There is neither beginning nor end to the imagination but it delights in its own seasons reversing the usual order at will"* (KH, 37). The "snake with its tail in / its mouth / rolls backward into the past" (P, 249). Presented in protean manner throughout the epic, this idea takes epigrammatic form in

> A ring is round
> but cannot bind
> though it may bound
> a lover's mind.
>
> (P, 192)

Williams meant to use the serpentine process of evaporation as symbol, as he shows not only in the Preface but in a letter which he wrote to Horace Gregory May 5, 1944, before *Paterson* had begun book publication. To Gregory he speaks about the interdependence of city and country, about the need for general ideas to be tested in local cultures:

It is in the wide range of the local only that the general can be tested for its one unique quality, its universality. The flow must originate from the local to the general as a river to the sea and then back to the local from the sea in rain.[17]

Only gradually did the poet realize that, like Whitman's *Leaves of Grass, Paterson,* if it were to represent a man's life, could not come to a predetermined close, since the time of death is unforeseen. Both he and his city continued their story after "the end" (the final words of Book IV), their experience a dream in reverse, to a degree, but also a progression. The Passaic fights backward in its course even as it thrusts ahead. To John C. Thirlwall, Williams explains why he feels a fifth book necessary:

If I believe that life ends at a certain time, with a certain completion of certain events, then there should be an end. But, as you recollect as you look back to find a meaning, nobody knows anything about death and whether it is an end. It possibly isn't an end.[18]

The pervading symbolic landscape in Part V comes from the Unicorn tapestry series in the upper-Manhattan medieval gallery. Saint Francis once said that the world was his cloister: the Cloisters are Paterson's world at this point, where art rather than physical virility expresses his creative urge. In trying to celebrate the particularity with which the twelfth-century embroiderers stitched their colored threads into the cartoons, Williams specifies twenty blossoms or ornamental shrubs as he pictures how "small flowers fill the scene" (P, 273). The long-since-vanished book of pressed plant specimens he prepared as a boy, his student visits to New York's Botanical Gardens, his liking for floral still life as a genre, as witnessed to by the Sheelers and Demuths he beheld daily in his Rutherford home, happy hours amidst iris and Japanese cherry in his yard when a respite from medical patients permitted—all helped to make this line from Book V an understatement in this regard: "Flowers have always been his friends" (P, 269). So wide was his knowledge of them that he had at his fingertips imagery enough to delete seventy-three varieties, listed in the YALC work sheets: chickory, wake robin, hepatica, Bouncing Bet, Queen Ann's lace, buttercup, whiteweed, fireweed, honey locust (the locust is mentioned in V but separate from the tapestries), trillium, steeplebush, cardinal flower, wild geranium, spring beauty, black-eyed Susan, pickerelweed, mullein, dogwood, water lily, sumac, thimbleberry, aster, bluebell, blackberry, pink yarrow, mint, burdock, bugloss, sorrel, milkweed, mallow, mustard, goldenrod, redbud, four-o'clock, heal-all, butter-and-eggs, hairbell, catnip, clover, shadbush, buckwheat, devil's-paintbrush, ironweed, wild ginger, boneset, witch hazel, blue-eyed grass, jewelweed, bee balm, quaker-ladies, rhododendron, crane's-bill (really another name for wild geranium), bellwort,

Solomon's-seal, tansy, blue flag, moccasin flower, arbutus, apple blossom, skunk cabbage, anemone, star-of-Bethlehem, laurel, cherry blossom, tiger lily, marsh marigold, creeping Charlie, honeysuckle, snake's-head, plaintain, snow-on-the-mountain, pennyroyal. This catalogue is only a dozen or so of the devices burlesqued in "The Rape of the Lock," epic conventions the investigation of which in *Paterson* would result in a most interesting book-length study.

As he finishes describing a springful of blossoms in his novel *The Build-Up*, Williams asks: "What can you do before such beauty but let your heart be softened?" (BU, 323). Having made the hard trip down the turnpike from Rutherford and across Manhattan lengthwise, he does just that as he gazes at the muted tones of the tapestry garden clinging to its stone walls. Gardens, like the company of those he loved, never failed to bring him joy and peace. In one section of the Unicorn series, oak trees brush a stag's antlers. A Breughelian touch to the landscape is the "rabbit's rump escaping / through the thicket" (P, 251). As is customary with Giotto and other pre-Renaissance artists, the Unicorn's appearance is multiple: in one place, penned in by a low wooden fence; in another, draped dead over a saddlebow. Returning to the collage method, Williams evokes an over-all, more generalized impression of birds, flowers, a castle half hidden in leaves, a pheasant and its shadow drinking at the fountain.

By the time *Paterson* V opens, it is spring again, a March different from and yet in its dreamlike spell somehow resembling that March with which the poem began. Williams seems to have left the Passaic River far behind; yet that central symbol is "changed, not taken away," as the Requiem Preface says of life. At first, he had entitled Book V "The River of Heaven," meaning to include in it the asphodel material now printed as another long poem. In its initial verses the mind-river analogy returns:

                    In old age
                      the mind
                        casts off
                      rebelliously
                      an eagle
                  from its crag
                        (P, 241)

Wildes, in his volume on the Passaic, calls the over-all shape
"an ill-drawn question mark," [19] a comparison interesting in
connection with the interrogatory passages of *Paterson* on the
sea as man's home. Earlier, Williams has attributed to his
symbol the power of solving this riddle harder than the
Sphinx's, "the riddle of a man / and a woman" (P, 130):

            Go where all
        mouths are rinsed: to the river for
        an answer
            for relief from "meaning"
                    (P, 135)

Others, even other poets, do not even see the question. Ginsberg's Book IV letter of June 6, 1949 (cf. YALC for its entirety),
composed in Newark, below the falls and thus not far distant
from where the Passaic's "mouth" is rinsed, shows that he as a
Labor journalist finds more absorbing than the elemental character of the place the world of politics in a neighborhood which,
as he writes, "has always had for me the appeal of the rest of
the landscape, and a little more, since it is the landscape alive
and busy" (P, 227). To him, the great Mill and River streets
upstream in Paterson are important because of the bars located
there. Unable to free himself completely from New Jersey,
he is equally unable to give it as "place" the prominence his
master does. By Book V, Ginsberg sends Williams this *apologia*
as he prepares to sail for the North Pole:

I have NOT absconded from Paterson, I do have a whitmanic mania

& nostalgia for cities & detail & panorama and isolation in jungle and pole, like the images you pick up. When I've seen enough I'll be back to splash in the Passaic again. . . . Paterson is only a big sad poppa who needs compassion (P, 248).

Unlike Williams, he could not consider the fields of home green enough for his Muse permanently, though he wished to keep them in reserve.

For his friend, however, Paterson was enough in art and Rutherford in life. How often he must have been asked why he continued to stay in the quiet little residential town outside New York City rather than move to Rapallo, Trieste, Paris, Ischia, San Francisco (at least for vacation)—glamorous places where his literary contemporaries were enjoying far more colorful landscapes than those of industrialized New Jersey, which each year surrendered more of their charm to an expanding economy. Surprisingly, he found comparable aesthetic delight without ever leaving home: "I have known days in Bergen co.—in February! / which were Italy to me," he records on a *Paterson* manuscript now at Yale University, changing in pencil the New Jersey place name to the simpler "at home." He explains his decision in "The Embodiment of Knowledge": "Why do I live in the town in which I was born? I who am a gypsy by inheritance and personal preference. Because one clarity is like another" (YALC).

William Carlos Williams was so much the spokesman for his enclave that two days after his death on March 4, 1963, the Bergen County *Record* in eulogizing him told how a poet, within his interior landscape, must go down to dangerous seas and up to precarious cliffs; its editor praises in this article Rutherford's late laureate as a prophet who like Thoreau believed that a man can travel much in his own Concord. Grateful affection and a simple, sincere pride entwine themselves yet about the name of Dr. William Carlos Williams when it is mentioned by Rutherford's citizens.

Paterson is another story. On the second anniversary of the poet's death, George James, feature writer for the Bergen County *Record*, encountered mass indifference about the greatest of Williams' poems—"one of the landmarks," he says, "that Paterson does not call to the visitor's attention." The city remains even yet, as in the poem, "unaroused"; it does not recall the lover who "climbed over broken rocks, through the twisted trees, around the trap rock walls of the chasm." [20] But outside its dream, where the people, as in *Paterson* I, walk incommunicado, a world within a world is beginning not only to hear but to listen to the New Jersey landscape of William Carlos Williams.

NOTES

1. "Williams, New Jersey," *Literary Review*, I (1957), 31.
2. Joseph Rydings, *Country Walks in Many Fields* (Paterson, N.J., 1934), pp. 305–306.
3. YALC, "The Clouds, The Men." I wish to acknowledge my deep indebtedness to the staff of the Beinecke Rare Book Library at Yale University for the courtesy extended me during the time I worked in its American Literature and Manuscript Collection.
4. Peter Archdeacon, *A Sketch of the Passaic Falls of Paterson, New Jersey* (New York, 1845), pp. 79–80.
5. *Ibid.*, p. 13.
6. "An Approach to the Poem," *English Institute Essays, 1947* (New York, 1948), p. 54.
7. Cited from George Santayana, *The Last Puritan* (New York, 1936), p. 116.
8. "Marsden Hartley—Painter of Mountains," *Creative Art*, III (June, 1928), xxxvi.
9. *Historic New Jersey through Visitors' Eyes*, ed. Miriam Studley (New York, 1964), pp. 101–102.
10. *Cf.* Archdeacon, p. 34.
11. "A Poet of the Quattrocento," *The Dial*, LXXXII (1927), 213.
12. *Paterson in Pictures* (Paterson, N.J., 1923).
13. John Littell, *Family Records* (Feltville, N.J., 1851), p. 478.
14. "An Essay on *Leaves of Grass*," *Leaves of Grass One Hundred Years After*, ed. Milton Hindus (Stanford, 1955), p. 27.
15. Harry Emerson Wildes, *Twin Rivers, the Raritan and the Passaic* (New York, 1943), pp. 227–228.
16. "And Many and Many a Time," *Forum*, II (Fall 1958), 19.

17. Cited by John C. Thirlwall in "William Carlos Williams' *Paterson: The Search for the Redeeming Language—A Personal Epic in Five Parts*," *New Directions 17* (New York, 1961), p. 225.

18. *Ibid.*, p. 281.

19. Wildes, p. 5.

20. George James, in Bergen County *Record*, March 5, 1965.

Ezra Pound: The Poet as Hero

M. L. ROSENTHAL

And Kung said, 'Without character you will
be unable to play on that instrument
Or to execute the music fit for the Odes.
The blossoms of the apricot
blow from the east to the west,
And I have tried to keep them from falling.'
(*Canto 13*)

I. AUTHORITY

Excitement attends almost all Ezra Pound's prose and poetry—
the excitement of the man himself, his urgency and cantanker-
ousness and virtuosity. Also, he has *authority*. In part this is the
irritating authority of the self-appointed leader, yet it is indisputable. One sees it in the reminiscences of his oldest friends,
still full of mingled admiration and resentment. "An uncom-
fortably tensed, nervously straining, jerky, reddish brown young
American," says Wyndham Lewis, describing Pound's arrival
in London in his mid-twenties. "He had no wish to *mix*; he just
wanted to *impress*." For the British, as for his own countrymen,
he was "an unassimilable and aggressive stranger." Still, the
authority was there despite the hostile response; he stood for
the most rigorous poetic dedication, and the best writers were
likely to recognize this fact. William Carlos Williams records
one such recognition:

He knew of Yeats slightly while in America but to my knowledge
did not become thoroughly acquainted with Yeats' work until he
went to London in 1910. There a strange thing took place. He gave
Yeats a hell of a bawling out for some of his inversions and other
archaisms of style and, incredibly, Yeats turned over all his scripts

of the moment to Pound that Pound might correct them. . . . Yeats learned tremendously from Pound's comments.[1]

Pound's criticism has a self-confidence that convinces, or repels, by main force. It is passionate lecturing, and impresses by its air of knowledge realized in experience. Behind it lies the absolute conviction that the poet—especially Pound himself—is a hero bearing the task of cultural salvation on his shoulders. His seriousness is unmistakable; he speaks of "our" problems. "We appear," he writes in his essay on Cavalcanti (Dante's friend and fellow poet), "to have lost the radiant world where one thought cuts through another with clean edge, a world of moving energies . . . magnetisms that take form, that are seen, or that border the visible, the matter of Dante's *Paradiso*, the glass under water, the form that seems a form seen in a mirror." Pound was precocious in early defining his proper aims and in rediscovering principles of practice from his studies of Romance literature, particularly of Provençal and Italian poetry. Very soon he was applying the religion of art to political and historical theory:

Has literature a function in the state? . . . It has. . . . It has to do with the clarity and vigour of 'any and every' thought and opinion. It has to do with maintaining the very cleanliness of the tools, the health of the very matter of thought itself. . . . The individual cannot think and communicate his thought, the governor and legislator cannot act effectively or frame his laws, without words, and the solidity and validity of these words is in the care of the damned and despised *litterati*. When their work goes rotten—by that I do not mean when they express indecorous thoughts—but when their very medium, the very essence of their work, the application of word to thing goes rotten, i.e., becomes slushy or inexact, or excessive or bloated, the whole machinery of social and of individual thought and order goes to pot. This is a lesson of history.[2]

But Pound's authority derives mainly from his verse. Even among the relatively imitative and "soft" pieces of his early twenties, we shall find work of distinction. Singing lines, often brilliantly compressed, mark the early pages of *Personae: The Collected Poems*. The young poet, seeking his continuities with a British and a European past as well as with his native American one, is moving toward some new fusion of melodic, visual, and intellectual elements. These poems are both exercises and momentary culminations, such as we find in "Ballatetta," a graceful blending of Provençal and Romantic idealism; in the vigorously colloquial "Cino" and "Marvoil" and the mystical "The Tree"; or in "Portrait d'une Femme," a compassionate yet satirical counterplay of matter-of-fact truths and imagined values. Ballad, sestina, *planh*, imitations of Villon and Browning—all these and similar efforts point up the poet's desire to repossess aspects of the consciousness of the past and to locate his own place in the tradition.

Then, rather suddenly, he is there. Among the poems of Pound's 1912 volume *Ripostes* we find two of the most striking lyric poems of the century, "The Return" and "The Alchemist." Of the former Yeats wrote that "it gives me better words than my own." In this poem he saw that same baffling, shifting relationship of waking mind to dream vision which he himself was forever seeking to interpret.

"The Return," indeed, is a superb realization of "the radiant world where one thought cuts through another with clean edge." The hero-gods of the ancient past, who "exist" for us only through literature, "return" without confidence:

> Sée, they retúrn; ah, sée the téntative
> Móvements, and the slów feét,
> The tróuble in the páce and the uncértain
> Wávering!

The "falling" rhythmic movement here is an organic aspect of this imagined picture. The extra light syllables break up the natural gallop of the dactyl, and there is further interruption by the bunching of accented syllables in "ah, see" and "slow feet" and by the iambic foot with which the third line begins. These modulations give an effect of startled wonder at the very start, immediately corrected by a slowing down of the rhythm which suggests a sympathetic, pitying identification with the shades that is both muscular and psychological.

But "they" *are* returning. The next stanza elaborates on their timidity and unsureness. However, it also accelerates the speed with which the hero figures come into focus. Greater sharpness is gained, too, by the addition of dramatic details and vivid similes, whereas the first stanza concentrated almost entirely on generalized impressions of hesitant motion.

> See, they return, one, and by one,
> With fear, as half-awakened;
> As if the snow should hesitate
> And murmur in the wind,
>   and half turn back;
> These were the 'Wing'd-with-Awe,'
> Inviolable.

In that last pair of lines we are swung sharply around, our attention thrust directly at the living past. Then the next stanza recovers the old sense of heroic being; in three swift, unbroken exclamations a whole world is repossessed:

> Gods of the winged shoe!
> With them the silver hounds,
>   sniffing the trace of air!

Finally there is the inevitable slipping away of the vision. Not at once, for the keener awareness is maintained through four more lines. But now the past tense is emphasized, and the song becomes a lament:

> Haie! Haie!
>   These were the swift to harry;
> These the keen-scented;
> These were the souls of blood.

As the poem ends, the wavering movement returns and we again see the hero-gods as they have become. The only reality left us is our awareness of the gap between vision and fact.

> Slow on the leash,
>> pallid the leash-men!

"The Alchemist" is a triumph of rhythmic "scoring" equal, as a piece of incantation, to the dramatic conjuring of "The Return." This "chant for the transmutation of metals" calls upon the female principle in all things to bring the gold to birth. It does so by invoking the names of goddesses, heroines of myth and literature, and historical personages, and with them the four elements and the realms of Paradise, Hades, and the physical universe. Images of light and burning, and of the life force, project the alchemist's desire to see the transmutation take place. As the poem progresses, we see recreated before us the mystic unity of thought and being, imagination and sense: the world seen through medieval eyes. But the range of awareness and of reference is also the poet's own. In the self-hypnotic prayer of his alchemist we can see his own desire to "transmute metal," to employ in his poetry both the heritage of the whole past and his own immediate consciousness of the present, transforming them into aesthetic gold:

> Selvaggia, Guiscarda, Mandetta,
>> Rain flakes of gold on the water
> Azure and flaking silver of water,
> Alcyon, Phaetona, Alcmena,
> Pallor of silver, pale lustre of Latona,
> By these, from the malevolence of the dew
>> Guard this alembic
> Elain, Tireis, Allodetta
>> Quiet this metal.

Imagism, a much-publicized phase of the fight of Pound and others to make organic form the aim of the best poets and the expectation of their best readers, is foreshadowed and surpassed in this passage. Pound's emphasis on the single image as "an intellectual and emotional complex in an instant of time" [3] is an aspect of his concern that the image, rather than some vague "thought," be recognized as the heart of poetic experience. From the pulsating centers called "images" the poem will gain its form; rhythm, sense effect, and structure must correspond to their guiding insight and emotion. It is characteristic of Pound that he should have taken the lead in this movement and that he should very soon have outgrown it and advanced to more complex problems.

Pound's experiments with translation added enormously to the authority of his tone and style. From the start translation afforded him the chance to sink himself into the poetry of the past and of other languages and societies. Responsive to tone and nuance, he could recover the sensibilities of others and find a voice for himself through them. His translations have the same basic virtue as his other poetry: intuitive grasp of the shape and emotional essence of his subject. Even if we do not know his originals, or are not equipped to read them, he convinces us that he has captured this shape and essence, has glimpsed "the form in the air" and approximated it through the "sculpture of rhyme." An obvious instance is his famous rendering of the Anglo-Saxon "Seafarer." Here Pound cultivates a heavy, lurching, even clumsy, pounding of sound. He makes certain repetitions of consonants and phrasing that the original does not have, to stress the function of the alliteration as a major structural aspect of the Old English poem's rhythm. The effect is "barbaric" and elemental, rhythmic as galley rowers are rhythmic; at the same time it underscores the rigors of seafaring life. While Pound actually stays very close to a literal translation of the text, he makes it a modern poem with archaic overtones. A sailor today would not quite feel the same way as "the seafarer" does, though he would grasp the feeling readily enough.

Even more ambitious is his work with Chinese texts, notably

with the Fenollosa manuscripts. Asked to put into poetic form the scholar's prose translations of Chinese poems in Japanese ideogram, Pound—working with Fenollosa's notes and educating himself in the process—accepted the challenge. Despite his initial ignorance of his materials and his mistakes, writes Hugh Gordon Porteus, Pound was able to grasp "the great virtue of the Chinese language"—namely, the way in which its written characters "contrive to suggest by their graphic gestures (as English does by its phonetic gestures) the very essence of what is to be conveyed." [4] The ideogram itself, a stylized picture or "graphic gesture" that has become the concrete manifestation of a sound and a concept, seemed to Pound the symbol *par excellence* of true communication, the kind that has not lost itself in abstraction. Because of it the poems of *Cathay* are by their very nature "imagistic."

In *Cathay* and elsewhere the word "adaptation" may be more appropriate than "translation." The latter term often conceals a literal unraveling of a text which destroys what it should reveal. If the original poet were alive today, writing in *our* language and with *our* experience behind him, how would he do this poem? This is the problem Pound sets himself in his translation-adaptations.

One of Pound's major adaptations is his *Homage to Sextus Propertius* (1917). His treatment of the subtle and difficult Roman poet of the first century B.C. is based on passages from the original elegies. Pound rearranges them freely, playing on sound and association from his own standpoint as well as from that of the original text. His aim was to make an original modern poem out of the light that Propertius' sensibility and his own seemed to cast on one another. The *Homage,* he wrote, "presents certain emotions as vital to me in 1917, faced with the infinite and ineffable imbecility of the British Empire as they were to Propertius some centuries earlier, when faced with the infinite and ineffable imbecility of the Roman Empire." [5] He thus identifies himself with the speaker in the poem, who is "not only Propertius but inclusive of the spirit of the young man of the Augustan Age, hating rhetoric and undeceived by imperial hogwash." Pound was thinking of the war rhetoric of his own moment and rejoicing in the weapons the ancient poet—"tying blue ribbons in the tails of Virgil and Horace" and "touching words somewhat as Laforgue did"—had handed down to him:

> Out-weariers of Apollo will, as we know, continue their
>   Martian generalities,
>   We have kept our erasers in order. . . .

Pound thus uses Propertius both to attack the rheorical sham of the Great War and to restate certain artistic principles in a larger context than before. It is clear not only from the *Homage* itself but from his other writings of the time that Pound viewed the classics as rekindlers of energy rather than as inert, soporific emblems of "education." "You read Catullus," he has observed, "to prevent yourself being poisoned by the lies of pundits; you read Propertius to purge yourself of the greasy sediments of lecture courses. . . . The classics, 'ancient and modern,' are precisely the acids to gnaw through the thongs and bulls-hides with which we are tied by our schoolmasters. . . . They are almost the only antiseptics against the contagious imbecility of mankind." [6] The twelve poems of the *Homage* are thus intended, not only as a faithful rendering of the Propertian spirit but also as a counterthrust against political and academic jargon and deception. "There was never any question of translation, let alone literal translation. My job was to bring a dead man to life, to present a living figure." [7]

That living figure, the Propertius who speaks in the *Homage*, foreshadows the protagonist of Pound's 1919 sequence, *Hugh Selwyn Mauberley*. Like Mauberley, he speaks for the true lyric tradition as opposed to the pretentious ponderosities of the day. He is a delicate ironist and devotee of Aphrodite rather than of Calliope, Muse of History. And he intermingles proud self-assertion and self-belittling much as does Mauberley, who typifies the modern poet. In his quick shiftings among moods and styles, too, he resembles the speakers in *Mauberley* and in the *Cantos*. To illustrate: Poem I, which in many ways parallels the opening "Ode" of *Mauberley*, begins with an entranced musical note, invoking the ghosts of the great Melic lyric tradition, then breaks off to jeer at the "Martian generalities" of would-be heroic poets. Next, Pound-Propertius jauntily prophesies that he will have "a boom after my funeral" and that all the "devirginated young ladies" will then love his work. But in the midst of this buffoonery, mythical allusion is woven into the poem's fabric in the purest evocative fashion. At last the opening poem ends on a graceful, serious note caught up from its opening theme:

> Stands genius a deathless adornment,
> > a name not to be worn out with the years.

In their final effect, all these shiftings make for a structural triumph revealing a complex sensibility. We must remember that Pound's adaptation is intended not as an exercise in translation but as a new work fully expressing Pound himself. He sets out to do deliberately what Yeats, through his "revision" of Arnold's "Dover Beach" in "A Dialogue of Self and Soul," did unconsciously: to bring the sensibility of the past into contemporary focus. The images by which this sensibility unfolds itself also define an ideal poetic personality and provide a symbolic argument made all-encompassing by the quick shiftings of the tone. In Poems VI and VII we reach the subjective center of the sequence. These plunge into deep erotic passion, the former poem drunkenly linking the themes of love and death (but also indulging in some wry speculation concerning the duration of Cynthia's mourning were her lover to die suddenly) and the latter rejoicing lustily in the "couch made happy by my long delectations" and idealizing the mistress as a Provençal *sirventes* might. Around the passionate center made by these two poems swirls the rest of the sequence, recapitulating its major "public" and aesthetic themes but also toying repeatedly with the motifs of jealousy and fidelity. Finally, at the very end, the poet puts all worldly cynicism aside, "taking his stand" with Varro, Catullus, and all other Dionysian poets. They are worshippers, not of Mars, but of Aphrodite—singers in the old way of their mistresses' beauty and their own desire, "bringing the Grecian orgies," as the first poem had said, "into Italy." And into England and America, for that matter.

II. Mauberley: Alienation of the Citizen-Artist

From the early poems, translations, and adaptations, we can see that the vast excitement of Pound's work is rooted not only in his own personality and abilities but in those artistic and intellectual revolutions which marked the first third of this century. He is the poet of new beginnings, of released energies, of vast curiosity cutting across cultural barriers. And tragically, the psychological symptoms of prolonged social crisis, that crisis which culminated in two wars as well as in the Fascist system he has defended, have found expression through him also. He is an epitome of a paradoxical era: a fighter for creative freedom and sanity who found himself, in old age, committed to a mental hospital "in a paranoid state of psychotic proportions" and only thus escaped trial for treason against the United States on behalf of Mussolini's government.

No layman can do more than speculate on the psychological causes of Pound's strange and frightening duality of spirit. Pound is hardly our only example of moral and intellectual as well as emotional hypersensitivity at bay. Many of his peers and near peers, Yeats for instance, have faced the same problems. But Yeats found saving symbols and masks and friends to keep him from running head on against the world. Pound, like Wilde and Lawrence and Joyce a self-exile, never heeded Yeats's whimsical warning to his "dear Ezra" to steer clear of naked politics.[8] One explanation we might offer is that Pound has committed one kind of fundamental Romantic error. He has tried to politicalize an aesthetic slogan—the slogan that it is the poet who protects the "whole machinery of social and individual thought and order" against catastrophe through his heroic tribal role as purifier of the language—its clarity, precision, and vigor. In his work we see the poet as citizen refusing to accept the alienation thrust on him as artist; the craftsman meets the challenge of cultural crisis by teaching the world the "secret" behind craftsmanship—its ideal of integrity. Here is one key to Pound's duality, a key to insight into his work. In *Mauberley*, for instance, as we shall see, the poet-protagonist first fights to recreate society in his own image and then, under pressure of the unequal struggle and his own self-knowledge, splits in two psychologically.

The basic political and social ideas which have entered into Pound's image of the good life and to which he has tried to accommodate his aesthetic methods are fairly easy to locate. He starts with self-evident premises, such as that the status and integrity of letters are vitally related to the condition of society— a relationship (as *Mauberley* tries to show) almost totally discounted since the eighteenth century. We need to look at certain moments in the historical past to find models of another way of life; thus, in *Canto 13* we see Confucius explaining:

> . . . when the prince has gathered about him
> All the savants and artists, his riches will be fully employed.

The medieval detestation of usury furnishes another model attitude, and who so gross as to defend usury as a public good? So does the behavior of certain Renaissance figures and institutions, and so does the distrust of bank profiteering expressed by Jefferson, Adams, and other American Founding Fathers. One of Adams' comments on the subject is emphasized and repeated in the *Cantos*:

> Every bank of discount is downright corruption
> taxing the public for private individuals' gain.

The "social-credit" theories of Gesell and Douglas, and the policies of Mussolini's government in its reorganization of credit financing and public works, appeared to Pound the logical culmination of past creative thinking concerning social problems. His *Jefferson and/or Mussolini* [9] presents fascinating (and fantastic) correlations of aesthetic and political-economic means and ideals. One quotation from its preface will demonstrate his confusion of these spheres of activity:

> By October 6, 1934 we find Mussolini putting the dots on the 'i's.'

> That is to say, finding the unassailable formula, the exact equation for what had been sketchy and impressionistic and exaggerated in Thomas Jefferson's time and expression.

"Sketchy and impressionistic and exaggerated"—these are familiar enough words, when applied to the writers against whom the most serious and accomplished modern poets waged their successful revolution in the decades after 1910. And the problem of "finding the unassailable formula, the exact equation" will also strike a familiar chord, particularly when we remember that the preface in which these words appear was originally a letter sent in 1934 to T. S. Eliot, then editor of *The Criterion*. Fifteen years earlier Eliot had used similar terminology in discussing the problems of finding in any given piece of work the right "formula for poetic expression of a particular emotion." [10]

But Eliot had been talking about art—poetic art, to be exact—and Pound was simply translating the language of artistic criticism into that of sociopolitical theory in rather naïve fashion. His whole book, indeed, is colored by aesthetic-centered thought, though its ostensible theme is ideological. Thus he compares the "artifex" of Mussolini's 1933 speech in Milan with the sculpture of Brancusi, and he talks of Jefferson's exaggerated "verbal manifestations" and of how "the fascist revolution is infinitely more INTERESTING than the Russian revolution because it is not a revolution according to preconceived type." Again, to show why the American system has in his opinion gone astray, he begins his explanation with an observation on *metrical* technique; and he defends Mussolini's methods as not unscrupulous but creative: "the opportunism of the artist."

Pound's political and economic attitudes, however eccentric, have had their hard meanings and consequences for him in the real daily world. He has revolted his contemporaries as often as he has taught them the difficult demands of a principled art. For our purposes the real question is not whether or not Pound's specific *ideas* are defensible in themselves, but whether or not they (and his "paranoia") have subverted his art. Their effect on his poetry after the honest self-examination of *Mauberley* raises subtle problems. The *Cantos* are as wrongheaded as they are brilliant. He has shot tendentiousness into them almost at will and has indulged his compulsion to be a professor-without-appointment insufferably. But the *Cantos are* a success, though very nearly a Pyrrhic one. They come close to disaster; only the creative *"direction of his will,"* to use Pound's phrase in comparing *Il Duce* with Confucius and with Dante, saves them from it in the long run.

Probably disaster or near disaster has been Pound's special risk from the beginning: the condition of his unique drive and influence. If we are to take some of his statements at face value, he seems to have set himself the task not only of living by what he called "vision of perfection" himself but of revolutionizing the taste of one nation—or perhaps two—through his literary activities. Despite his striking achievements, he alienated many confederates and grew much disturbed over his "failure" to bring about a cultural revolution. Out of his brooding self-analysis grew the two-part sequence *Hugh Selwyn Mauberley*, the first part dated 1919, the second 1920. "A Farewell to London"—and to the United States as well—it presents the now mature poet at the crucial point of rejecting the culture he has failed to change and at the same time, obliquely and almost "secretly," rejecting himself in a social role and seeking, through gestures of withdrawal and through the most unyielding irony, to redefine himself in all his relationships. Pound has said that *Mauberley* is merely a sort of simplification of the *Homage*, for readers without sufficient literacy to follow what he was doing in the earlier work. That is partly true and partly a joke. It may also be an attempt to conceal the confessional aspect of the later sequence.

Mauberley is a quasi-fictional but basically autobiographical account of a young American poet's effort to find himself within the English literary tradition and at the same time to affect the tradition himself. Like Propertius, he is a bold critic of current pomposities, a lover of the Beautiful for its own sake, and above all a conscientious craftsman. But he is a more troubled and introspective figure than Propertius by far. Even more than the *Homage, Mauberley* is constantly varied in mood and tone: now polemical, now richly self-revealing or lyrical, now cold and polished, now scholarly in its allusiveness, now relaxed and bawdy or jeering. The title of the opening poem, *E. P. Ode pour l'Élection de Son Sepulchre* ("Ezra Pound, Ode on the Occasion of Choosing His Burial-Place"), echoes the sixteenth-century poet Ronsard, as the French in the closing stanza echoes the *Grand Testament* of the fifteenth-century poet Villon. The echoes associate the speaker with the lyric traditions of premodern Europe. They also suggest he is pondering his own self-exile and symbolic death and comparing his own dedication to his art with that of the masters of the past. The "Ode" as a whole raises the question whether he has, literally, exiled and sacrificed himself to no purpose—failed—or whether he has triumphed in his own fashion. Pound's vigorous denial that Mauberley is Ezra Pound [11] is justifiable enough in its way; *no* created speaking character, even when called "I," is identical with its creator. The distinction, however, does not obviate the fact that Mauberley is *one* psychological image of "E.P."—an aspect of his self-awareness. We shall not be far wrong if, following the lead of the first poem, we call the speaker "Mauberley-Pound."

Mauberley's "story" may be retold briefly, if with some inevitable oversimplification. For three years, the opening "Ode" tells us, he has sought to revive the classical spirit of poetry in obstinate Britain. This was his Odyssean mission, and, wishing to perform it in a modern way, he has held before him as a contemporary model of the Grecian ideal the precision and formal perfectionism of Flaubert. But he has been more like Capaneus, who defied Zeus and was struck down, than like Odysseus; or if like Odysseus, he has been a variant one, less shrewd, who allowed himself to be tricked by the Sirens and then forgotten.

As in the *Homage*, though, the confession of error is tempered by its ironic tone, by the way in which the speaker allies himself with Grecian heroes and great writers, and in the ensuing four poems by the wholesale Propertian assault on the degraded state of contemporary civilization. Ugliness, crudeness, and mass production, the second and third poems say, are what is now demanded. The heritage of pagan myth, of Classical art and thought, and even of primitive Christianity is now washed away by a mushy, formless, leveling secularism. The decay of value has already, Poems IV and V insist, betrayed the youth of the world into mass slaughter. The civilization professes faiths it no longer understands and traditions it no longer cares to preserve save as rhetorical incentives in war:

> Quick eyes gone under earth's lid,
>
> For two gross of broken statues,
> For a few thousand battered books.

The succeeding seven poems shift to a historical review, with cinematic close-ups, of the modern literary scene since the 1880's. When Pound was born (1885), poetry and the other

arts were already on the defensive in England, the alienation of
the artist having reached a sort of dead end after a century
or more of deterioration in his status. "Painters and adulterers"
—society had come to regard the two terms as virtually
synonymous, and the Muse herself seemed reduced to beggary
and whoredom. Some of Yeats's fellow poets of the nineties are
summoned up as admired figures who remained true to the
tradition of craftsmanship despite neglect and "failure" like
Mauberley's own. A Mr. Nixon, very possibly modeled on
Arnold Bennett, advises the young poet to "give up verse, my
boy," for "there's nothing in it." At the very end of the 1919
portion of the sequence, the poem "Envoi," modeled on Waller's
"Go, lovely rose" but thoroughly "modern" in its rhythmic
variations and in the character of its thought, reasserts his creed
of Beauty. It symbolizes the poet's intention to continue along
the chosen path of dedication to craft in the old sense despite
every disillusionment and defeat.

The "Envoi" serves as a kind of purgation of forensic ambitions
and rhetorical warfare. The second part of the sequence,
Mauberley (1920), departs decisively from that arena, becoming
almost entirely subjective. Though the early themes are
still echoed, it is the personal counterpart that is the theme.
Where in the opening "Ode" he had stressed his conflict with
an unresponsive world, in the first poem here he stresses the
limited, if genuine, character of his own skill. In the second
poem he reviews the three "wasted" years, seeing them as a
time of drifting amid "phantasmagoria."

> Drifted . . . drifted precipitate,
> Asking time to be rid of . . .
> Of his bewilderment; to designate
> His new found orchid. . . .
>
> To be certain . . . certain . . .
> (Amid aerial flowers) . . . time for arrangements—
> Drifted on
> To the final estrangement. . . .

Entranced in his dream, he had ignored or neglected the real possibilities of poetry and of life and had not yet discovered the true implications of his vision of perfection ("orchid"). The language suggests a relationship between this failure and one in love or in sexual experience; he had not yet learned the lesson Apollo read to Propertius.

It is as if the poet were saying that behind his attempt to "conquer" Britain through art and argument—that manifestly quixotic and presumptuous task he had set himself—had lain a suppressed recognition of his inadequacies as artist and as man. Mauberley had avoided the simple, crucial issues of his own life in favor of enterprises so grandiose they would hide his privately feared inadequacies. Usually so cocksure, Pound came closer in these poems of *Mauberley* (*1920*) than almost anywhere else in his work to opening up to himself and to the world the terrible uneasiness behind his sense of persecution and his epic declaration of purpose:

> By constant elimination
> The manifest universe
> Yielded an armour
> Against utter consternation. . . .

Yet even in these five poems, breakdown and retreat behind verbal armor are not the poet's *final* answer. As many other poets have done, he uses the semblance of disorder to help himself get his bearings. Irony toward the age and its demands continues simultaneously with the new turn of the sequence, though the language has become indirect and inward. Mauberley-Pound had not believed in his exclusion from the world of letters before, and he does not believe in it now. As he develops the imagery of the poet-wanderer's drift into escape and (in Poem V) of his continuing vision—however self-defeating—of Beauty, the sheer brilliance of the writing, together with the fact that he has *not* after all "given up verse," is qualification enough of the self-doubts he has expressed.

> Tawn fore-shores
> Washed in the cobalt of oblivions. . . .

and:

> The sleek head emerges
> From the gold-yellow frock
> As Anadyomene in the opening
> Pages of Reinach.

That image of the modern mind which Yeats sought has, clearly, several manifestations in the personality of Mauberley-Pound. He is an Odysseus with an epic cultural mission; a prophet whiplashing a decadent social order; a creative dreamer lost in reverie, heir to the best in the entire poetic tradition. And he is also the exposed and vulnerable sensitive spirit who doubts himself, undercuts his self-respect by questioning his own motives, but then—like Yeats—accepts the burden of the Self, the whole bundle of failures, delusions, limitations, and comes up surprisingly tough and springy at the last. In this multiple image Pound closes off all possibility of reconciliation with a world which cannot respond to him on *his* terms and which he will not serve on *its* terms.

III. SOME NOTES ON THE "CANTOS"

The composition of *Mauberley* and the *Cantos* began about the same time. The two works have basically the same protagonist and similar perspectives, but the two segments of the former sequence were completed by 1920, while the *Cantos* has been a work in progress for more than forty years.[12] As the *Cantos* developed, it became clear that the work would be a complex proliferation involving many more motifs, characters, and clusters of ideas than *Mauberley*. The similarity and difference between them is well illustrated by the opening poem of each sequence. Although in both instances the protagonist identifies himself with Odysseus, in *Mauberley* the identification is clearly figurative, while in *Canto 1* the speaker seems literally to be the Odysseus of Homer until we approach the end of the poem. *Canto 1,* indeed, is a compressed translation of Book XI of the *Odyssey* (the *"Nekuia"* or "Book of the Dead"), one of the most brilliant translations from Classical literature in the English language. Pound employs certain Anglo-Saxon effects magnificently to catch the tone of primitive terror and the movement in Homer:

> Souls out of Erebus, cadaverous dead, of brides
> Of youths and of the old who had borne much;
> Souls stained with recent tears, girls tender,
> Men many, mauled with bronze lance heads,
> Battle spoil, bearing yet dreory arms,
> These many crowded about me; with shouting,
> Pallor upon me. . . .
>
> And Anticlea came, whom I beat off, and then Tiresias Theban,
> Holding his golden wand, knew me, and spoke first:
> 'A second time? why? man of ill star,
> Facing the sunless dead and this joyless region?'

But Tiresias' question shows that the protagonist is not really Homer's Odysseus after all. Odysseus summoned up the dead only once. The figure repeating his invocation and experience in this canto is Pound's actual protagonist, the "I" of the *Cantos,* just as the "he" of *E. P. pour l'Élection de Son Sepulchre* is the protagonist of *Mauberley.* Momentarily, in this first canto and at various points thereafter, he wears this Odyssean mask; it is one sign among many that he has now accepted the heroic role he was uncertain he could manage in *Mauberley,* and without the self-lacerating irony of that poem. Like the great epic heroes before him, the "I" of the *Cantos* must visit the dead and be guided by prophetic voices from the past. Before the sequence is ended, he put on numerous masks to identify himself with many other heroes of myth, history, and literature. Figures like Confucius and Malatesta and John Adams speak out of their worlds as men striving to establish creative order. Thus they resemble Odysseus, whose task it was to restore right order in his homeland and then to carry its values to the hinterlands. Their active wisdom is like that of Odysseus and also partakes of the procreative energy of the life force, which the Homeric hero so clearly symbolizes. In Homer he is an almost impersonal embodiment of the cosmic male principle Pound describes in *Canto 99:*

> . . . man's phallic heart from heaven
> a clear spring of rightness. . . .

Women and goddesses are drawn to him inevitably, and when at last he returns to Penelope it is the great bed carved out of living oak which best symbolizes their reunion. In Pound, as in Yeats, this tradition is combined with the more modern search for self-definition and creativity. (It is appropriate, for this reason among others, that Pound should have based his version of "The Book of the Dead" on a sixteenth-century Latin translation by Andreas Divus. He thought that Divus had so captured the Homeric text as to provide a vital connection between it and the possibilities of modern English verse.)

From this beginning and from these implications extend the lines of thought and the underlying oppositions of value that hold the *Cantos* together. If the vivid repossession of the Homeric spirit in *Canto 1* symbolizes what the poem "stands for," it does not wholly provide its range of identification. Throughout the *Cantos* we experience moments of realization, each contributing to the fusion of values from various times and cultures. *Canto 13,* for one instance, presents with beautiful lucidity the Confucian spirit in a dialogue between Kung (Confucius) and his disciples. Rational discourse, anger, lyrical reverie, succeeded each other; formal speech is played against the colloquial. The primal force of Odysseus' confrontation with the dead gave the poem one dimension; this canto adds a spirit of enlightened secularism and of philosophical nonconformism. Political, economic, and social dimensions are added elsewhere. And again and again we have passages in which, out of the materials of his wide reading and his longing to hold intact his vision of an Earthly Paradise, the poet brings the gods back to life:

> The light now, not of the sun,
> > Chrysophrase,
> And the water green clear, and blue clear. . . .
>
> Zagreus, feeding his panthers,
> > the turf clear as on hills under light
> And under the almond-trees, gods,
> > with them, *choros nympharum*. Gods. . . .
> > > (*Canto 17*)

Pure, clear light and color, light especially, are inseparable from Pound's Paradise. He often returns to the picture just given when he wants the sense of divine beauty and tranquility. It sometimes seems he literally believes in Zagreus, the god of generation, who after dismemberment was healed in Hades and reborn as Dionysus. The condition of Zagreus resembles our modern plight and hope for reintegration. His name also suggests creative frenzy and sexual energy. So, then, Pound's Odyssean-Dantean hero must penetrate the hell of the modern world before he can reassert the wholeness that certain individuals and societies in the past knew. Associated with his search for prophetic truth and a right knowledge of the beautiful is that related sexual symbolism we have already noted. Pound seeks to restore the sexual mysteries that are the wellsprings of religion and art and that have suffered centuries of neglect because of the rise of "usury" and commercialism. The sexual theme is the theme of self-realization and renewal:

> Hast thou found a nest softer than cunnus
> Or hast thou found better rest
> Hast'ou a deeper planting, doth thy death year
> Bring swifter shoot?
> Hast thou entered more deeply the mountain?
> > (*Canto 47*)

By the same token the great crime of usury balks and blights the procreative cycle that is the source of all life's innocent ceremony, all its joys and values. Pound uses the Latin term *usura,* which carries more of the medieval connotation of moral depravity than the modern English equivalent. The money corruption Pound-Mauberley saw behind the alienation of the artist and his degraded status is the chief blight on the modern spirit.

> Usura slayeth the child in the womb
> It stayeth the young man's courting
> It hath brought palsy to bed, lyeth
> Between the young bride and her bridegroom
> CONTRA NATURAM
> They have brought whores for Eleusis
> Corpses are set to banquet
> At behest of usura.
>
> *(Canto 45)*

In the "Hell Cantos" (14–16) Pound uses the foulest images and invective he can think of to describe a civilization ruled over by this Usura. He includes as its representatives not only profiteers and exploiters, but also a whole range of hypocritical moralists—repressers of all that is instinctual—and "perverters of language":

> the soil living pus, full of vermin,
> dead maggots begetting live maggots,
>   slum owners,
> usurers squeezing crab-lice, pandars to authority . . .
> and above it the mouthing of orators. . . .
>
> *(Canto 14)*

The poet is inspired by the procreative principle as Dante was by the force of Divine Love, and there is a rough parallel between the progression of the *Cantos* and that of the *Divine Comedy* (as between that of the *Cantos* and that of the *Odyssey*). Just as Dante summons up all his hatred and revulsion to depict the various punishments of the damned, so Pound hurls his disgust at the people and conditions he considers the befoulers of life. We have spoken before of poetry in its process of "revision" over the generations by what seems at times only a single poet. No one has a keener sense of this process than Pound at his best, and one of the triumphs of the *Cantos* is the way in which poets of the past are worked into its fabric. Pound sometimes repossesses them through translation or adaptation, often with the kind of implied transference of the speaking voice we observed in *Canto 1*. Sometimes he assumes another poet's tone or method, as in the Dantean "Hell Cantos." Sometimes he creates a scene which puts the poets he most admires completely within the context of thought of the *Cantos,* yet at the same time brings out their unique qualities. An outstanding instance is the portrait of William Blake in *Canto 16*. He is pictured running on the Purgatorial Mount, painfully overcoming the road that winds about the mountain "like a slow screw's thread." As he runs toward his own salvation, he keeps his eyes full on the horror of the hell man has made for himself. The picture has the sharp visual detail of Dante, though its effects are developed "presentatively," in the post-Imagist manner. And it interprets for us exactly the moral vision of Blake (the post-Renaissance poet whose sexual emphasis most resembles that of Pound and Yeats):

> And the running form, naked, Blake,
> Shouting, whirling his arms, the swift limbs,
> Howling against the evil,
>   his eyes rolling,
> Whirling like flaming cartwheels,
>   and his head held backward to gaze on the evil
> As he ran from it. . . .

The scope of the *Cantos*, as with epic structures generally, is the whole of being, both real and imagined: the natural and the supernatural, life and death, human experience and the dream of the divine. Like *Mauberley,* the work has deep implications of self-analysis for the poet himself, but it rarely invites our attention to them. Rather, it centers on the clash and interplay of the modern Inferno and the ideal world. Its many "voices" (the poets, the heroes, the leaders, the thinkers), in contrast to Mauberley, can and do say what Pound cannot say in his own right. Similarly the shifting rhythms and styles of the writing broaden and deepen Pound's scope immensely and contribute to the poem's historical and cultural inclusiveness. Published in "installments," as it were, since 1919, the *Cantos* has been a gigantic experiment of a new kind, its growth in time essential to its very nature. Each of its larger units extends our range of consciousness concerning the relevance of the central perspective: a universal sensibility gauging the depravity of a usury-ridden world and setting against it the ideals of rational thought, rational economic practices ("rational" in the view of such Social Credit thinkers as Douglas, Gesell, and Pound), and a "pagan" aestheticism. As each unit is developed, it recapitulates the root themes in a new context; ordinarily the refocusing is not at first clear to the reader, but the pattern does emerge.

The method Pound employs is an outgrowth of his preoccupation with sensuous presentation through the concrete image, the precisely appropriate rhythm, and the ideogram—that is, with communication that grows on the reader as a series of experiences. The opening two cantos introduce fundamental motifs: first, the inclusive sensibility that is the poem's hero, and its purposes; and second, the ideal of creativity in action, whose patron deity is Zagreus. Succeeding cantos show the rich implications of these motifs. The Cid, for instance, adds chivalric overtones to the Odyssean hero, and the echoes of such poets as Sappho and Catullus further define the poetic tradition whose values the *Cantos* seeks to reassert. Pound's ingenuity in perceiving and delineating new dimensions, new aspects, is one of his most intriguing qualities throughout the sequence. Thus, his conception of sentimentality as a fraudulence of feeling and expression that destroys standards of value and therefore abets Usura is brought out with all his virtuosity at the beginning of *Canto 30*. The goddess Artemis is heard complaining (her song is a "compleynt," and the form and diction suggest medieval verse) that the soft-mindedness of our professedly humanitarian age prevents all correction of abuses and genuine purification of society. "Pity," she cries, "spareth so many an evil thing" that "all things are made foul in this season." The result is that

> Nothing is now clean slayne
> But rotteth away.

Similarly, the rendering in English of Cavalcanti's *Donna mi prega* adds the Platonic idealism and intellectual eroticism of that poet to the ideal vision developed in so many facets in the course of the sequence.

If we think of each group of cantos as one of a number of hard centers around which the basic motifs are constantly in motion, while the whole work plunges cumulatively ahead, we shall have little trouble grasping the main outlines of what Pound is doing. Once we have these outlines, we are less likely to be thrown off by the many surface aspects that must confuse even the best-educated reader: the Greek and Chinese phrases, the allusions to books most of us would not in the normal course of things have read, the Joycean punning, and so on. To Pound the specific connotations of a given language seem often too idiosyncratic to be sacrificed. Even the *appearance* of letters and words has its idiogrammatic particularity, conveying something of value otherwise forever lost.

The major groups of cantos can readily be summarized. The first six or seven establish the basic axes. *Cantos 8–19* center on the Renaissance and its relation to the modern triumph of Usura. *Cantos 30–41* bring the origins of the United States, the economic and social views of the Founding Fathers (Jefferson, Adams, and Madison in particular), and the struggles over the form the American banking system and money policies should take into the foreground. *Cantos 53–61* take up Chinese history (a motif foreshadowed in *Canto 13*), finding conflicts and ideals that parallel those of the Renaissance and of eighteenth-century and modern America and England in a civilization totally unlike that of the West. *Cantos 62–71* center on the figure of Adams again. *Cantos 74–84* (the "Pisan Cantos") show the poet at the end of the war, in an American prison camp near Pisa, sizing up his life and achievement in the light of the various themes and ideals projected by the poem so far. (In this section, as elsewhere, a defense of the Fascist system is implied, its ideals and practices being compared with those of Adams on the one hand and of Confucian Chinese rulers on the other.) *Cantos 85–95*, called "Rock Drill," sum up the bedrock convictions and discoveries of the voyager-hero. *Cantos 96–109* ("Thrones") gradually prepare us for the protagonist's final encompassing vision of the secular-paradisal potentialities of man. At this writing the presumption is that there will be a final group of eleven poems.[13]

From this very elementary summary it will be clear that the structure of the *Cantos* has a rhetorical emphasis as well as a narrative organization. Its method of presentation, however, is based on Symbolist, Imagist, and stream-of-consciousness techniques: the juxtaposition of scenes, images, lyric passages, evocative moments of every sort without conventional transition, preparation, or formal consistency. Furthermore, while the "argument" progresses on ever-widening fronts and the protean protagonist wanders through every kind of experience, the poet deliberately inserts passages at certain intervals that are intended to recall the earlier sections and suggest their connection with the motifs introduced later. He also sets passages that contrast sharply with the tone of everything around them in strategic places—as when he puts the calm discourse of Kung and his disciples just before the violent "Hell Cantos"; or the vision of Circe's isle (*Canto 39*) in the midst of the first Jefferson-Adams-Madison group; or the incantation to all the goddesses (*Canto 106*) in the "Thrones" group, which as a unit is devoted to bringing into a single focus the interpenetrating Occidental and Oriental motifs followed out in the *Cantos* as a whole.

Ezra Pound rarely achieves the kind of self-transcendence within a short space which is the mark of Yeats's greater genius as a dramatic lyricist. But he is unrivaled in sheer poetic courage, in breadth of conception, and in the intensity of his music and imagination at peak moments. No one has surpassed him in conveying the death throes of a civilization or in summoning up the radiance and frankness of the boldest creative spirit. The fact of Pound's commitment to a free imagination disciplined only by its own traditions and knowledge is surely more fundamental to his art than are the terrible distortions into which that commitment has at times misled him.

NOTES

1. *The Selected Letters of William Carlos Williams,* ed. John C. Thirlwall (New York, 1957), pp. 210–11. See also Yeats, *Essays* (London, 1924), p. 178.

2. *The Literary Essays of Ezra Pound,* ed. T. S. Eliot (New York, 1954), p. 21.

3. *Ibid.,* p. 4.

4. Hugh Gordon Porteus, "Ezra Pound and His Chinese Character: A Radical Examination" in *Ezra Pound,* ed. Peter Russell (London, 1950), p. 215.

5. *The Letters of Ezra Pound, 1907–1941,* ed. D. D. Paige (New York, 1950), p. 231.

6. *Ibid.,* p. 113.

7. *Ibid.,* pp. 148–149.

8. *A Vision* (New York, 1956), pp. 26–27.

9. Ezra Pound, *Jefferson and/or Mussolini* (London, 1935; New York, 1935).

10. T. S. Eliot, *Selected Essays* (New York, 1950), pp. 124–125.

11. Pound, *Letters,* p. 180.

12. The first published canto appeared in 1919; volumes of cantos have appeared in 1925, 1928, 1930, 1934, 1937, 1940, 1948, 1956, and 1959.

13. Many of the cantos not mentioned in this summary are transitional or recapitulate motifs already developed. *Cantos 72–73* have so far been withheld from publication.

A Sovereign Voice:
The Poetry of Robinson Jeffers

ROBERT BOYERS

A generation of critics and observers has agreed to bestow upon Robinson Jeffers the gravest sentence the critical imagination can conceive, the conclusion of ultimate irrelevance for both his life and work. And though Jeffers, dead now since 1962, never gave a damn about either criticism or the critical imagination, nor for that matter about responses to his own poetry, those of us who continue to find in Jeffers a good deal to study and admire ought a little to speak out in his behalf from time to time. The propitiatory ritual need not always be wholly gratuitous, after all, and one has reason to fear that the inevitable decline in Jeffers' reputation may not contain within it the seeds of some future revival.

Already the figure of Jeffers as a kind of gloomy apparition haunting the parapets of the stone tower he built and lived in has come to assume nearly mythical dimensions, and his isolation from the movements, whether artistic or political, of his time has been too easily attributed to savage intemperance or to idiotic philosophic ideologies relating to the doctrine of inhumanism. Indeed, more than any other poet of the modernist or post-modernist periods, Jeffers has served as a whipping boy to a variety of well-placed poets and critics who have found it stimulating to deal with him exclusively on their terms, though never on his. Thus, for Yvor Winters, Jeffers' poetry presented a simple spectacle of "unmastered and self-inflicted hysteria" working upon concerns that were "essentially trivial." For Randall Jarrell, an infinitely more gifted and judicious writer than Winters, Jeffers' poetry demonstrated that "the excesses of modernist poetry are the necessary concomitants of the excesses of late-capitalist society," and what is more set up "as a nostalgically awaited goal the war of all against all." For Kenneth Rexroth, whose championing of the most defiantly mediocre talents on the west coast is notorious and might at least have extended to a major talent like Jeffers', Jeffers' poetry is "shoddy and pretentious," with "high-flown statements indulged in for their melodrama alone."

There is no single source for such misstatements and half truths, and it would seem clear that any correctives would lie in the direction of Jeffers' verse itself, illuminated in part by the interesting documents that have been recently brought to light. And in turning to Jeffers and his work it is also useful to acknowledge that distinctions must be made and retained, in discussing what is fine and what is not, for Jeffers wrote a great deal in the course of a professional career that spanned fifty years, and he was not always a meticulous or especially prudent craftsman. Clearly he did not linger over brief passages to the degree Ezra Pound might have urged him to, and he felt none of the urgency to revise and refine his work that is charac-teristic of modern poets as diverse as T. S. Eliot and Marianne Moore. Not that Jeffers is crude or simple-minded, for he is not. Jeffers knew his gift and trusted his ability to give it adequate expression. As to whether that expression were sometimes more than adequate, he would leave it to others more anxious about such questions than he to decide.

In fact, the ferocity of the critical reaction against Jeffers that really began to set in after the end of World War II is in certain respects explicable in terms of the adulatory sympathies his earlier verse inspired in a number of people who might have been expected to know better. One of Jeffers' most consistent admirers, Mark Van Doren, in the foreword to Jeffers' *Selected Letters,* concludes with the line: "Homer and Shakespeare. In what more fitting company could we leave him?" Such conjunctions are not likely to sit well with more balanced observers of our poetry, and there is no doubt that Jeffers was frequently embarrassed by attempts to claim more for his achievement than it could realistically support. No doubt there is in Jeffers' best work a peculiarly sovereign quality— peculiar in our time, at least: an ability to make large statements on large questions with little of the customary qualification and caution we have come to accept as almost obligatory in our serious literature. Only Jeffers' concerns are so much less varied than Shakespeare's, the range of his poetic devices so limited by contrast with not only Shakespeare's but Eliot's and Yeats's and Auden's, the generosity of his commitments so restricted by his fear of excessive involvement with other human beings as reflected in his poetry and in personal documents. Even in the case of Jeffers' characters in the long narratives, which would seem to confer some degree of similitude with Homeric figures, Jeffers' creations do not really warrant such a comparison, for the memorable characters are largely maniacal, gripped by obsessions that never really evoked what Jeffers thought they would: unable clearly to distinguish his own views from those of his characters in ambitious works like "The Women at Point Sur," perhaps because he never fully considered the long-range implications of his sentiments and avowals, Jeffers could do no more than "look grim" when confronted by articulate critics of his narratives "and assure them that my hero was crazy but I am not." The Homeric perspective can by no means be equated with such a muddle.

In a way it is unfortunate that Jeffers wrote any long narratives at all, for none succeeds, and for reasons that need hardly be elaborated in detail. Structurally, they are sound enough, but the texture of these poems is swollen by effusions of philosophizing and by attempts to impose representative signification on characters and actions which are so extraordinary as to be either ludicrous or simply shocking. Not that any serious reader is going to rush shrieking from the room at the mention of a little incest at a time when every perversion has been relieved by repetition and familiarity of its capacity to extract from readers even a bit of a chill. What is shocking in Jeffers' narratives, from *Tamar* through the later poems, is the author's contentions of symptomatic and representative status for the perverse obsessions of his characters. Obviously the single-mindedness of Jeffers' pursuit of his themes in the long poems ought to dispel any notion that he indulged his fantasies in the interests of melodrama alone, as Rexroth claimed. Jeffers simply thought he had hit upon a fruitful means for engaging the most profound problem he could imagine: the relationship of the individual to his time, and the uses and limitations of human freedom. Jeffers was mistaken in that his means were not adequate to the task he set himself. Never a good judge of the work of other poets, Jeffers really was incapable of criticizing his own poetry, even after a period of years had gone by to provide a measure of detachment. Attempts to justify the narratives on philosophical grounds held but mild interest for Jeffers, who could barely force himself to breeze through books written on his work, and none of these succeed in justifying the narratives as poetry in terms that Jeffers himself could have admired. The bravest attempt we have had is the chapter on "Point Sur" by Brother Antoninus in *Robinson Jeffers,* his book-length defense of the poet, but I do not imagine that most readers of poetry will any longer find the poem tolerable, if ever they did.

Only "Roan Stallion" among Jeffers' narratives would seem to provide the consistently varied texture that is requisite in a long poem, but even here one finds it difficult to accept Jeffers at his own estimate and in the terms of his advocates. While the entire poem is powerful and not at all absurd, as some have claimed, the whole fails to sustain particular elements in the imagery. The magnificent evocation of the roan stallion as a symbol of male potency is quite as fine in its way as D. H. Lawrence's comparable use of horses in his novel *The Rainbow,* published ten years before Jeffers' poem. But the eroticism in these passages of "Roan Stallion" is not clearly related to the basic thrust of the poem, which cannot be taken to be an indictment of male potency in general. If, as Jeffers wrote in a letter, "the woman fell in love with the stallion because there was no one else she could fall in love with," why is her attraction to the horse evoked in literally sexual terms? Unabashed sexuality the woman had had a good deal of, and there was no reason for her to be drawn to the horse for more of the same. Familiarity with Jeffers' universe, with the universe created by his many poems, suggests that the stallion was to call to mind qualities quite distinct from pure sexuality, though related, and yet these qualities are never sufficiently identified. The figure refuses to yield its latent connotations and is distinguished by an opacity that characterizes the image rather than the symbol. In this respect Jeffers' failure has a good deal in common with much of the narrative poetry produced in the Romantic period. In each there is a strong lyrical element which calls into question the poet's center of interest and the consequent interest of readers. While the structure of the work naturally tends to focus attention on the unfolding of events in the phenomenal world, the poet's interest seems always elsewhere, in the emotions that give rise to action, and in abstract conceptions of fate and will. Poets find themselves more immediately and intimately involved in their characters than they ought to be in narrative poems, unable to decide where their creations begin and they leave off. W. H. Auden has lately described Byron's failure in poems like *Childe Harold* in such terms, and post-Romantic critics like Bradley have been similarly concerned with these matters.

In short, then, for a number of reasons, Jeffers devoted a great deal of his time and energy to the cultivation of a sub-genre—narrative poetry—to which his gifts were not especially adaptable. What is also distressing, though, is that the attention Jeffers has received has been so disproportionately weighted in the direction of these failed narratives and that his stock has fallen so badly as a result. What more signal instance have we of the capitulation of criticism to what is most gross and obvious in a man's work, and in a generation that has had the temerity to exhume and to sanctify an Emily Dickinson, a body of work at once fragile, restrictive, and yet upon examination singularly exotic and intense both in formal and human qualities? It is as though there had been a tacit agreement among all influential parties that Jeffers' shorter poems should be looked upon as nothing more than an adjunct to the narratives, perhaps even as something less, as filler for the volumes his publishers issued with remarkable regularity for so many years. As it is, Jeffers' short poems, many of them rather lengthy by standards of the conventional lyric, will fill an enormous volume when they are collected, and an impressive volume it will be; for at his best Jeffers could blend passion and restraint, image and statement, contempt and admiration, as few poets of any time have been able to, and often with a music so ripe and easy that it is able to impress itself upon our senses without our ever remarking its grace and majesty, its sureness of touch. How better to know what we mean when we speak of such qualities than to locate them in those poems whose perfection of form and control of tone set them apart from the rest of the poet's work? I would select the following as representative of Jeffers at his best, in an order I might recommend to a skeptical and rather hard-nosed student whom I especially wanted Jeffers to reach: "Ossian's Grave," "The Broadstone," "The Low Sky," "Antrim," "A Little Scraping," "November Surf," "Hurt Hawks," "Fire on the Hills," "Ante Mortem," "Post Mortem," "Credo," "Rearmament," "Haunted Country," "Return," "The Treasure," "Practical People," "The Maid's Thought," "To the Stone-Cutters," "The Cruel Falcon."

No doubt I have neglected someone's favorites in drawing such a list, but consensus is not what matters here. I am sure that responsible arguments might be made for poems like "The Purse Seine" and "Shine, Perishing Republic," which have been frequently anthologized, or for a sobering longer poem like "Hellenistics," so earnestly extolled by Brother Antoninus; but each of these has a ponderousness that is somehow too reminiscent of the longer poems, an indulgence of the explicit statement that runs against the grain of the hard, oblique quality we are given to demand of the poetry we admire. Of course, there are many fine things in many of the poems I have rejected, if we may use so strong a word: one thinks of the weaving of exclamations in and out of "The Purse Seine," the parallelisms binding the otherwise loosely flowing open-ended line structures, the colorful images sheathed in the poet's wonder, quietly unfolding a vision of entrapment that is to stand in analogy to our own:

I cannot tell you
How beautiful the scene is, and a little terrible, then, when the crowded fish
Know they are caught, and wildly beat from one wall to the other of their closing destiny the phosphorescent
Water to a pool of flame, each beautiful slender body sheeted with flame, like a live rocket
A comet's tail wake of clear yellow flame; while outside the narrowing
Floats and cordage of the net great sea-lions come up to watch,
Sighing in the dark; the vast walls of night
Stand erect to the stars.

How starkly these fine lines contrast with Jeffers' attempts to draw his analogy, with the crude simplifications of a political and social reality that leads to confusion and a blunting of those energies the poem had quietly released: "I cannot tell you how beautiful the city appeared, and a little terrible. / I thought, we have geared the machines and locked all together into interdependence; we have built the great cities; now / There is no escape. We have gathered vast populations incapable of free survival, insulated / From the strong earth." What can one say to all this as poetry, except that it is disastrous to use inflated rhetorical expressions of the sort represented in this sampling without some sense of irony, of the disparity between the more poetic language one familiarly relies upon and the gross sociologisms Jeffers would permit to roughen the texture of the verse.

There is, we have been given to understand, a certain ignominy readily to be associated with the use of the term "poetic language," and it ought perhaps to be justified in connection with a poet like Jeffers, who has been accused of shoddy versification and pretentious inflation of imagery and rhetoric. Clearly, it would seem, what is shoddy can never be poetic, since what is poetic is always to some degree conscious, restrained, elegant, and delivers up its meanings in terms that are pleasurable wholly apart from what is being delivered or represented. The experienced reader of poetry will usually have little difficulty in distinguishing what is shoddy from what is not. In the matter of pretension, there may be a good deal of difficulty that will be less securely resolved. Pretension, after all, has to do with qualities that may be largely extrinsic to the poetry itself, with an attitude or pose that may be justly or unjustly presumed to have dictated not only the broad contours of a poem but its particular words and images. Often, one may safely predict, the presumption of general attitudes by readers will have little to do with what actually inheres in a given body of work, but will be used to explain or to justify an antipathy which may have more to do with the limitations of a reader than with the failings of a poet. Surely Yvor Winters' abstract identification of mysticism with muddle is fundamentally responsible for his inability to achieve even an elementary understanding of Jeffers, whose poetry evinces a materialism that is distinctly removed from the kind of mysticism to which Winters so objected. Given his constitutional incapacity to apprehend as genuine any perspective on human life other than his own, Winters found in Jeffers' work a muddle, and it was inevitable that he should then seek to wither his adversary by the positing of mysticism as the source of his defection from authenticity.

But as to the question of what does and does not constitute poetic language, one may concede that critics of Jeffers have on occasion found fruitful grounds for argument. There is a good deal of pretension in the narratives, where prophetic rant frequently mounts to a kind of hysteria that has very little to do with the appeal poetry is to make to our senses. John Crowe Ransom has written that "the poetic consideration of the ethical situation is our contemplation and not our exercise of will, and therefore qualitatively a very different experience: knowledge without desire." I am not certain that I like the Aristotelian antithesis between *knowledge* and desire, but Ransom's formularization will do for our purposes. What is pretentious in the work of art, Ransom's statement suggests, is its attempt to be more than it can be, to *do* where its function is primarily to be. Which is not to say that a work of art, in particular the poem, cannot represent a position, take sides, for obviously it can; but if it does, it must do so almost in spite of itself. What is important about it is the metamorphic flexibility which facilitates the passage of our imagination into and out of a number of conditions of being, for without such passage, and without real variety, there will be no tension and no intensity of concern on our part. One thinks of Keats's famous letter in which he describes the poetical character: "it is not itself—it has no self—it is everything and nothing." That is to say, the poet is conceived in terms of a neutrality that permits him to assume qualities of the objects he contemplates.

What does such speculation lead us to conclude about those elements in Jeffers' work which have been vigorously assailed? Again, distinctions must be kept in mind. In what sense can Jeffers' work be said to suffer from pretension? It is pretentious when it ceases to control those elements of will that stand behind any creative act—elements which for the most part cannot be permitted to govern the nature or intensity of the poet's expression. Only the precise materials the poet uses can legitimately determine the intensity of expression and the poet's posture, for in its own terms the poem posits a world of its own, a word-world, if you will, which stands not so much in imitation of the phenomenal world we inhabit as merely in analogy to it. Given such a relationship, degrees of intensity and tonal qualities of a poem cannot be said to issue legitimately from contemplation of a reality which is not that poem's authentic reality. We take for examination a brief poem from Jeffers' final volume, entitled "Unnatural Powers":

> For fifty thousand years man has been dreaming of powers
> Unnatural to him: to fly like the eagles—this groundling!
>   —to breathe under the seas, to voyage to the moon,
> To launch like the sky-god intolerable thunder-bolts:
>   now he has got them.
> How little he looks, how desperately scared and excited,
>   like a poisonous insect, and no God pities him.

The poem has the merit of focusing in brief compass what may be said of Jeffers' failures in a great many short poems. The poet here stands not within his poem, as Keats would have had him, not dissolved in the terms of his saying; nor does he stand beside his materials, gently or fiercely ordering, arranging them as Wallace Stevens would characteristically reveal himself handling the creatures of his own imagination; nor even does Jeffers stand here above his materials, for to stand above would be to retain some manner of relation. Jeffers here stands without the substance of his poem, not above or aloof, but apart. The words are connected by a will that is in no way implicated in the words themselves, so that the ordering, the structuring of sentiments cannot be judged except by reference to that will, which we can have no way of knowing. The poem calls neither for understanding nor for contemplation, but for simple assent, for a process of suspension in which the reader ceases to be himself and gives himself wholly, not to the poem, but to the poet. To abandon one's self-possession temporarily, as to suspend disbelief, is to participate in a ritual which calls upon our instincts of generosity in the interests of a pleasure and enlightenment that are ideally to repay our gesture. The work of art requests, as it were implicitly, that we be generous in the interests of our senses. At his worst, and even to some extent when he is not writing badly at all, Jeffers insists that we agree to heed what he says though there be nothing in it for us, not even the extension or stimulation of our imagination. Utterly without art, and without sympathy either for us or for the materials he manipulates, Jeffers coldly mocks our foibles, our dreams, our delusions. The ideological content of Jeffers' fine poetry here hardens into a mannered response to experience, so that no valid experience is lived through in the poem. What we have is a system of response, but nothing valid or poetically real to respond *to*. Confronted by such poems as "Unnatural Powers," we can have no alternative but to speak of arrogance and pretension.

How much less we are disposed to object to Jeffers' poetry when he reminds us of his mortality. We remain wary of prophecy in general, and of false prophets in particular, but we consent nonetheless to attend to Jeffers' prophetic rigors on occasion, perhaps even to be a little moved by the spectacle of a man obviously concerned for a purity of spirit, an integrity so hard for any man to come by. We are moved, for example, by "Shine, Perishing Republic," a poem too familiar to quote. It is not one of Jeffers' best things, but there is a fine tolerance for humankind in this poem that is attractive and that we respond to repeatedly. The theme of the poem is, after all, not so very new or terrible, having to do with the corruption of institutionalized life in the modern world, the tendency of mass culture to absorb protest and distinction and to heighten vulgarity in its citizens. Yeats had no less to say of such matters than Jeffers, and one need only think of those unbelievably awful poems of Lawrence's on the beastly bourgeoisie to realize how conventional among recent poets these concerns of Jeffers' have been. In fact, what is most responsible for the effectiveness Jeffers' poem has is the relatively understated quality it shares with some of the leaner lyrics that are not so well known. It is as though Jeffers were here dealing with realities too long pondered and accepted to fight over, and the assimilation of these contemporary realities to the perspective of eternal recurrence, ripeness, and decay allows Jeffers to speak of them with a calmness we admire. The poet's accents are firm, rather than petulantly defiant, as he counsels his children on the course he would have them follow: "Corruption / Never has been compulsory, when the cities lie at the monster's feet there are left the mountains." There is something almost plaintive in those words, "there are left the mountains," the procession of weak accents falling toward the final unaccented syllable, suggesting the encouragement of an option that is to be embraced only after others have been definitively abandoned, as they had been perhaps too casually by Jeffers himself.

What "Shine, Perishing Republic" lacks is a richness of sound and of metaphor. The language of the poem is not very interesting at all, dealing rather broadly in abstractions which yet do not confound, but which evoke, really, only other abstractions. If America is settling, as the poet claims, "in the mould of its vulgarity, heavily thickening to empire, / and protest, only a bubble in the molten mass, pops and sighs out, and the mass hardens," we can be expected to feel nothing more than modest dismay, for our sympathies have not been engaged by anything more than an issue, nicely stated, but hardly made manifest. And nowhere does the poem improve upon this initial evocation, the poet settling for modest effects, again largely concerned with assent rather than with intensifying our experience of a reality we are presumed to recognize as pertinent to our own.

I have no doubt whatever that Jeffers was more than aware of his inclination toward prophetic abstraction, toward the hollow exclamation patently ringing with WISDOM, as he was aware of a solemnity in his own demeanor that could degenerate into sententiousness in the poetry. But a brief sonnet like Jeffers' "Return" is so perfect in its way that to read it, again and again, is to forget Jeffers' faults and to wonder how a hard-boiled materialist often abused for the purple pride of his verse could manage to sound so much like Whitman, and yet like the Jeffers who was always so different from Whitman.

> A little too abstract, a little too wise,
> It is time for us to kiss the earth again,
> It is time to let the leaves rain from the skies,
> Let the rich life run to the roots again.
> I will go down to the lovely Sur Rivers
> And dip my arms in them up to the shoulders.
> I will find my accounting where the alder leaf quivers
> In the ocean wind over the river boulders.
> I will touch things and things and no more thoughts,
> That breed like mouthless May-flies darkening the sky,
> The insect clouds that blind our passionate hawks
> So that they cannot strike, hardly can fly.
> Things are the hawk's food and noble is the mountain, Oh noble
> Pico Blanco, steep sea-wave of marble.

Here at last is a poetry of sensation, of touch, in which form is meaning and substance, in which a restless and mobile imagery is the very whole and perfect embodiment of emotion. Here the poet feels not about his materials, but into and through them—things are his message, and as the poet thinks things he makes a poem. He has seen that to the degree that he thinks primarily thoughts he will cease to be a poet and become a philosopher, a spokesman, a critic, anything but a poet. Does it matter that there is a minimum of paraphrasable content in such a poem, as Winters argued against Jeffers' output generally? I think not, for then, what would we do with a Herrick, or with a lyricist like Hardy, were we forced to consider the content of a poem as the quantity of ideas to be gathered therefrom?

And indeed, what more is Jeffers saying but "no more thoughts," not absolutely and forever, but now, when we embody a poem, allow an image to course through and work upon our sensibilities, when we would be reverently humble, and grateful to life for what it is, which is more than we usually deserve. How marvelous Jeffers' image of thought as a swarm of "mouthless May-flies," and we need hardly remind ourselves how often our poets have railed against the intellect that darkens the possibilities of human feeling, that distracts and weakens both passion and pleasure. Are such commonplaces banal? Not as Jeffers has them in "Return" and in his better poems, for Jeffers here proceeds through an intuition that is more than an assertion of will. He is a poet, not of the world, but of a world *he* knew well, a world partial at best, but firmly gripped and eagerly loved, and his ability to make it known and real for others is a measure of his success as a poet.

Who among us that has read Jeffers with devotion, though critically, will not confess to an admiration for a man who could so charge a created universe with a network of images so consistently developed, so densely woven into the very fabric of the verse? Who more earnestly than Jeffers has confronted the frailty of our lives and engaged more desperately the attempt to reorient our customary perspectives, to take us beyond pain into praise and wonder? Jeffers knew all too well how men could suffer, and did; and he knew why they suffered, and his awareness rarely failed to leave him either angry or amused, or both, for he felt that most human suffering was the result of unwarranted expectations, foolish illusions. His entire career was dedicated to the chastisement of a pity he felt and knew others felt, for he did not believe that pity was an essentially human quality, though for the most part peculiar to our kind. He felt that pity, and the suffering it often implied, was a product not of human emotion, but of human civilization, and with this he had no sympathy at all. Against this civilization, the pride of Western man with its "little empty bundles of enjoyment," Jeffers set the figure of the hawk, the eagle, the falcon, the vulture, predators all, and cast them winging alternately amidst towering rocks and seething waters, landscapes of permanence and of violent energy. The ambience of Jeffers' poems is characteristically stark, though rarely barren, and one has in them a sense of granitic harshness, as of objects tempered in a flame so blazing as to burn away all that is ephemeral and soft and pitying—everything, in a word, that is simply and merely human. But Jeffers' poetry is neither antihuman nor inhuman. It plainly works itself out within a system of values which includes much that is human, in terms of what we are capable of responding to at our most intense. As one would expect in a created universe of considerable density, though not of great complexity, there is a recurrence of specific symbols within the pervasive imagery of the poems and a consequent cross fertilization of meanings, so that we are presented a vision of experience that is everywhere interfused, a frame of reference that cuts across entire groups of poems. Everywhere meanings seem to beckon away beyond themselves, so that in Jeffers' achieved works there is rarely an impression of a static quality, despite the weight of particular images.

Here is an irregular sonnet entitled "The Cruel Falcon," which ought to help us with some of the things we have been saying:

> Contemplation would make a good life, keep it strict, only
> The eyes of a desert skull drinking the sun,
> Too intense for flesh, lonely
> Exultations of white bone;
> Pure action would make a good life, let it be sharp-
> Set between the throat and the knife.
> A man who knows death by heart
> Is the man for that life.
> In pleasant peace and security
> How suddenly the soul in a man begins to die.

> He shall look up above the stalled oxen
> Envying the cruel falcon,
> And dig under the straw for a stone
> To bruise himself on.

With this extraordinary performance we move more securely into that created universe which we know with every accent as Jeffers'. The setting is harsh, the features of the landscape characteristic in the marmoreal coldness of their surfaces, the poetic energies intensely abiding in the carefully chiseled phrases. What we have here is the movement and vitality, not of life, but of an art that enhances life by appropriating its features in the interests of a vision at once more passionate and more lovely than any vision of life itself. Here is not that looseness of texture even discerning readers like Brother Antoninus have sought to legitimize in their defenses of Jeffers, for Jeffers knew that as a poet and as a man he could achieve liberation only through scrupulous concern for style, for form. There are no paradoxes in this mature vision, so finely wrought, no telling nuances to qualify the poet's commitment; but everything is precisely placed, distributed its proper weight, and there are elements of style so subtly woven into the poem's basic structure that they largely escape observation. Notice the delicacy with which Jeffers effects shifts of tense and mood in this poem, moving from the conditional into the hortatory, to the present indicative, to the future tense where he rests his case. It is a little triumph of the prophetic voice, urging without sinister overtones, stealthily proclaiming its insights without violence, for it has earned the privilege of prophecy by the substantiveness and accuracy of its representations in the course of the poem.

The language of "The Cruel Falcon" is, as we have intimated, perfectly accurate, and if this language is without that exotic strangeness we so admire in a Stevens, its dismissal of abstraction and of the commonplace routines of experience is impressive enough. And what precisely does Jeffers mean when he admonishes us to "keep it strict," to speculate on the contours of a "pure action," to abandon the "pleasant peace and security" that are the extinction of the soul? I do not know why critical observers have found it so difficult to explain these admonitions, why they have resorted to the interpretation of inhumanism to explain the work of a man all too frail, too human, and in his way enamored of a beauty our best men have long sought to capture and identify. Jeffers' concern in his poems is with the liberation of spirit from what is gross. Human flesh is gross: the conventions by which men cultivate the pleasures of flesh utterly ingenious and thoroughly destructive of alternative values. Jeffers' concern is with a resurrection of spirit out of the ashes of human display, a religious concern, and is frequently expressed in terms that have their source in religious archetypes. The chastisement of flesh has, after all, been a staple feature of religious practice for any number of millenniums, though Jeffers' extension of this tradition has its unique attributes. For Jeffers the god who creates and observes his universe cares not what we do, so long as we do it well, so long as life is clean and vibrant with energy and possibilities of renewal, so long as it is whole, sufficient unto itself like the rocks Jeffers loved to contemplate, like the white bone of the desert skull in his poem, freed of gross desire, liberated to "lonely exultations."

If Jeffers is truly a religious poet, he can be said to worship largely at the altar of art, for his resolution of the problems of spirit is really an aesthetic resolution, just as his politics, if he did indeed have a politics, is fundamentally determined by an aesthetic response to the world. Jeffers disparaged not human life, but the ways in which human beings could destroy their world and each other. There is nothing barbaric or Fascistic about these lines from "November Surf," generated by the poet's disgusted observation of the summer refuse that litters the clean surfaces of his beloved shoreline, with its smoldering waves and granite promontories:

The earth, in her childlike prophetic sleep,
Keeps dreaming of the bath of a storm that prepares up the long
  coast
Of the future to scour more than her sea-lines:
The cities gone down, the people fewer and the hawks more
  numerous,
The rivers mouth to source pure; when the two-footed
Mammal, being someways one of the nobler animals, regains
The dignity of room, the value of rareness.

It is distressing that at this late date one should feel it necessary
to defend such writing, when its intentions are so clear and so
fundamentally decent. Perhaps the crucial words in the passage
are "childlike," "dignity," "rareness." Yeats would have understood Jeffers' meanings without any difficulty whatever, and
though the Irish poet could speak in certain poems of "all hatred
driven hence" and of the blight that is arrogance, he knew the
value of passions bordering on violence and of sudden purgation. And just as Yeats could speak of ceremonies of innocence,
so Jeffers sanctifies the "childlike prophetic sleep" of the
elemental, innocent in its contentment with the wholeness, the
unity, of all things. For Jeffers the cities of man, representing
industrial civilization, are a violation, an index to the dishar-
mony and spurious competitiveness that have always distinguished our species. In the perspective of Jeffers' poems,
human life is a defilement of all that is dignified and whole, and
we are to listen to him not because he says we should, but
because the poetic manifestations of his vision are sufficient to
his message. How easy it is to ridicule Jeffers, to parody his
preference of a hawk to a man; but given the terms of his
vision, there is nothing in this to mock. For poetry is not a
program, not a series of proposals which are literally to be
carried over into the domain of normal human activity. Brother
Antoninus has written eloquently on these matters in his book:
"We must not shut ourselves off from the archetypal sources in

[an artist's] vision by virtue of [our] revulsion from their social consequences when attempted politically in our time." The poet "makes his vision permanent by virtue of its inherent aesthetic, which protects it from misapplication in the phenomenal world, because once it is translated into another idiom it vanishes."

Jeffers' exaltation of the hawk, then, is not an exaltation of a naked violence that will see the destruction of man by man, but an exaltation of nature, of need, of instinct. For Jeffers the instinct of the hawk is tolerable, even majestic, because it does not seek to aggrandize itself at the expense of creation—it strikes according to its need and within a framework that does not threaten the fundamental harmony of other things. Its rarity he saw as a quality intrinsic to its nature, associated also with its reasonable relationship to its surroundings. At the point where the environment could not support increasing numbers of the species, the species by a law intrinsic to its nature would cease to multiply: not a matter of will but of nature. How different is man, clamoring for a little space, killing for programs and ideologies. And anthropological investigations into the similarity of human and animal aggressions, explanations of territoriality as a fundamental impulse of all life, would have left Jeffers no less secure in his mounting of the distinction, for Jeffers' thesis was not developed as fact, but as intuition. In the development of an ideal of what is beautiful and can authentically be meaningful to men, Jeffers' vision resists the disparagements of scientific critiques.

Jeffers does not succumb, it must be said, to pure aestheticism. His indictments of mass man, which is to say of man in our time, are not without a measure of conventionally *human* sentiment, and a number of the poems evoke a tension in which the resort to aestheticism is viewed as an element of necessity rather than of will or choice. The conflict in Jeffers is powerfully dramatized in the poem "Rearmament"—a poem in whose broadly undulating rhythms and the sweep of its long line the very quality and substance of Jeffers' message is embodied and reflected:

These grand and fatal movements toward death: the grandeur
   of the mass
Makes pity a fool, the tearing pity
For the atoms of the mass, the persons, the victims, makes it
   seem monstrous
To admire the tragic beauty they build.
It is beautiful as a river flowing or a slowly gathering
Glacier on a high mountain rock-face,
Bound to plow down a forest, or as frost in November,
The gold and flaming death-dance for leaves,
Or a girl in the night of her spent maidenhood, bleeding and
   kissing.
I would burn my right hand in a slow fire
To change the future . . . I should do foolishly. The beauty of
   modern
Man is not in the persons but in the
Disastrous rhythm, the heavy and mobile masses, the dance of the
Dream-led masses down the dark mountain.

The rhetorical aspects of this poem are not as subdued as they might be, but a poem dealing with the disastrous currents of an entire civilization heading toward ruin need not apologize for a vocabulary that includes such terms as "fatal," "tearing pity," "monstrous," and "disastrous." It is a poem that teaches us a good deal about the function of art, or at least of an art that would transcend our sufferings and the evils we promote. It is an example of an art that through identification with the impersonal roots of all human behavior, of all activity in this universe, permits us to contemplate the reality of our foolishness and mortality without much pain, but with praise forming at the lips. Here, perhaps more clearly than in any other poem, Jeffers makes clear what we ought to have known even in his lesser work. To attribute, as Jeffers does, foolishness to the instinct to "burn my right hand in a slow fire / To change the future" is not to consign oneself to the perdition of the heartless, but to seek to forge out of futility a perspective in which futility can be relieved of its manifest failures, purified, rhythmically interpolated into a pattern in which it has meaning as part of that process that is life on this planet. The detachment that makes most great art possible is not heartless, nor is the distancing that is the process of the historical perspective, and that consigns to men the relative insignificance they deserve in the scheme of things, without its virtue. Throughout his career Jeffers tried to resolve the ambiguities of his vision in a direction that would take him further and further from concern with his fellows. How successful he was we can see in "Rearmament," with its persisting ambiguities and unresolved tensions. What is unmistakable, though, is the poet's steadfast refusal to counsel violence among men and his ability to achieve a perspective wherein the violence men would and did commit could be made tolerable, in a way even absorbed into the universe as an element of necessity. It is nothing less than a tragic vision; and if Jeffers in his poetry could not sufficiently examine and evoke the larger potentialities of man within his limitations, as could a Shakespeare and a Yeats, he did at least project a vision worthy of our attention and capable of giving pleasure. The felicities of Jeffers' poetry ought no longer to be denied, but received with gratitude. If he was not among our supreme poets, they have been few who were his equals.

The Experience of the Eye:
Marianne Moore's Tradition

Miss Moore has told *viva voce*, and surely more than once, the story of her supervised visit to the zoo. She had consented to be accompanied there by a man from *Life*, to be photographed in acts of guarded friendship with such beasts as might offset, by their bizarre aloofness, her innocent self-sufficient face and cartwheel hat. She had nothing more to say, though *Life* later had a few hundred words to say, about her dealings with the photogenic beasts. What she remembered was a man expounding the snakes to a group of children. She had heard what he said and noted what he neglected to say: a libel by omission, which she saw it was her duty to correct. So, "You must be sure to tell those children," she said, "that snakes are not cold and not slimy; that they are dry and just as warm as their surroundings. One need not hesitate to touch them." The man from *Life* saw his cue; he caused a large snake to be passed into the hands of Miss Moore. He was obeying the tradition by which journalism was governed as long ago as Boswell's famous question to Dr. Johnson: "What would you do, Sir, if you were shut up in a tower with a baby?" It is the tradition of Pécuchet's laboratory: supply some incongruous reagent, and see what happens. It is the molecular unit in the only American tradition for dealing with genius, which is to write a biography.

Miss Moore did not flinch from her principle, though she had never handled a snake before. She accepted it. She was immediately asked what it felt like. And then, faithful to a tradition of her own, she consulted her fingers and the memories to which her fingers gave access, and pronounced simply, "Like rose petals." It was perhaps too poetic a remark to make its point, but she has never allowed a fear of being thought poetic to deter her from accuracy. For she meant the resemblance of snakes to rose petals neither as a fancy nor as a simile, but as a virtual identity of tactile sensation: a species of wit gone into the fingertips: a tactile pun.

In her poems, things utter puns to the senses. These, registered in words, make odd corrugations of the linguistic surface. Thus her words note a certain sleepy cat's "prune-shaped head and alligator eyes" and identify in his whiskers "the shadbones regularly set about the mouth, to droop or rise / in unison like the porcupine's quills," and register him, awake, "Springing about with froglike accuracy": the frog and the cat being two creatures that land where they meant to.

This policy of accurate comparison, bringing, if need be, the prune, the alligator, the shad, the porcupine, the frog to the service of a discussion of a cat, does not worry about congruousness just as Braque does not worry about perspective, being intent on a different way of filling its elected spaces. Congruity, like perspective, deals in proportions within an over-all view. Miss Moore's poems deal in many separate acts of attention: optical puns, seen by snapshot, in a poetics normally governed by the eye, sometimes by the ears and fingers, ultimately by the moral sense. It is the poetics of the solitary observer, for whose situation the usual meanings of a word like "moral" have to be redefined: a poetics whose effort to define itself has for two centuries constituted a tradition of some centrality. To understand that tradition is to perceive Miss Moore's place in the story of the mind of Europe neither as eccentric nor as peripheral, as she is sometimes made to seem.

Not more than two centuries' weight, though two centuries of continuous revolution, lies behind the ideal of describing accurately the thing seen. The art of doing that was developed, so far as it has been developed, almost wholly in the nineteenth century. Hardly anyone had wanted to do it earlier. It was a thing that Boswell felt he wanted to do, when the Hebrides

offered ruins, rocks, and grandeurs, but the despairing *Journal*
note in which he confesses to being very weak at it points less
to his private inadequacies than to the fact that there existed no
descriptive tradition from which he might have learned. Words
can set things seen before the mind only by a system of
analogies, and no one had thought to want analogies for the
experience of the eye, as it passes along the contours or across
the surfaces of the seen world.

This is not a question of what is called "visual imagery."
When Shakespeare has Romeo say,

> Night's candles are burnt out, and jocund day
> Stands tiptoe on the misty mountain-top,

he sets before our minds visual imagery, but imagery that offers
no analogy for the experience of the eye; rather, for our icono-
grams of effortless power. If you commission an artist to draw
what Shakespeare is setting before the mind, you get Blake's
painting "Glad Day," which looks like a jocund youth but not
like the sun rising. In the same way "night's candles" suggests
the elation of the mind, but not the experience of the eye with
a field of stars. Nature, from the time of Homer to the time
of John Donne, had been apprehended according to forms of
personal analogies, as a field of wills and forces which, written
down as analytically as possible, generated the physics of things
seeking their places and vacua abhorred; and written down
according to a less exigent discipline, the world of moonlight
sleeping on banks, winds cracking their cheeks, and the stars
keeping their courses. So pervasive is this tradition that even
the austerity that merely names things is apt to commit the
things named to fields of mythological force. In the little poem
attributed to Sappho which begins *Deduke men a selanna*
we are apt to find what no doubt H.D. found, pioneering
Imagism:

> The moon is gone down,
> and the Pleiades,

> time passes, and at midnight
> I lie in my bed alone.

But almost certainly a Greek reader would have thought of the moon going down to sleep with Endymion, and the Pleiades with Ocean. Far from being numbed, as we Copernicans feel, by the heavens' chill otherness, the poet feels deserted while they are fulfilled. Delicate arms enfold the beings of the sky; all things complete their couplings save myself.

In a world which was felt in that way the mere testimony of the eye had negligible power to declare the otherness of the visible; and after the world had ceased to be felt in that way, sometime in the seventeenth century, after the New Philosophy had put all in doubt, the eye did not instantly enforce such assertions. Rather poetic diction continued to trace the old paths, informing us that restless Sol had shone his ardent ray, and justifying itself by claims about sublimity and about fancy. Already by the 1720's Pope had sensed that the old language, in enlightened times, could only make fun of itself in a complicated fashion, the real world, as distinguished from the one poetry inhabits, having been created by Sir Isaac Newton. Pope at his most solemn remains a tireless personifier—

> Another age shall see the golden ear
> Embrown the slope, and nod on the parterre.

It was not until the 1790's that the universe of Newton, about which in detail there is much to record but really little to say, was admitted to English poetry.

Wordsworth, of course, admitted it—Wordsworth whose very model was Newton, the unspeaking sage: not generating utterances (except perhaps afterward, in tranquility), but rather "voyaging through strange seas of thought, alone." And Wordsworth seeking to come to terms with a world where no restless Sol puts forth an ardent ray, but rather people are "Roll'd round in earth's diurnal course / With rocks, and stones, and trees," sensed at once that in the presence of such a universe one's traditional language could register no more than one's feelings about it. And Wordsworth's is the traditional language. His diction, by which he maneuvers himself from one end of a poem to the other, retains the trick of personifying, but a trick now suffused by "as if":

> The city now doth like a garment wear
> The beauty of the morning;

and what is not personified will be merely listed:

> silent, bare,
> Ships, towers, domes, theatres, and temples lie
> Open unto the fields, and to the sky,
> All bright and glittering in the smokeless air.

The Westminster Bridge sonnet is partly about the bare city and partly about the observer's emotions:

> Ne'er saw I, never felt, a calm so deep!

For this universe, as he was to reflect repeatedly, is one whose meaning you half-perceive and half-create. Moreover, it half-creates you; and Wordsworth's principal subject became "The Prelude, or The Growth of a Poet's Soul." And there, for some decades, the matter rested.

Or there poetry let it rest. The task of mediating with a universe now merely visible, now merely *there,* was carried on, since no work of the imagination is ever abandoned; but not carried on by poets, who contented themselves with the orchestration of passion. It was carried on by painters and scientists. Wordsworth's immediate successor is John Constable, whose theme is quite simply a drama perceptible in the experience of the eye, experience imitated by the brush. Next, with less drama but much narrative about field work, the art of natural description was pursued by geologists, who had two objectives, both practical. Their first objective was to present in a printed book an array of visual evidence, at a time when getting an accurate picture onto the page involved laborious collaboration between observer, artist, and engraver. The observer had maximal control over his discriminations and emphases if he could somehow learn to make his point with unassisted language. Their other objective was to educate the reader's eye, so he could learn to see things for himself. The finest energies of the nineteenth century flowed into teaching people to see what was around them, reading in a new way, intimate, surprising, the Book of Nature. By the time Sherlock Holmes was damning "the great unobservant public, that could hardly tell a weaver by his tooth, or a compositor by his left thumb," the tradition had become accessible for vulgarization in the *Strand* magazine. It was a Scottish geologist, Hugh Miller, who composed the phrase Stephen Dedalus was to draw from his treasure house, "a day of dappled seaborn clouds." It was a Swiss naturalist, Louis Agassiz, who carried the mimesis by words of the experience of the eye to such a pitch that Ezra Pound, in whose visual world "light shaves grass into emerald," was to set him in the sphere of the fixed stars and remark that he could teach "even a literatus" to write. And a principal amateur geologist of the nineteenth century, who spent some thousands of pounds on a collection of rocks and gems, and gave his attention by turns to the experience of the eye amid natural things and the experience of the eye amid the painted forms of a Constable or a Turner, was of course John Ruskin.

Two quotations from Ruskin will bring us to the threshold of Miss Moore. Here is what he says about the moral attributes of perception:

The greatest thing a human soul ever does in this world is to see something, and tell what it saw in a plain way. Hundreds of people can talk for one who can think, but thousands can think for one who can see. To see clearly is poetry, prophecy and religion all in one.

This tells us that Nature does not teach us by dramatic example, as the Renaissance supposed, or by stealing into our hearts in a wise passiveness, as Wordsworth supposed, but by guiding an act of perception and enunciation entered into with the whole being: which act is a moral act and exfoliates legitimately into moral reflections. Here is Ruskin describing a fir tree:

The Power of the tree . . . is in the dark, flat, solid tables of leafage, which it holds out on its strong arms, curved slightly over them like shields, and spreading towards the extremity like a hand. It is vain to endeavor to paint the sharp, grassy, intricate leafage until this ruling form has been secured; and in the boughs that approach the spectator the foreshortening of it is just like that of a wide hill-country, ridge just rising over ridge in successive distances.

The moral reflection Ruskin derives from this is that painters have an obligation to look. For the passage is specifically an education of the eye for painters, who without Ruskin to instruct them in seeing are apt to paint fir trees constructed like chandeliers. He is tracing the tree's visible gestures. The strong arms his fir tree holds out betoken no act of facile personification, in the manner of the tiptoe posture of Romeo's dawn. They are analogies for the eye retracing the gesture made in three-dimensional space by piney branches. These arms hold out "dark, flat, solid tables of leafage," and these tables curve over the branches "like shields," and spread out toward the extremity "like a hand." They are foreshortened, furthermore, as they approach the spectator, like the ridges of "a wide hill-country." Arms, tables, shields, hands, hills, are so many analogies for the experience of the eye, by which the painter's eye is to be educated, and the art critic's also. They do not constitute a recipe for a painter, who if he were to paint what Ruskin names would arrive at surrealism. He is to learn what Ruskin names, and paint the tree, having learned at last how to see it; and this putting down of what he has learned to see will not be copying, but "poetry, prophecy and religion all in one."

This tree of arms, shields, tables, hands, and hills, like Miss Moore's cat of porcupine, alligator, shad and prune and frog, is a tree of language, not of painting, existing only on Ruskin's printed page. It got there by an effort of attention, commanding the resources of the whole being, that devised and traversed a half dozen analogies—analogies not for a tree but for a tree's fancied kinetic act, and the eye's act responding. And Miss Moore's focal discovery, aligning her with Braque, not with Dali, has been simply this: that poetic cats exist only on the page. Ruskin himself did not know this, being content to impersonate Isaiah.

Like prophecy since Isaiah, poetry since Homer has imitated a voice crying, and the literary imitation of the visual was involved, when the problem finally arose, in endless compromises occasioned by the fact that the visual is voiceless. Wordsworth dropped his voice to a murmur without quite availing, and poetry ceded the theme pending the discovery of some poetic medium as physical, as detectable as John Constable's pigments. This medium proved at last to be something as uncompromisingly mute as cats and trees: the printed page itself.

In Miss Moore's time—she was born thirteen years before Ruskin died—the poet has found it indispensable to work directly with the printed page, which is where, and only where, his cats and trees exist. Constable in the same way worked directly with his pigments, and not by transmitting directions to an accomplice. We may say that this became possible when poets began to use typewriters. And we may note three of the things that Miss Moore has been in her lifetime: a librarian; an editor; and a teacher of typewriting: locating fragments already printed; picking and choosing; making, letter by letter, neat pages.

Her poems are not for the voice; she senses this in herself reading them badly; in response to a question, she once said that she wrote them for people to look at. Moreover, one cannot imagine them handwritten; for as Ruskin's tree, on the page, exists in tension between arboreal process and the mind's serial inventory of arms, shields, tables, hands, and hills, so Miss Moore's cats, her fish, her pangolins and ostriches exist on the page in tension between the mechanisms of print and the presence of a person behind those mechanisms. Handwriting flows with the voice, and here the voice is as synthetic as the cat, not something the elocutionist can modulate. The words on these pages are little regular blocks, set apart by spaces, that have been generated not by the voice, but by the click of the keys and the ratcheting of the carriage.

The stanzas lie on the page, one after another, in little intricate grids of visual symmetry, the left margin indented according to complex rules which govern the setting of tabulator stops. The lines obey no rhythmic system the ear can apprehend; that there is a system we learn not by listening but by counting syllables, and we find that the words exist within a grid of numerical rules. Thus *The Fish* has 27 syllables per stanza, arranged in five lines on a three-part scheme of indentation, the syllables apportioned among the lines 1, 3, 9, 6, 8. And since a mosaic has no point of beginning, the poem is generated from somewhere just outside its own rigidly plotted field: generated not merely by ichthyological reality but by two words, "The Fish," which are part of the first sentence, but not part of the pattern, being in fact the poem's title. Therefore:

THE FISH

wade
through black jade.
            Of the crow-blue mussel-shells, one keeps
            adjusting the ash-heaps;
                        opening and shutting itself like
an
injured fan.

To begin this sentence we read the title, and to end it we read three words (four syllables) of the stanza: for the single stanza is a patterned zone specified within, but not coterminous with, the articulation of the sentences. The single stanza exhibits, in fact, an archaic disregard of the mere things human desire does with sentences. The voice shaping sentences is anxious to be understood; the stanzas are cut and laminated in severe corrective to that anxiety, posing against it their authority of number (1, 3, 9, 6, 8) and typography. They even invade the sounds of speech with their rhymes, not performing, however, the traditional offices of rhymes, not miming a symmetry, clinching an epigram, or caressing a melodic fluid, but cutting, cutting, cutting, with implacable arbitrariness: "like / an / injured fan."

It is a poem to see with the eye, conceived in a typewriter upon an 8½ x 11" sheet of paper. If metric is a system of emphases, centered in human comfort, human hope, syllable count is a system of zoning, implied by the objectivity of the words, which lie still side by side for their syllables to be counted. If the stanzas of "Go, lovely rose" are audible, created by the symmetries of the uttering voice, the stanzas of "The Fish" are visible wholly, created by the arrangement of words in typographical space, the poem made for us to look at. And it is amusing to notice that Miss Moore can revise a poem from beginning to end without changing a word in it. The first three times "The Fish" appeared in print its stanzaic system grouped the syllables not 1, 3, 9, 6, 8, but 1, 3, 8, 1, 6, 8, and in six lines, not five. What we have been looking at since 1930 is a revised version. The poem was twelve years old when the author made this change, and it is not, despite the mechanical ease of retyping with newly set tabulator stops, a trivial change, since it affects the system by which pattern intersects utterance, alters the points at which the intersections occur, provides a new grid of impediments to the overanxious voice, and modifies, moreover, the obtrusiveness of the system itself; the new version actually relents a little its self-sufficient arbitrariness and consigns more leisurely fish to only half as many winking little quick monosyllabic turns. One can nearly say, putting the first and second versions side by side, that we have a *new* poem, arrived at in public, without changing a word, by applying a system of transformations to an existing poem. One remembers Charles Ives's statement that American music is *already written* (so that he had no need to invent tunes), and his pendant outburst on sound ("What has music to do with sound?"), as who should ask, What has poetry to do with people's anxiety to make themselves understood?

It contains, of course, the rituals generated by that anxiety, as music contains sound. Miss Moore's poems deal with those rituals as music dealt with them before the clavichord's mathematic was supplanted by the throb of the violin. She will not imitate the rising throbbing curve of emotion, but impede it and quick-freeze it. One impediment is the grid of counted formalisms. Another is the heavy system of nouns.

> The Fish
> wade
> through black jade. . . .

The black jade got onto the page by the same process as Ruskin's arms, shields, and hills, but without benefit of the syntactic lubricants that slide us past a comparison: simile becomes optical pun. "Black jade" is an optical pun. So are the "ash-heaps" of the "crow-blue mussel-shells." Optical precision has brought these ash heaps and crows into the poem; a moment later it will bring in a fan, to swell the bizarre submarine population; and before the poem is over we shall have taken stock of spun glass, turquoise, stars, pink rice grains, green lilies, toadstools, an iron wedge, a cornice. Each of these optical puns a moment's thought will assimilate; yet each such moment interrupts the attention (which simply does not expect to encounter such objects under water) and interrupts also the expected mechanisms of the English sentence, which has two places for nouns, before verbs and after them, actor noun and patient noun, "John threw the ball," but not "move themselves with *spotlight* swiftness." Miss Moore's sentences, unlike those of Olson or Creeley, are formally impeccable; but that impeccability, like the straightness of the horizontal lines of a graph, takes some searching out, interrupted as it so constantly is by repeated intersections with different systems entirely for dealing with nouns.

Just as idiosyncratically the poems deal with quotations. These lie on the page with as arbitrary a look as the nouns wear, set off by quotation marks, yet none of them familiar quotations: not allusions therefore but found objects, slivers of excellence incorporated into the *assemblage*. One function of the notes to these quotations is to persuade us that they are genuine found objects, that Miss Moore has not been fabricating found objects by setting quotation marks around phrases of her own devising. The notes are not, like the notes to *The Waste Land*, part of our education; we are certainly not meant to look up the sources; the author says she hopes that we will "take probity on faith" and disregard them. And it is probity, of course, that these poems most obviously enact, creating, according to rigorous self-imposed rules, a crystalline structure, bristling with internal geometry, which (1) exhibits patent optical symmetries; (2) reassures us, if we take the trouble to trace out its syntax, by rigorously fulfilling any syntactic law we care to apply; (3) maneuvers through this system, with a maximum of surface discontinuity, some dozens of surprising words and phrases, treated as objects, laid end to end; and (4) justifies each of these objects by a triumphant hidden congruity, usually based on some acute visual resemblance. The poem is a system, not an utterance, though one can trace an utterance through it.

The poem is *other* than an utterance, other than what the poet "has to say." And this otherness is doubled by the presence within the poem of some autonomous envelope of energies, a fish, a cat, a ballplayer, to which the poem conforms its oddly depersonalized system of analogies. This autonomous thing is always represented as fulfilling the laws of its own being by minding its own business, which is not ours. It also fulfills laws of the poem's being, serving frequently as a point of departure, left behind. Thus the poem headed "An Octopus" is really "about" a glacier, probably the only glacier in literature that not only exists but behaves, and in a way means to earn our approbation.

AN OCTOPUS

of ice. Deceptively reserved and flat,
it lies 'in grandeur and in mass'
beneath a sea of shifting snow-dunes;
dots of cyclamen-red and maroon on its clearly-defined pseudopodia
made of glass that will bend—a much needed invention—
comprising twenty-eight ice-fields from fifty to five hundred feet
    thick,
of unimagined delicacy.
'Picking periwinkles from the cracks'
or killing prey with the concentric crushing rigor of the python,
it hovers forward 'spider-fashion
on its arms' misleadingly like lace;
its 'ghostly pallor changing
to the green metallic tinge of an anemone-starred pool.' . . .

The icy octopus has by this time torn up and carried toward us not only the normal detritus of the landscape but five separate quotations, being in this respect as "deceptively reserved" as the poet. And the poem continues to edge forward glacially, picking up and shifting periwinkles, pythons, spiders, lace, anemone. In fact, by the time it has drawn toward its close (having incorporated, *inter alia,* the Greek language, Henry James, and numerous citations from the National Parks Rules and Regulations), it appears to be discussing its own decorum as much as that of the glacier-octopus:

    Relentless accuracy is the nature of this octopus
    with its capacity for fact.

'Creeping slowly as with mediated stealth,
its arms seeming to approach from all directions' . . .

It resembles, in its "capacity for fact," the capacity of the imaginary garden, in the celebrated example, for real toads. Miss Moore's subjects—better, perhaps, her fields of preoccupation—have these two notable characteristics among others: that they are self-sufficient systems of energy and that they can appropriate, without hostility, almost anything that comes near. They are generally animals; they feed and sleep and hunt and play; they are graceful, without taking pride in their grace. They exemplify, as nearly as possible, the qualities of the poems in which they are found.

This is the point to invoke one last tradition and make one last discrimination, for we are on treacherous ground. When the moral of a poem is its own aesthetic, aesthetics have become at least continuous with morals, a continuity human experience has recurrently tested and seldom found reliable. Miss Moore, causing her poems to enact with such rigor the moral virtues they celebrate, skirts the tradition of the dandy, whose life was a controlled thing and whose norms of conduct were stylistic. The tradition was detached from that of fancy dress and made available to art by the "Tragic Generation" among whom Yeats passed his youth; its principal modern celebrant, a descendant of the nineties in that as in so much else, was Ernest Hemingway, whose bullfights and lion hunts were aesthetic gestures and whose descriptions of clear water running over stones were moral achievements. It is Hemingway who most dramatically fulfills, in our time, Ruskin's precept that to see something, and tell what one saw in a plain way, is "poetry, prophecy and religion all in one," though the second word would have made him uneasy. We can see in his career one apotheosis to which the discipline of describing natural objects was tending during many decades.

But Hemingway's conception of style as the criterion of life, which he had from the tragic dandies of whom Lionel

Johnson may serve as the type, contains one element totally alien to any poetic effect of Miss Moore: *self-appreciation.* To take satisfaction in one's achievements, and to undertake the achievements in quest of that satisfaction, these are the great temptations by which such a poetics is beset; and the theme of many poems of Miss Moore is precisely the duty to resist such a temptation. Her black elephant utters an opening vaunt not immune from self-congratulation:

> Openly, yes,
>   with the naturalness
>   of the hippopotamus or the alligator
>   when it climbs out on the bank to experience the
>   sun, I do these
>   things which I do, which please
>   no one but myself . . .

but midway through the poem it is making a crucial discrimination:

> . . . nevertheless I
>   perceive feats of strength to be inexplicable after
>   all; and I am on my guard: external poise, it
>   has its centre
>   well nurtured—we know
>   where—in pride; but spiritual poise, it has its centre where?

To offer behavior which is "inexplicable after all" is to take no credit for it. The "beautiful element of unreason" has its uses. Another poem in the same way recommends "unconscious fastidiousness," and having surveyed with some astringency the behavior of a swan and of an ant, asks,

>   . . . What is
> there in being able
>   to say that one has dominated the stream in an attitude of self-
>   defence;
>   in proving that one has had the experience
>   of carrying a stick?

These last words delimit our present theme. To "prove that one has had the experience" of playing with a cat, or seeing a fish, or pretending to be an elephant is just what a poetics of visual experience is likely to find itself engaged upon: even as Ruskin tended to be intent on proving that he alone had ever really seen a fir tree. We have seen some of the formal obstacles Miss Moore lays across the assertions of her sentences, in part to avoid implying that a cat or a fish has never really been looked at before. The remaining problem is how to avoid seeming to assert that one has had the experience of overcoming formal obstacles. It is here that her habitual preoccupation with otherness comes to her aid.

For those autonomous envelopes of energy she so admires are adamantly *other,* in a way that Wordsworth's Nature never was. Where Hemingway imitated bullfighters, she is content to admire ballplayers. Her cats, her jerboas, her pangolins and elephants, are not beings she half-perceives and half-creates. Their accomplishments are wholly their own. It is not the poet who notes that the jerboa is sand-colored, but the jerboa that "honors the sand by assuming its color." Similarly the verse, without an excess of mimetic virtuosity, follows the little creature toward its burrow:

> By fifths and sevenths,
> in leaps of two lengths,
>> like the uneven notes
>> of the Bedouin flute, it stops its gleaning
>>> on little wheel castors, and makes fern-seed
>>> foot-prints with kangaroo speed.
>
> Its leaps should be set
> to the flageolet;
>> pillar body erect
>> on a three-cornered smooth-working Chippendale
>>> claw—propped on hind legs, and tail as third toe,
>>> between leaps to its burrow.

It is the animal that has discovered a flute rhythm for itself, "by fifths and sevenths / in leaps of two lengths," and to play the flageolet in its presence is not our ingenuity but our obligation. Similarly the formal ingenuities of the poem, each stanza opening with a 5-syllable line and closing with a 7, are a tribute the jerboa earns. So when, as normally, we find that the poem is itself enacting the virtues it discerns in its subject, we are not to say that what it is doing is commenting on its own aesthetic, as in Hemingway's celebrations of the way one works close to the bull; rather that its aesthetic is an offering to the virtuosity of the brisk little creature that changes pace so deftly, and direction so deftly, and keeps intent, and keeps alert, and both offers and refrains from flaunting its agility.

The subject is other, exacting tribute; Miss Moore's descriptions are not feats, but homages. She herself, finally, is other; and saying with the elephant, "I do these / things which I do, which please / no one but myself," she is fulfilling a nature of her own, in whose presence the merely curious are meant to be disarmed. For the unclubbable cat she offers this defense:

> As for the disposition
> invariably to affront, an animal with claws wants to have to use
> them; that eel-like extension of trunk into tail is not an accident.
>   [To
> leap, to lengthen out, divide the air—to purloin, to pursue.
>   To tell the hen: fly over the fence, go in the wrong way in your
>   [perturba-
>   tion—this is life; to do less would be nothing but dishonesty.

In the same way, a being with an eye wants to have to use it; and so does a being with a memory, and a being with a typewriter. So by a long way round, by way of a poetics that dislocates, seemingly, each nuance of normal utterance, this rendition of the experience of the eye comes to be natural after all, an instance of commendable behavior. It imitates, in Aristotle's strictest sense, without congratulating itself on having thought to imitate or on having found the means. It compels our minds to move across an opaque and resistant surface, that of the printed language, in emulation of the eye's experience moving across the contours of a pangolin's armor; and it impedes the facilities of the conclusion drawn, the thing said, the instance appropriated into a satisfactory system, on the principle that while psychic experience flows naturally into utterance, optical experience requires to be carefully anatomized before we can too readily allow it to be psychic. For the supreme insult—this is its final claim—the supreme insult to that which is other than we, that which, perceived by the eye, is *therefore* other: the supreme insult we can offer to the other is to have, on too little acquaintance, something to say "about" it.

T. S. Eliot: The Transformation
of a Personality

GEORGE T. WRIGHT

I

To understand the personae of any writer we must first have
an idea of the characters who inhabit the world of his poetry,
for it is from these characters that the personae, the speakers,
will be drawn. Some writers, perhaps because of the genres they
usually explore, use few characters, others use many; some use
vaguely defined people, others define them with great precision; some poets change their tactics in the course of their
career, greatly increasing or decreasing the number or the
exactness of their people, without usually abandoning the
qualities that hold all the characters together. For every poet
we sense a range of persons who represent in part the poet's
view of human life.

Probably on no other score has Eliot's work been so condemned as for its choice and treatment of people. Yet the
number of characters who, directly or by immediately understood allusion, make their way into his poems is phenomenal.
Because of the peculiar allusive structure of his verse, it is
difficult to draw a line between who is and who is not actually
in his poems. In one sense, only the old man, his boy, and
his housekeeper inhabit the world of "Gerontion"; in a second
sense, it is inhabited also by the jew, Christ, Mr. Silvero, Haka-
gawa, Mme. de Tornquist, Fräulein von Kulp, De Bailhache,
Fresca, and Mrs. Cammel; in a third sense, it is inhabited
by characters whom the old man's phrasing recalls—Vindici,
Beatrice of *The Changeling*, Everyman, Tennyson's Ulysses,

Judas, and others, all of whom are, when the allusions are perceived, hardly more shadowy than the second-level characters or, indeed, than the boy, the housekeeper, or even the old man himself. In the same way *The Waste Land* employs a small army of characters either present or recalled, all of whom contribute to our impression of Eliot's treatment of people. And other poems, especially those written no later than 1922, introduce people almost as multitudinously as Hardy's *The Dynasts*.

But the peculiarity of number is not the only distinguishing mark of Eliot's characters. Their kind of actuality is rather different from that of any other poet's people. In the first place, the poet cares little for their individual qualities; what he cares about is their relationship to certain enduring archetypal roles. They act, consequently, if they act at all, in conformity to the demands of their roles rather than from what we should call personal motives. The details of their talk, of their manners, of their gestures, are idiosyncratic rather of their roles than of themselves. The shifting of the candles by Mme. de Tornquist, the entrance of Doris from the bath, the successive actions of the typist and the clerk, all reflect nothing individual in these persons—no charming inconsistency, no personal diabolism—but are clearly ritual actions that they perform in order to fulfill their roles in a ritual drama.

It is this ritual aspect of his characters which makes them so different from the people we usually know. We are accustomed to thinking of people as individuals, or at least as types familiar to our culture, but, for the purposes of his poetry at least, Eliot gives us people whose archetypal roles characterize them more fully than do their cultural and individual peculiarities. Occasionally what we think of as a human face breaks through the archetypal mist—Prufrock, the Lady, sometimes even Sweeney, and the poet himself in *Four Quartets*. Such characters as these are exhibited in their culture in somewhat more detail; the poet permits them greater local definition. But they still retain their roles in the ritual drama, still speak and act in response to ritual demands. The typical character in Eliot's poetry is like the Lady at the beginning of "A Game of Chess," identified only by her room and the objects it contains, by her perfume and by the disembodied words she utters. We see everything in her setting, but of her nothing but her hair. Naturally enough: *she* is not important; what is important is the role that she plays, a role defined more fully by her environment than by anything peculiar to herself.

At the same time, though, the contemporaneity of the archetypal is stressed. Most of Eliot's characters are drawn from modern European culture, and much of the point in their actions lies in the juxtapositions within them of contemporary and eternal human qualities. This arrangement enables Eliot to present the modern world as merely one of an infinite number of disguises that permanent human reality may wear. And just as individual qualities are slighted, so the culturally accidental fuses into the humanly essential.

Since Eliot's characters do not usually receive substantial individuality, and since even their cultural characteristics give way to their human ritual roles, they are often unstable. Different persons who play the same archetypal role tend to "melt" into one another, and even the different roles merge into abstract humanity. In Eliot's verse a comparison of one character with another is often, to a degree unusual even in poetry, an identification; because of the scanty individuation, the distinctions between persons and between levels of actuality are unstable. Agamemnon appears not merely as a figure comparable to Sweeney; he *is* Sweeney, or at least the two men are not altogether distinct. The women in *The Waste Land* are all one woman, as Eliot tells us plainly, the men all one man, and "the two sexes meet in Tiresias," who is man in the archetypal role of quester. Personality is shadowy and tentative; the human, not the individual, occupies almost all the poet's attention. The characters are like unconscious immortals who, in the fashion of Tiresias, change shape, setting, culture from age to age and repeatedly perform the same ritualistic functions in Egypt, in Greece, in England, from behind masks that betray nothing of the distinctive face.

Among all the possible roles, Eliot has chosen mainly to portray that of the quester, man in his role as seeker for meaning, truth, reality, virtue, the good life. All the events of Eliot's verse take their meaning from their relationship to this quest, and all the characters must be interpreted according to the ways in which they fulfill this role. Those who continue to pursue the goal either have or do not have the requisite qualifications; those who fail to pursue it at all, or who give up the pursuit, are damned. Virtually every character can be evaluated in terms of his reference to this central situation. Since the pursuit may be attempted through various human activities—mainly love, poetry, political and economic activity (history), and religion—some characters are treated only or mainly in terms of the search as it may be made through one of these areas. Most of the women of *The Waste Land*, for example, are reprehensible for their degrading attitudes toward human love, which in Eliot's verse never turns out to be a very profitable path for the quester. The quester in *Ash Wednesday* works through religion, in *Four Quartets* through several of the possible activities, but in *The Waste Land* the protagonist's search is more general: it is *the* quest, whatever its specific form.

This use of poetry reflects Eliot's beliefs about the nature of human life. He sees man as primarily engaged in a quest, seeking, through the various modes of conventional activity, satisfactory terms on which to live with the cosmos. But as characters melt into each other, so selves melt into the world that they define. Value in Eliot's verse resides not in the self or any qualities thereof, but in the reciprocal working out of a relationship between self and world. They define one another in such a way that the self's action alone cannot establish value. The world around the self enters into it as fully as the self enters into the world, so that the establishment of a

satisfactory relationship between them is a reciprocal enterprise, hardly manageable by the self alone, which must know
when to take action and when to wait for action to be taken:
"Teach us to care and not to care / Teach us to sit still" (CPP,
67).* Passion and perception are insufficient equipment for
the quest, because the quest is really a quest of the world to
come to terms with all its parts. It is in this coming to terms
that value lies, in the working out of a form of conduct, a
process signified by ritual disciplines and realized in the making
of a poem.

His poetry is thus concerned with *being*, rather than presenting, a form symbolic of the conditions of human life. In a
sense, the world, not the poet, writes the poem, just as the
world, not the self, achieves value at one moment or another.
Since value is still inseparable from human selves, however, they
must form the principal instances through the articulation of
which poems come to *be*. And the reciprocal process, dramatized
in the fact of the poem but also dramatized in the instances
of the poem, can be approached from several points of view.
Sometimes speakers tell us their stories and so reveal their
moral situations; sometimes they direct our attention to other
selves and other parts of the world. But always in revealing
one they reveal the other. The confession of experience reveals
the world implicated in the experience; the observation of a
world reveals the implicated self of the observer.

But specific human personalities are only one dimension of
Eliot's treatment of people. Any objective account of the world
must show the presence not only of human selves but also of
the marks they have left upon it. Any physical setting, such as
those of *Four Quartets,* is suffused with the almost palpable
meaning (obscure as it may be) of the consciousnesses that

* Unless otherwise noted, references are to *The Complete Poems and
Plays, 1909–1950* (New York, 1952) (CPP); *Selected Essays, 1917–
1932* (New York, 1950) (SE); and *The Sacred Wood* (London, 1948)
(SW).

have lived or worked there or merely passed through. Earth, air, water, and fire are so suffused with the human quest that the quest has become an objectively discernible aspect of these elements. History is present, and so is the future. And as men transform the physical universe into something objectively more than physical, that something more enters again into every subjective self. Each pervades the other in a constantly renewing and reordering process.

If, then, the poem is to be a reproduction of that process, it must not limit its account of human personality to the occurrence of specific personages. The poem itself is an instance of the world, or rather a verbal symbol of it. It, too, is a palpable physical reality, but, like the world, it is suffused with the mark of both past and present human consciousness. Thus the poem recapitulates the tradition of poems both by containing specific allusions and by echoing in form and tone the poetic achievements of the past. It further reproduces the humanness omnipresent in the world by the multiplicity of authors and characters whom it recalls or vaguely echoes and who give to the world its own specific character. At the same time, a single present directing consciousness fills the poem and moves among its words with the same powers and limitations with which men move about the world. The presence of the poet in the poem is as objective and as difficult to formulate as the presence of man in the world. But each gives to what he inhabits the color and the tone that we recognize as its effect. The poem symbolizes the world, and the poet fulfills the coördinate role of man.

II

To portray his specific personages, Eliot employs in his early work a technique comparable to sculpture; his later work recalls the motion picture. Like Browning's dramatic monologues, Eliot's early poems present personae whose motions are arrested. Like the figures on Keats's urn, these personae are caught permanently in certain attitudes. The poems are portraits of souls in various conditions, of souls who do not advance or recede in their quest. As in Dante's *Inferno,* all progress in the poem is not of the soul portrayed, but of the reader and poet toward a sense of the fixity of that soul's condition. The personae do not grow wiser, but only more confirmed in the attitudes with which they began; such events as take place only reinforce their positions. Prufrock, the protagonist of "Portrait of a Lady," Gerontion, and the "I" of most of the other poems unify the world they present by the attitudes they take toward it, attitudes that do not change but which it is part of the purpose of each poem merely to present.

The same is true of much of Eliot's later work—of the Ariel poems, *The Waste Land, Ash Wednesday,* and *Four Quartets.* Yet in these poems the poet is concerned to present souls rather in attitudes of movement than in attitudes of stasis. The points of development portrayed are sometimes phases, sometimes moments of change. Certainly Eliot's technique remains largely the same—he is always essaying an unmoving portrait of a soul. But the souls of the early speakers remain still for the sitting; the souls of the later speakers are in the process of significant transformation, are, in effect, in Purgatory. Prufrock, Gerontion, and the "I" of "Lady" survey the circumstances, internal and external, which have made them what they are. Pericles, Simeon, and the Magus do likewise, but the attitudes they now take are tentative and characteristic of a stage in their spiritual progress; they contain at least a potentiality for movement absent in the earlier work. Furthermore, our attention is called more briefly to the *person* who progresses, and more fully to the nature of the progress. *The Waste Land* had already begun this tendency; *Ash Wednesday* continues it; and in *Four Quartets* the journey is almost completely depersonalized. The stages of the journey are revealed by a persona largely detached from his revelation; the stages are not stages in *a* progress of someone, but stages in the progress: the poem memorializes moments of transformation, moments of change, in virtual isolation from any person who experiences them. From the personal experience of Prufrock and Gerontion we have shifted at last to abstract experience, to the moving points around the still center of the poem or the static journey, from the *Inferno* through the *Purgatorio* to the *Paradiso*.

The validity of these observations is not reduced by the fact that the early poems vary in the degree to which their personae are circumstantially identified. Only a few personae in the early volumes are so clearly delineated as Prufrock, and these early poems can easily be divided into two kinds—those that pose a persona who talks mainly about his own situation, and those that pose a persona who talks mainly about the state of the world outside him. The personae of "Preludes," "Rhapsody on a Windy Night," and of most of Eliot's "metaphysical" poems survey the world in which they live mainly by watching the progress or lack of it in a world external to the speaker. Nevertheless, any evaluation of the world functions also as an evaluation of oneself. In "Rhapsody" the "I" is clearly implicated in the pointlessness he has described. And in other poems the poet's personae, though anonymous, are usually implicated less directly; they stand for the modern questing soul, looking upon the disorder of the world and involved in that disorder along with all other people. As a human being, the persona cannot merely observe the world; he must also evaluate it and lament it.

For observation, evaluation, and lamentation are the inevitable experiences of any perceptive persona. Even the more clearly individuated personae must, in the process of telling us about themselves, also tell us about their world. Their world is full of persons who have forgotten their purposes—English countesses, Mr. Silveros—or of institutions or great men whose achievements have been perverted—Chopin, Lazarus, Hamlet, Christ. The differences between Eliot's personae in the early poems are largely differences in the degree to which they are circumstantially identified in this world of corrupted purposes. When they are clearly identified, it is usually *their* corruption that the poem emphasizes as emblematic of human and modern corruption; when they mostly observe without participating, the emphasis is on the world's corruption. But no one is not implicated. Self is involved in the world's corruption; world is involved in the self's. The theme is the same, and only the point of view changes. And throughout all the poems both world and selves remain fixed in their damnations.

After 1925, however, Eliot's emphasis is less on corruption than on possible redemption. And his two points of view persist. In "Marina," "Song of Simeon," "Journey of the Magi," and *Ash Wednesday* he examines the experiences of spiritual progress from the point of view of the experiencer. In "Animula" and *Four Quartets* he examines the same experiences, but from the point of view of a more detached but by no means unimplicated persona. All these poems examine both world and self, and in the experiences central to each poem the persona is implicitly or explicitly involved. But he moves, or is about to move; his being is impermanent, suffused with what he is on the edge of being.

III

Such are the general characteristics of Eliot's personae. But how does he handle them in order to relate them intelligibly and effectively to the reader, to the poet, and to the poem? To answer the last two parts of this question, modern criticism supplies an abundance of theory; but matters of point of view and tone, which largely define the relation of persona and reader, have rarely been adequately analyzed. All poetry is a kind of speech; insofar as it is poetry, it is all one kind of speech; but it draws on, even mocks, and certainly imitates other categories of human utterance. The words of poetry are variously imitative of the sounds and meanings made by different sorts of men in different sorts of circumstances. "Tone" is the catchall word we use to describe this aspect of poetry, and it is the tones of his discourse which mainly define the relation of a persona to his reader.

What does tone tells us, and how? It tells us what kind of man the speaker is generally, and it lets us see from time to time some of his specific feelings; it further tells us the kind of audience he is addressing and his purpose in addressing them. To a large extent, poetic tone is conveyed through the audience's detection of certain conventional rhetorical patterns of speech, which make clear either the nature of the speaker himself and his various mental and emotional phases or the nature of his audience. These conventional rhetorical patterns of speech are themselves analyzable into patterns of sound and meaning— into, first, a diction, syntax, sentence structure, appropriate to, say, casual conversation and not oratorical address; and second, into intricate patterns of pitch, volume, and tempo, the general harmonics of which may be appropriate to lyrical, elegiac, or other kinds of utterance.

Whatever the neural justifications for these conventions of sound, we distinguish even in our silent reading of poetry between sounds of one order and sounds of another. A good reader of verse can, by the skillful manipulation of the musical dynamics of his voice, make even a reading of nonsense syllables dramatic. But in most writing the variations of tone lie in our understanding the melodic force of specific words, phrases, and syntaxes and, even more, of their intricate combinations. We grasp their melodic force because we have heard them before, or something so close to them that they have a familiar ring. We thus accept writing as not only composed of devices of wit, imagery, plot, and other intellectually assimilable elements but as also including sound and even as relying for much of its effect on our knowledge of conventional correlations between the sound patterns of speech and various human situations. The sound patterns themselves are conventional, peculiar to language, age, and culture; the various human situations are similarly restricted to those conventionally recognized as possible or typical in any society; and the correlations between them are also imposed on a poet by the poetic and social traditions of his contemporaries.

During any day spent in the company of people, one hears an almost infinite variety of tones; and the tones of any good poem of a few pages' length are hardly less various. Poetic personae characteristically use different tones to convey different emotions—fear, horror, love, pity, anger—and to convey these emotions with a thousand variations in shading; or they mix these emotions with each other—love mixed with anger, pity mixed with love, resentment mixed with pity, and infinite others. At the same time, personae traditionally take up, even in the same poem, different relationships with their audiences, now cajoling them in friendly fashion, now warning them on the basis of superior perception, now commanding them with authority, now chatting with them, now berating them, mocking them, scorning them, ignoring them, now disposing of them with gentle superiority. Indeed, any long poem, composed throughout in a consistent verse form, must necessarily vary not only the emotions of the persona but also the attitudes of the persona toward whomever he addresses, in order to avoid dullness.

Throughout most English poetry these changes in tone have been conveyed largely by musical means—by the management of pitch, volume, tempo, within a continuing scheme of versification. Many modern poets continue this practice, and all do to a certain extent, but several modern poets—notably Eliot—frequently alter the verse form along with the change in tone. *The Waste Land* is certainly the most stunning example of this. Instead of writing the whole poem in blank verse, or even in his own kind of liberated blank verse, Eliot uses a variety of meters and forms, which constantly break in upon one another with violent irruptions of tone. On the other hand, his changes in verse are, in a sense, secondary to the changes in tone which they support. And other modern poets have made frequent use of the poem that, without disturbing the metrical formula of the verse, still wrests the persona from one point of view to another—or, differently interpreted, juxtaposes two very different personae who speak in tones that clash. Yeats in particular does this in the refrains of some of his later poems, and his device has been widely imitated.

But the structure of Yeats's refrain poems is quite revolutionary and in its arrangement of tones differs even from the structure of Eliot's juxtapositional poetry. In some at least of Yeats's late poems the structural principle is quite Hegelian: two conflicting personae, or attitudes, or tones, are juxtaposed— and dropped! The reader must grasp the whole poem that emerges from their confrontation. This is a technique reminiscent of satire, but one hardly ever used in other poetry; it is only dimly anticipated by such works as *The Canterbury Tales* and is common among English poems only in certain ballads. It is not the technique of Eliot, whose poetry in this respect as in many others follows a traditional course. For in Eliot's work there is always one dominant tone to which the persona consistently returns.

The tone which dominates most of his poems is that of the progressing or defeated quester reviewing his experience for the benefit of an almost casual audience. From "Prufrock" to *Four Quartets* the dominant tone is a conversational tone. The variations, to be sure, have an almost incredible range, and they are largely responsible for the obscurity with which Eliot is so often charged; the verse changes, and transitions are omitted in this poetry of juxtaposition. But even in *The Waste Land* the persona returns from his wanderings among other speech patterns to resume the tone of casual (and usually gloomy) reminiscence:

April is the cruellest month, breeding
Lilacs over the dead land, mixing
Memory and desire . . .

Under the brown fog of a winter dawn,
A crowd flowed over London bridge, so many,
I had not thought death had undone so many.

The hot water at ten.
And if it rains, a closed car at four.
And we shall play a game of chess . . .

A rat crept softly through the vegetation
Dragging its slimy belly on the bank . . .

I Tiresias, old man with wrinkled dugs
Perceived the scene, and foretold the rest—
I too awaited the expected guest.

Phlebas the Phoenician, a fortnight dead,
Forgot the cry of gulls, and the deep sea swell
And the profit and loss.

Who is the third who walks always beside you?

I have heard the key
Turn in the door and turn once only

I sat upon the shore
Fishing, with the arid plain behind me

These tones are not the same by any means, but in each passage the diction is that of a smooth and easy English. They are supplemented by many passages of actual conversation—some intense, some merely animated, but phrased mostly in the language of common conversation. Indeed, if the poem is at all unsuccessful, it may be partly because, skillfully as most of the tones are assimilated to the basic one, a few of them remain not totally assimilated, notably the cry to Stetson, the gnomic laments of the Rhine maidens, the Hindu mutters, and the excessive allusiveness in the last few lines. All of these, at least to the ear of this reader, are insufficiently harmonized with the tone of the rest of the poem, a tone that, like all of Eliot, is basically, but not continuously, conversational.

Within his basic conversational tone the speaker of *The Waste Land* ranges widely. Most frequently, as the above passages indicate, his tone is serious, if not somber. But he is occasionally capable of other feelings. At his vision of the affair between the typist and the clerk, the persona shows an ironic amusement that includes his vision of himself. There is wit in the presentation, too, of Mme. Sosostris, of Lil, and of Sweeney and Mrs. Porter. And an occasional intensity rises above the conversational in the reminiscences of the protagonist's relationships with the Hyacinth girl, with Stetson, and with the Thunder.

In fact, the persona changes so much that his unity constantly verges on incoherence. Sometimes within one role he changes tone; sometimes his change of tone signalizes also a change of person: he becomes Ferdinand or the Fisher King or the modern husband. And these quick changes raise the question of the relationship between changes of tone and changes of persona. To a degree, all of us become different persons when we change our moods and the tones that go with them; our emotions as well as our social positions are roles, masks, that we take up and discard. At every moment we play different parts, and the changing tones in our words reflect the most minute changes in our attitudes. The more extreme these changes, the less coherent is our own unity; but extreme changes may also result in an increase of scope. The man or the persona capable of moving among widely different roles demonstrates the rich multiplicity of human possibility, provided he still somehow remains single. The singleness of Eliot's persona in *The Waste Land* is sometimes doubtful, but he consistently returns to his role of quester recounting in a casual but often intense English the phases of his perception.

This easy conversational tone persists, too, throughout the poems in which the "I" is more observer than participant.

The diction and tone of "Preludes" are dryly conversational, as are those of "Rhapsody" and the other minor poems of Eliot's first volume. His "metaphysical" poems continue witty and casual in their tone, even though they at times, as at the end of "Sweeney among the Nightingales," attain a greater elevation. *Ash Wednesday* adapts Eliot's usual tone to the purposes of prayer, confession, supplication, and thanksgiving, but the manner is still easy. And in *Four Quartets* virtually all the varying tones are adapted, with a skill superior even to that employed in *The Waste Land*, to the basic tone of a man talking to various auditors—to a few friends, to God, and perhaps to himself.[1] In *Quartets* the few lines that stand out as not quite right are mainly lapses in tone; the author has not fully assimilated these tones to his basic one. The "Garlic and sapphires" passage is notably deficient in this respect: the tone of a gnomic riddle is out of place. So are such lines as

I do not know much about gods . . .

or

I sometimes wonder if that is what Krishna meant. . . .

In the first the pose of intellectual innocence fails to convince, and the casual phrasing of the second cannot, for the ordinary reader even of Eliot, contain the word "Krishna" without absurdity. In each case the attempted variation of the conversational tone has failed to connect suitably with the picture of the persona given by the rest of the poem.

In summary, then, we can say that one principal unifying force in Eliot's poetry is the tone that underlies each poem, and the tone in turn defines the level at which the persona meets the reader. As a rule, Eliot holds his persona firmly to a conversational level, but because of this firm base can allow him to explore an assortment of other audience-defining tones—prophecy, lyric apostrophe, formal lamentation—so long as he always returns to his base. The result is a richness and variety of tone rare in any nondramatic verse and, indeed, seldom achieved in traditional drama. In his plays Eliot has been held too closely to a one- or two-tone drama, with the consequence that the rich textures of his verse, founded on the freedom to range almost at will among tones, are lost to him on the stage. Among his longer poems only *The Hollow Men* has a base not that of conversational language, in consequence of which perhaps its texture is thinner than that of his more successful works, and its almost unrelieved dreariness more a triumph of wit than of poetry.

The conversational tone of most of Eliot's work invites the reader to accept the persona in a more or less equal relationship. The persona does not speak down to the reader—even in *Four Quartets* he addresses the reader as a friend except in a few falsely humble, rather patronizing lines that tend to weaken the equal relationship. But while the conversational base defines the rapport between reader and persona, within the conversational tone the persona reveals a pattern of emotional response appropriate to his role as questing man. The talk of *The Waste Land* reflects in turn the speaker's aspiration and despair, his capacity for ecstasy and humor, his union of sense and sensibility which makes him a representative man. The tones reveal the man, his cosmic situation, and his relation to the reader; it might even more accurately be said that a definition of each of these includes a definition of the others. The persona is involved in the same world as the reader; as his world defines his own role, his own self, so it defines both the reader's pattern of responses and his involvement with all other men in a human world. In fact, the deliberate reproduction of the tones of casual speech, of what Wordsworth called "the real language of men in a state of vivid sensation," has been felt in our century and the last to signify the commonalty of all human experience. Yet because in Eliot there exists no real discontinuity between the self and its cosmic situation, the reader's identification with the persona is doubtfully pure. Reader and persona are emblems of each other. The poet and the reader share the persona's situation—his traffic among tones, his quest. As the following pages will show, however, they share with each other more than the persona shares with them. The "hypocrite lecteur" is assuredly the persona's "semblable," but he is also more fully the poet's.

IV

In his criticism Eliot has repeatedly discussed the relation between the poet and his personae. He has been especially concerned to distinguish between the poet's emotions and the emotions of the characters he presents. "No artist," he writes, "produces great art by a deliberate attempt to express his personality" (SE, 96). And again: "Poetry is not a turning loose of emotion . . . it is not the expression of personality" (SE, 10). Emotion—even the poet's emotion—has its place in a poem, but it is not *directly* expressed. "What every poet starts from is his own emotions" (SE, 117), but:

It is not in his personal emotions, the emotions provoked by particular events in his life, that the poet is in any way remarkable or interesting. His particular emotions may be simple, or crude, or flat. The emotion in his poetry will be a very complex thing, but not with the complexity of the emotions of people who have very complex or unusual emotions in life (SE, 10).

The process by which the artist's emotions become poetry is subtle and indirect:

It is suggested, then, that a dramatic poet cannot create characters of the greatest intensity of life unless his personages, in their reciprocal actions and behaviour in their story, are somehow dramatizing, but in no obvious form, an action or struggle for harmony in the soul of the poet (SE, 172–173).

The soul of the poet, and not merely his emotion, is the

source of the struggle and of the harmony. The soul presumably includes the entire psychic life, and between its dynamics and the events of the poem a subtle correlation exists. We have to remember, however, that it is a correlation between totalities, a transformation of the psychic life into the very different terms of art, not merely a point-by-point translation into discrete linguistic symbols. Goethe's Mephistopheles, for example, is unsatisfactory because he "embodies a philosophy. A creation of art should not do that: he should *replace* the philosophy" (SW, 66). Dante, on the other hand, "has succeeded in dealing with his philosophy, not as a theory . . . or as his own comment or reflection, but in terms of something *perceived*" (SW, 170–171).

Is the method of *Faust* really different in kind from the method of *The Divine Comedy,* or does the latter simply excel in the degree to which it translates the psychic life into symbolic wholes rather than into allegorical pieces? Where does literature cease to be literature and become merely imaginative language? As one can see even from his apparently unfair but significant comparison of the character Mephistopheles with the whole of *The Divine Comedy,* Eliot's answer appears to depend on the context in which the poetic elements figure. Not symbols so much as how they function together is his main criterion for judging poetry. Even in the individual sections of a work Eliot is more concerned with the concord between elements than with the immediate representational function of each element. Thus, his idea of the objective correlative is phrased in terms that reveal his contextual point of view:

The only way of expressing emotion in the form of art is by finding an 'objective correlative'; in other words, a set of objects, a situation, a chain of events which shall be the formula of that *particular* emotion; such that when the external facts, which must terminate in sensory experience, are given, the emotion is immediately evoked (SE, 124–125).

Not an object, but a *set* of objects; not an event, but a *chain* of events. Every unit in the poem, analyzable into specific images, words, and sounds, has meaning *as a whole*. The specific elements do not translate immediately into meanings and then add up into larger meanings. They work together *in the poem* and translate as wholes into meanings. Even though we must grasp the meanings of individual words and sounds, we instantly, as it were, send those meanings back into the poem until they have taken their place in larger units that are then retranslated back to us as wholes.

If this is true for the small units, it is also true for the larger units and ultimately for the whole poem. Behind the whole poem lies the fundamental emotion or feeling or complex of feeling—the psychic structure—of which the poem is a symbolic realization. All the conventions and devices of poetry—the plot, the characters, the imagery, the verse form—exist to be manipulated in such a way as to provide in their totality the "formula" of the poet's feeling. So in the metaphysical poets a "telescoping of images and multiplied associations" is used because the poets "were, at best, engaged in the task of trying to find the verbal equivalent for states of mind and feeling" (SE, 243, 248). States of mind and feeling are larger than emotions. And, as Eliot says, looking into the heart "is not looking deep enough. . . . One must look into the cerebral cortex, the nervous system, and the digestive tracts" (SE, 250). In order to express the whole man, not merely his emotions, the poet's mind must be "constantly amalgamating disparate experience" (SE, 247). His "perceptions," like those of any "really appreciative mind," do not "accumulate as a mass, but form themselves as a structure" (SW, 15). The various elements in verse must be used in drama

to get upon the stage [a] precise statement of life which is at the same time a point of view, a world—a world which the author's mind has subjected to a complete process of simplification (SW, 68).

And this is possible because

To create a form is not merely to invent a shape, a rhyme or rhythm. It is also the realization of the whole appropriate content of this rhyme or rhythm. The sonnet of Shakespeare is not merely such and such a pattern, but a precise way of thinking and feeling (SW, 63).

In this process the whole life of the author is transfused into the work:

The creation of a work of art, we will say the creation of a character in a drama, consists in the transfusion of the personality, or, in a deeper sense, the life of the author into the character. This is a very different matter from the orthodox creation in one's own image (SE, 137).

To support his position Eliot quotes Rémy de Gourmont's description of Flaubert:

Flaubert incorporait toute sa sensibilité à ses œuvres. . . . Hors de ses livres, où il se transvasait goutte à gouette [sic], jusqu'à la lie, Flaubert est fort peu intéressant (SE, 193).

And Eliot adds that we can say of certain poets that they, too, "se transvasaient goutte à gouette" [sic]. Since the process is one of transfusion and not of direct expression, "A poet can express his feelings as fully through a dramatic, as through a lyrical form"; and, consequently, "for a poet with dramatic gifts, a situation quite remote from his personal experience may release the strongest emotion" (SE, 290).

The poet, then, is to be thought of as a whole man, directing his whole self, with all its ideas, prejudices, emotions, and attitudes, toward one subject or problem after another in one poem after another. The whole self is one whole, and the whole poem is another; and the poem is the objective correlative, the poetic equivalent, of the whole man. It is his "personality" that does, in fact, confer a unity on the poem and, indeed, on the whole body of a poet's work:

The whole of Shakespeare's work is *one* poem. . . . A man might, hypothetically, compose any number of fine passages or even of whole poems which would each give satisfaction, and yet not be a great poet, unless we felt them to be united by one significant, consistent, and developing personality (SE, 179).

A poet's work is usually distinguished by a "tone," or series of tones, which is peculiar to him:

Every writer who has written any blank verse worth saving has produced particular tones which his verse and no other's is capable of rendering. . . . Shakespeare is 'universal' because he has more of these tones than any one else; but they are all out of the one man (SE, 101).

Every poet thus has his own tonality, which is to be associated with a unique way of looking at life. As Eliot says of Ford's verse,

Even in so late and so decayed a drama as that of Ford, the framework of emotions and morals of the time is only the vehicle for statements of feeling which are unique and imperishable: Ford's and Ford's only (SE, 189).

And he says in the same essay that an involved style "should follow the involutions of a mode of perceiving, registering, and digesting impressions which is also involved" (SE, 187). Since Massinger's feelings and ideas are conventional and derivative, so ultimately is his verse. "Marlowe's and Jonson's comedies," on the other hand,

were a view of life; they were, as great literature is, the transformation of a personality into a personal work of art, their lifetime's work, long or short. Massinger is not simply a smaller personality: his personality hardly exists (SE, 192).

Of Jonson's drama he says elsewhere: "what holds the play together is a unity of inspiration that radiates into plots and personages alike" (SE, 134). And of Shakespeare:

It has been said that Shakespeare lacks unity; it might, I think, be said equally well that it is Shakespeare chiefly that *is* the unity (SE, 119).

Heywood's work is another matter: "to inform the verse there is no vision, none of the artist's power to give undefinable unity to the most various material" (SE, 152). In his contemporaries "there is at least some inchoate pattern; there is, as it would often be called, personality" (SE, 153).

By finding, in both the detail and the design of a work, the appropriate correlative of the poet's feeling (his soul, his ideas, his attitudes, his whole self), the poet will transfuse himself into his poem and so confer on it the unity of his own personality. On one level, then, the poet's aim is to make a total verbal equivalent for his total feeling; in effect, one purpose of the poet in writing *is* to express his personality. But this is personality in the largest sense, and its expression in the poem is less an aim than an inevitable product. Eliot believes the poet has other, more immediate purposes in composing any poem. These purposes appear to have little to do with the reader:

The poet does not aim to excite—that is not even a test of his success—but to set something down; the state of the reader is merely that reader's particular mode of perceiving what the poet has caught in words (SW, 170).

But what has the poet caught in words besides his own personality? Again Eliot writes:

The emotion of art is impersonal. And the poet cannot reach this impersonality without surrendering himself wholly to the work to be done (SE, 11).

But what is the work to be done? It is evidently not the expression of one's own emotion; this gets done, but it should not be the poet's intention to do it. The work to be done, according to Eliot, is the presentation of a "statement" or a "vision" of life.

A "vision of life" sounds very much like a "personality." The former is inevitably dependent on the latter, or even a part of it. But they are, more accurately, two sides of the same coin and not the same side. A poem is a formulation of the poet's sense of the world in which he lives. Such a formulation must reflect the psychic structure of the poet, but so, to one degree or another, does all writing. The writer's personality is merely implicit in poems as in other written work. If a writer discusses his own personality *in* his writing, we should presumably interpret this first as significant for our understanding of his view of life; but our sense of his total personality, of the form of his mind, will be extractable rather from the form and the manner of the discussion than from anything we are explicitly told.

For it is in the choice and arrangement of his materials, not in his explicit statements, that the poet most fully reveals himself. Affirmations and disavowals that the persona makes more or less directly serve only to clarify the poet's attitude toward life. But an attitude is not a mind; the poet's psychic life is larger than his view of life; and we understand his soul only as we understand both the view of life presented in the poem and the way in which it is presented. In any final analysis, perhaps, the two are inseparable; their interpenetration is thorough, and we cannot comprehend either the mind without knowing the view of life, or the view of life without the structure of its presentation.

But for the duration of the poem the poet's mind makes no overt intrusion. Eliot regards the poet's position as almost a passive one: he is a catalytic agent, a "finely perfected medium in which special, or very varied, feelings are at liberty to enter into new combinations" (SE, 7). And, consequently, "the progress of the artist is a continual self-sacrifice, a continual extinction of personality" (SE, 7). He does not feel the emotions of his personae, though he may at some time have felt emotions like them. In fact, the more perfect the artist, the more completely separate in him will be the man who suffers and the mind which creates; the more perfectly will the mind digest and transmute the passions which are its material (SE, 7–8).

But although the personality of the poet should be kept out of the parts of the poem, it enters the poem as a whole. It is visible in the total form, the total style, of the completed work. The artist is freed from the necessity of having emotions and personality, at least for the time of composition, and his job is to concentrate so on the work to be done—the finding of a verbal equivalent for his feeling—that his whole experience fuses into a new thing, the poem, the work of art.

For it is not the 'greatness,' the intensity, of the emotions, the components, but the intensity of the artistic process, the pressure, so to speak, under which the fusion takes place, that counts (SE, 8).

For example, in *The Waste Land,* although the protagonist's quest is essentially the same quest as Eliot's, it is inside the poem instead of outside, and at no particular point in the poem is Eliot participating in the emotions of his personae. What we have is "an artistic conscience arranging emotions," not feeling them out loud; or "the transformation of a personality into a personal work of art, [one's] lifetime's work, long or short" (SE, 187, 192). Of the sudden transitions and juxtapositions of modern poetry Eliot has said: "Whether the transition is cogent or not, is merely a question of whether the mind is *serré* or *délié,* whether the whole personality is involved" (SE, 446).

Thus, neither the persona nor his statements are to be interpreted as directly representative of the poet and his psychic life. Taken outside the poem, the poem's statements of belief might be shared by the poet; but as the poem stands, the statements are within it, and the total beliefs that the poem expresses are inseparable from the form that contains them and are modified by that form; and the form that contains and modifies the beliefs reflects as a whole the total personality of the poet, and, more importantly, asserts the poet's total view of life.

Not only, then, is Eliot the poet to be considered as separate from characters like Prufrock and Gerontion and Tiresias but he is also distinct from the speakers of such poems as "Preludes," *Ash Wednesday*, and *Four Quartets*. In every poem certain situations, certain sets of objects, certain chains of events, as well as the characters themselves and the sounds and meanings of the words, the lines, the sections—all work together to form a whole pattern whose immediate implication to a sensitive reader is a formulation of a view of life and whose further implication, deeper but more incidental to the apparent purposes of the poet, lies in the reflection of the poet's whole personality. Even the direct statements of *Four Quartets* and *Ash Wednesday* have a double function: they must be understood as units of meaning, but, once understood (whether or not they are assented to), they must be sent back into the current of the poem so that the reader will grasp their context, the total statement that the poetic form adumbrates.

Eliot tells us, in his early essay on "Dante," "The aim of the poet is to state a vision, and no vision of life can be complete which does not include the articulate formulation of life which human minds make" (SW, 170). The vision *includes* the formulation by particular personae, but it is larger; it is itself a larger formulation in nonexplicit, in poetic, form. The ritual performers, the conversational tones, are merely the result of Eliot's choice, largely deliberate, among possible techniques for presenting his view of reality. That he chooses these techniques tells us much about his view of reality and about his own mental being. The various poetic materials reflect his conscious poetic intelligence as well as the structure of his personality. But the poem is the thing, and in the poem the statement of belief is presented, not confessed; the feelings of the speaker are depicted, not shared; and the persona is a point of view *in* the poem, not the point of view of the poet.

Thus, although the reader may be inveigled into reading a poem by his tentative identification with its persona, he must, if he is to grasp the poem, encounter the poet elsewhere, at a point where reader and poet together can see the poem as a whole. Everything in the poem must be clarified by reference to the world outside the poem, but this system of repeated reference is a technique of the poem, not a series of valid truths. Each denoting element, including the persona, must take its meaning from the world that is the poem. And just as Mephistopheles should not embody a philosophy, but, like *The Divine Comedy,* replace it, so Prufrock and Gerontion and the "I" of *Four Quartets* are incomplete if we take their message to be what they more or less tell us it is. Not what the personae say, nor what they embody, but what the poem *is,* is the point. Instead of presenting an instance of human experience, the poem provides an experience, is, in its role of artifact undergone, an experience itself. Poet and reader *have* the experience together; and it is in the having of it—not in the seeing of it, as in Browning, nor in the pretending to have someone else's, as in the Romantics—that poet and reader coincide. The experience is neither simulated nor observed, though both simulation and observation may enter into it as functions of the persona; but the experience is immediate and actual.

But why is the experience of reading a poem valuable? Immediately, perhaps, because its substance is the world we compose, and the poem is a recreation of the pattern of our own life. Ultimately, perhaps, because poems are instances of one mode of comprehending meaning, and hence one mode of making meaning; thus, while to use the mode is valuable, to contemplate it in its instances is to penetrate not merely the patterns of our social existence but also the pattern of experience which underlies the artistic formulation of that social existence. In experiencing the poem, in short, we experience art as well as art's vision of life. Possibly this is why critics enjoy modern poetry more than other people do; critics come to the poem with their minds already full of poetic theory. And an Eliotan poem gives them not only a vision of life but an instance of art, an instance that the poet deliberately arranges to give, as one of his most important aims in writing his poems. To understand a poem by Eliot, we must leave the persona and grasp the poem at the level at which it asserts both the world and itself, and, through itself, the value of artistic expression—the value of singing.

NOTE

1. In his 1931 essay "Charles Whibley," Eliot notes that "there are only four ways of thinking: to talk to others, or to one other, or to talk to oneself, or to talk to God" (*Selected Essays*, 447). By 1953 Eliot had come to limit the number to *The Three Voices of Poetry*, but *Four Quartets* may use these four voices without clearly discriminating among them. In a way, the poem is addressed to all four audiences at once, so that the four voices "melt" into one another, like "music heard so deeply / That it is not heard at all, but you are the music / While the music lasts."

The Organ-Grinder and the Cockatoo: An Introduction to E. E. Cummings

JOHN LOGAN

"Because only the truest things always are true because they can't be true." This is the meaning of the stars proffered by a Fourteenth Street organ-grinder's assistant, Mr. bowing Cockatoo, who presents "with his brutebeak / one fatal faded . . . piece of pitiful paper." The fortune on the piece of paper offered by the bird in poem No. 25 of E. E. Cummings' *95 Poems* (1958) is as enigmatic as the message engraved on Keats's Grecian urn: "Beauty is truth, truth beauty,—that is all / Ye know on earth, and all ye need to know." It is enigmatic because it is written on the hidden heart, but must be read in the open eyes. Such reading requires the paradigms of love as well as those of language. The meaning of the cockatoo's remark is the meaning of the poem in which it is found. The nature of truth, the nature of art, the nature of love, and the paradox of the *via negativa*—all resonate about it. But the cockatoo is a figure of the poet, and the "pitiful paper" he offers is the whole meaning of the life's work of one of the most gifted and most prolific poets of our language.

Cummings published more than a dozen volumes of poetry between 1923 and his death in 1962. His monumental *Poems 1923–1954* (1954) contained more than six hundred poems and received a special mention from the National Book Awards Committee. It was followed by *95 Poems* and the posthumous *73 Poems* (1963). Their combined titles represent an odd, uninventive conclusion to a series of books whose art and fun usually began with the names Cummings selected for their spines. His first poems were called *Tulips and Chimneys*

249

(1923), which meant girls and boys. Later, one met the algebraic poetics of *1 x 1* (1944) and *is 5* (1926), the first suggesting the multiplication which results in love as a product and the second suggesting the product of an extraordinary and inventive multiplication of 2 x 2. *No Thanks* (1935), said another of his books, speaking the name given it as a tribute to the fourteen publishers who had refused to bring it to birth and whom Cummings names vindictively in "dedication." *XAIPE!* (Rejoice!) commands the cover of his 1950 volume. In addition to these books of poems, Cummings published a novel of World War I, based on his experiences in a prison for technical offenders in France, *The Enormous Room* (1922); a journal of a visit to Russia, *Eimi* (1933); two plays, *Him* (1927) and *Santa Claus: A Morality* (1946); a collection of his drawings and paintings, *CIOPW* (1931); a collection of his six addresses given at Harvard University under the Charles Eliot Norton Professorship, *i: six nonlectures* (1953); and more. George Firmage's *E. E. Cummings, A Bibliography* (1964) lists twenty-eight titles or "persons" in the Cummings canon, and it is indeed proper from Cummings' point of view to think of these books as "persons." He said once in conversation that he hoped *Him* would exist in the way that people do and agreed with Rainer Maria Rilke that "works of art are of an infinite loneliness and with nothing to be so little reached as with criticism. Only love can grasp and hold and fairly judge them."

Thus, the long-laboring (grinding) musician of Cummings' poem is also a figure for the poet, and in presenting us with an oracular white cockatoo, the poet holds out to us himself. However, as the poem makes clear, the organ-grinder will not tap the creature's cage unless we ask him to. We seldom ask. I think it is because even if we understand this—that if we let him the poet gives us himself—still we may not understand the truth behind: that what the poet offers us is not so much himself (who cares, we may say), but by a self-transcendence, *our*selves. But nearly everyone cares about that. If we really knew the truth of this we would be more interested in poetry. One's first impulse is to think, "Nonsense. What mysticism! It can't be true. No one can give us ourselves." Well, let us agree. What I have said can't be true. Still, as Cummings writes, "the truest things always are true because they can't be true."

My father used to tell me that you have to take a Dutchman for what he means, not what he says. All poets are Dutchmen. Why can't you take a Dutchman for what he says? Because, my father insisted, "They can't speak splain for splutterin'." To shift the image, paraphrasing a Hindu poem, the poet is the lover who "utters senseless sounds out of the fever of his love." We have to listen to poetry with that little-known, almost vestigial organ, the inner inner ear (in contrast to the outer inner ear, known to anatomists, which is made of bones). I believe it was bequeathed to us by our prehuman ancestors, who perhaps were cockatoos. We ourselves are the faded pieces of "pitiful paper" they brought forth. Yet in us is the meaning of the stars! It is Hamlet's dilemma, the mystery of the creature crawling between heaven and earth. It is the puzzle of the Incarnation. There is sadness to it. There is grief and loss. Like the fortune seeker of Cummings' poem we weep, and Fourteenth Street disappears as our vision blurs. The organ-grinder vanishes. The cockatoo is gone. But not only are our eyes full of tears, our "tears are full of eyes," and in these many-surfaced mirrors we ourselves appear, gesturing perhaps with love, hatred, frustration, awe, praise. The poet, whom I have already described as Dutchman, lover, organ-grinder, and cockatoo, I now assert is one who weeps with tears full of eyes. Do I make him sound like a tragic hero? Well, it is true the organ-grinder is a "melancholy fellow." But when one of us says, "I want a fortune," he stops grinding, and he smiles. One of the refreshing things about Cummings is that so many of his poems are in the role of the organ-grinder *anticipating* that we shall ask him for our fortune. He is, therefore, a profoundly optimistic poet, more so than any other American poet of stature, and he is certainly the funniest poet who ever lived. But he laughs with tears in his eyes in his tears.

The gaunt, melancholy face, somewhat arrogant with the sense of a long labor well done, brilliantly transformed by a smile, was Cummings' own. He was personally a vivacious, quiet, charming, solemn, funny, serious man with the look of a gentle skull about him. He was bald, and the bones of his face were high and very symmetrical, set for the most part with a certain hauteur, which his wife, Marion Morehouse, has caught in a number of famous portraits. A man with an immense gift for story telling, Cummings was a total delight as a conversationalist, and his talk was formed both with an extraordinary comic gift and with a blessed compassion, which his nervous companion felt as the easing gesture of the great, of the natural nobleman. A Cummings tea was a memorable, cockle-warming human joy. Mrs. Cummings, gracious, startlingly young (she is a former fashion model), pouring at table— Cummings nimbly hopping about, alternately the seer and the pleased small boy, serving his guests cake and jam and brandy for their tea and telling his riotous stories, as of the 1929 Ford which he used to drive around his summer home in New Hampshire.

The Ford was one of Cummings' few concessions to our mad age. He felt that machines had destroyed man's sense of himself, had by some heartbreaking rhetoric usurped to themselves as objects the energies by which man was meant to relate to other human beings. Furthermore, in order to develop machines man had exalted the values of technology and science-making over those of feeling:

(While you and i have lips and voices which
are for kissing and to sing with

who cares if some oneeyed son of a bitch
invents an instrument to measure Spring with? (No. 23) *

Cummings did not own a TV or radio and would not use the telephone—although it was the Cummings home in Cambridge which sported the first telephone in that city! It is the kind of paradox one comes on again and again looking at the man and his work.

In that huge, three-story home which still stands on Irving Street in Cambridge, Massachusetts, Cummings was born on October 14, 1894. His father was a Unitarian minister and an instructor at Harvard, where the poet himself later took a master's degree in classics (prior to his war experience as an ambulance driver). Contrary to current fashion (Cummings was a rebellious fellow), he freely claimed to have had a happy childhood and to have loved *both* his parents. He has written a number of poems about both, including the famous elegy, "my father moved through dooms of love" (No. 62), which he included in every public reading. One of Cummings' poems for his mother placed her in "a heaven of blackred roses" (No. 31). Considering the number of roses in his poems, we may wonder whether Cummings was not trying to construct such a heaven himself—or perhaps to recreate the "garden of magnificent roses" which he tells us flourished beneath one window of his room.

In the first critical biography of Cummings, *E. E. Cummings, The Magic Maker* (1957), Charles Norman quotes a completely winning memoir of Cummings' childhood, written by his sister Elizabeth Qualey. Here we learn of the toolroom on the third floor where the children played, of the roof with a railing where the boy mounted a windlass for his box kite, and of the tree house built by himself and his father, complete with porch,

---

* Unless otherwise identified, the numbers I cite refer to *100 Selected Poems* (1959). Cummings himself made this remarkable selection, which includes work through *Xaipe!* (1950).

bunk, stove, where he went to be alone and frequently in summers to spend the night. Mrs. Qualey tells of the local balloon man who came in the spring, to stay forever in one of Cummings' best-loved poems (No. 4), and of the circus whose animals and performers he never ceased writing of. We get in this memoir a glimpse of the spirit of the boy, Cummings, who, during a whooping-cough epidemic formed a Whoopers Club of which he was president and whose paper he edited! Members had to be veterans of the illness and were required to write stories. "We had badges and mottoes too," Mrs. Qualey writes, "and we all played together and had so much fun that children tried to get exposed to whooping cough so they could join."

In the work, Norman quotes correspondence relevant to every major event in Cummings' career, his incarceration during World War I, the publication of his books, his appointment to the Charles Eliot Norton Professorship in 1952, his sad, hilarious, ironic part in the Boston Arts Festival in 1957, for which he originally wrote, but was not allowed to deliver, the strong poem for the Hungarian Revolution entitled "Thanksgiving (1956)"; it concludes with the lines

> so rah-rah-rah democracy
> let's all be as thankful as hell
> and bury the statue of liberty
> (because it begins to smell)

Norman publishes some magnificent photographs of Cummings' paintings, his work sheets, and himself, the last series beginning in 1918 uniform and finishing with a marvelous photograph by Mrs. Cummings, taken at his house in the Village. Norman writes occasionally with verve, especially about the Village in the twenties and thirties and its legendary folk, as Joe Gould, of whom Cummings drew a portrait in verse (No. 39). He writes always competently and *con amore*, telling the story of Cummings and his novels, plays, poems, painting. He shows intelligence and feeling about the poems, is a good defender on points where Cummings comes under fire. One is grateful for many aspects of the book and for the fact of celebration (long overdue) which its happy existence implies. But it is true that the words of the book which stick best are those of other people, and not only of Cummings: Pound's squib about Cummings' Russian diary, *Eimi;* Carl Sandburg and Marianne Moore on the *Collected Poems;* Cummings' sister's account of their childhood; Burton Rascoe's fine report on a chilly fall afternoon in Paris in 1924 when Cummings visited the Archibald MacLeish's.

But perhaps the best existing introduction to Cummings' poetry is his own *i: six nonlectures.* Certainly one comes from it with a heightened respect for both the Cummings rhetoric and the poetry. One will not forget in reading the book that it is the work of one of the greatest lyric poets in our language; it is a master's examination of himself and his writing, done when he was over sixty years old. And this is the most exciting possible kind of book. It begins with a wonderful yarn about a child of remarkably loving, remarkably intelligent, and remarkably heroic parents. It tells of his education in "cerebral Cambridge" and "orchidaceous Somerville" (Massachusetts), and in the "little barbarous Greenwich perfumed fake," where he says he first breathed, and in Paris ("love rose in my heart like a sun and beauty blossomed in my life like a star"). It is the story of his first friends, such as Harvard's Professor Royce, his first books, and his first singing. In the last group of three lectures, since for the adult Cummings "The question 'Who am I' is answered by what I write," we are given his own selection of his poems and prose (largely from *XAIPE!,* *1 x 1, Eimi, Him,* and *Santa Claus*) with his comments on them. The whole is supplemented, as were the last fifteen minutes of each of the "nonlectures" when they were given at Harvard, by his own selection of the poetry which has formed him.

The book, which is marked by the poetry of the inner inner

ear, is also about it. It is about it because it is about self-transcendence, which is why it is called *i*. I suspect that it would also have been called *i* if it had been about selfishness, but this would be less accurate, and Cummings is, well, careful with words. As proof of both Cummings' care and pre-occupation, he writes in the fifth of his six "nonlectures":

Let us make no mistake: Him of the play so named is himself and nobody else—not even Me. But supposing Him to exemplify that mythical entity "the artist," we should go hugely astray in assuming that art was the only self-transcendence. Art is a mystery; all mysteries have their source in a mystery-of-mysteries who is love . . . nor could all poetry . . . begin to indicate the varieties of selfhood; and consequently of selftranscendence.

Later, to stress this self-transcendence, Cummings closes the "fifth lesson" with the great serpent scene from *Antony and Cleopatra* and the hymn to the blessed Virgin, composed by Dante to open the final canto of the *Divine Comedy* (I translate the first two verses to show Cummings' point):

> Virgin mother child of your son
> More low more high than any creature
> Fixed end toward which all plans run
>
> Your self transcended human nature
> So well its maker did not shun
> To take His self its shape and feature.

One may add little on the possibilities of selfhood in the high sense. However, we may note the connection between the notion of transcendence ("climbing over") oneself and the notion of ecstasy ("standing outside"); the one follows the other, and without both, there is neither love nor art. Thus Cummings gives us a sixth and final lesson whose subjects are "ecstasy and anguish, being and becoming; the immortality of the creative imagination and the indomitability of the human spirit."

Allied to this celebration of the individual human spirit are Cummings' apparent antipatriotism and his apparent anti-intellectualism, which are large themes of *i*. Both are signs of fundamental affirmations. The apparent antipatriotism is a goad to a higher notion of self than is usual, hence a goad, as well, to a higher sense of the ends of freedom. The apparent anti-intellectualism is basically an affirmation of the *mystery* of things which Cummings believes to be more compatible with "feeling" than with knowing, supposing the latter activity to be a kind of "measuring" that excludes love. At heart, the quarrels of Cummings are a resistance to the small minds of every kind, political, scientific, philosophical, and literary, who insist on limiting the real and the true to what they think they know or can respond to. As a preventive to this kind of limitation, Cummings is directly opposed to letting us rest in what we believe we know; and this is the key to the rhetorical function of his famous language.

Resisting every kind of compromise and scornful of literary tyranny, Cummings' work contains two kinds of purity, one of art and one of the heart. The first is signified by his heroic un-concern for tyrants (such as money, "Mostpeople," various isms, and the laws of inertia as they apply to literature); the second, by the constant compassion in what he makes. The two together have always distinguished him. Thus in his first book, *The Enormous Room,* one finds the language he invented, "The Zulu . . . shoulderless, unhurried body, velocity of a grass-hopper, soul up under his arm-pits, mysteriously falling over the ownness of two feet, floating fish of his slimness half a bird . . ." One also finds an immense compassion: such a book is, in fact, best understood as an incantation, I should like to say prayer, offered for persons he loved in the war—both in hope of their well-being and as a reparation in human art for those times of inhumanity when, as another of his "criminal" and confined friends wrote, "the hoar frost grip[s] thy tent." This compassion issues in his work in a direct, feeling fashion so that one has in him little sense of the dichotomy between the artist and his art—I mean that quality whereby one senses that he writes his poems in his own voice instead of adopting a series of masks. When masks are apparent in his poems, he is using them for portraiture and still maintaining his own point of focus for selection, as in the poems which begin "rain or hail / Sam done / the best he kin" (No. 78) and "next to of course god" (No. 24).

It is this characteristic of speaking with his own voice that has put off a number of critics who, following the obiter dicta of T. S. Eliot, are embarrassed by the idea that a poet has his own feelings and that it is these which appear in his writing. It has also led to the kind of statement one often reads, that Cummings has been saying the same thing in the same way since he started to write. This is quite false. For example, he abandons quite early the Poundian archaisms which give a poem like "Puella Mea" its remarkable and exquisite flavor. Again, there are poems in *No Thanks* which, like the stunning Nos. 2, 9, 13, and 48 of that volume, employ a greater range of invention than those of any previous volume. And the last three volumes of *Poems 1923–1954* contain pieces more profound than anything he wrote earlier; among them, "hate blows a bubble of despair into" (No. 83), "one's not half two. It's two are halves of one:" (No. 74), "nothing false and possible is love" (No. 80), "my father moved through dooms of love" (No. 75), "no man,if men are gods;but if gods must" (No. 92), and "i thank You God for most this amazing" (No. 95). Reading these latter poems, one smiles at the term "charming," so often applied to his work, frequently as a technique of damning. Such a term does not touch the depth of these poems or the conjugal mystique of "somewhere i have never traveled,gladly beyond" (No. 35) or "o by the by" (No. 89) (which looks as though it is about kites). And even less does such a term meet the violence, the anger, the bawdiness, the bitterness of some of his most memorable work.

The other purity of Cummings' work, that of art, has put off still others who concentrate on the craftsmanship rather than on the feeling and find themselves irritated or puzzled or intimidated by the well-known Cummings experiments with syntax, spelling, and the appearance of the poem on the page. Early a rather remarkable hostility in academic circles against the work of Cummings set in, a feeling seen archetypically in R. P. Blackmur's never altered nor recanted condemnation of Cummings' work as involving a kind of "baby talk." Much of this hostility seems to me based on a deep-laid, partly superstitious resistance to what might be called the fracturing of the word. Some of it is based on the same inveterate taboo which D. H. Lawrence and James Joyce suffered under: the banning from serious writing of certain Anglo-Saxon expressions and a feeling against the literary portraiture of certain kinds of people, such as drunks (unless they can afford it), homosexuals (whom Cummings always portrays unsympathetically), and whores (who are usually portrayed sympathetically). Their biases, of course, are far less strong in our time than they were when Cummings' earlier books were appearing. Blackmur's study, which has so heavily influenced academic critics in this country, was based on Cummings' vocabulary, which is admittedly the least imaginative aspect of his work (coinages and composites aside). The freshness Cummings has brought into the language as such has come from the unexpected qualities he has turned up in common words by shifting their usual syntactical function and by introducing various classified (viz., tmesis and grammatical synthesis) but little analyzed practices into the language of poetry. Freud's analyses of the punnings, splittings, and composings in the language of dreams and jokes provide an insight into some of Cummings' effects, which to my knowledge no student has yet followed out.

As the figure in Marianne Moore's poem "Poetry" announces, "We do not admire what we cannot understand." Fortunately, the case for understanding Cummings has improved a great deal in recent years. The promise of earlier studies by people like Theodore Spencer and Horace Gregory has been reassuringly fulfilled in Norman Friedman's *E. E. Cummings: The Art of His Poetry* (1960), which has fine, lengthy expositions of Cummings' devices and their development in his work. He has begun to be studied seriously and at length as an inventor, and there is a growing literature of Cummings research. I need only add in this connection Friedman's second book on Cummings, *e. e. cummings: The Growth of a Writer* (1964), Robert Wagner's *The Poetry and Prose of E. E. Cummings* (1965), and S. V. Baum's edition of *Cummings and the Critics: Collection of Critical Articles* (1960).

Generally we may say that Cummings' typographical inventions are instruments for controlling the evocation of the poem in the mind of the reader; they are means of mitigating the temporal necessities of language with its falsification of the different, temporal rhythms of experience itself. Cummings is a painter, of course, and most of his poems are two things, auditory art and visual art, nonrepresentational pictures whose appearance on the page is essential to the artist's intention. (His correspondence with his publishers confirms this.) There is, typically, an intimate connection between the poem's appearance and the proper control of reading rate, emotional evocation, and aesthetic inflection. Indeed, one has the sense, reading these "picture poems" (his phrase) aloud, that one is translating inadequately from one language to another, with proportionate loss to the mere listener. This is an especially striking realization when one remembers that Cummings himself read his poems memorably, indeed read his own work better than any other living poet. One wonders what the greatness would be if he could hear in Cummings' voice what is added in the eye.

It is impossible, for example, to hear what happens in the first poem of *95 Poems*. This poem achieves a simple beauty, good as anything of its kind Cummings has done, when the word "loneliness" emerges, austerely, rending the heart, simultaneously with the slow appearance to consciousness of the phrase "a leaf falls," with which it intertwines or spirals round, or is spiraled round, leaflike, falling. This small work brings about an artistic happening unique to this poet.

l(a

le
af
fa

ll

s)
one
l

iness

One of the most gaining tour-de-force pieces which demonstrate the importance of the visual as a determining aspect in the reading of a poem is "r-p-o-p-h-e-s-s-a-g-r" (No. 13 in *No Thanks*), where the energy of the piece is coiled in the language so as to dramatize the leap of a grasshopper, a momentary thing. For the most part, Cummings did not choose "picture poems" for his *100 Selected Poems* (1959), but visual regulation is apparent in Nos. 4, 6, 17, and 20.

The problem of bridging the gap between the time qualities of language and of experience is one of the oldest which the art of poetry has had to deal with. However, the idea that the poet has a right to use visible, printed (as well as the older, auditory) means to solve this problem comes hard to some, as does the solution of another general problem of poetry, its rhetoric: that of breaking up the usual patterns of response so that the poet may exercise some direction over the way in which his materials are received. The reader must not be allowed to bask in the ease of what he thinks he knows or feels lest he be denied the reality of the occurrence of a new poem. There is a certain destructive element which enters the technique of poetry at this point, aimed at dynamiting the cliché patterns of response. Cummings' orthographical and typographical inventions are his great lingual explosives. A reader must *react* to Cummings; he cannot dismiss him willy-nilly. It happens that one of the possible reactions is hostility, or perhaps more accurately, anxiety. One has the impression that a critic like Yvor Winters is simply made very uncomfortable by Cummings' work. I wonder if there does not operate in the response of such a critic the notion I mentioned before of language as fetish, with the setting up of taboos against tampering or touching. Cummings treats words as though they were objects which could be transplanted, split, caressed, injured, brought into existence or out of it—as though they were servants subject to the feeling and control of the master, who therefore emerges as a kind of genie of language, sometimes benevolent, but possibly dangerous.

Cummings, for the most part, does not employ shapes literally related to the sense of his poems (as did George Herbert in a number of fine poems) or symbolically related ones; rather he employs shapes we would be likely to call abstract, that is, nonrepresentational. Cummings' noteworthy alternate profession as a painter is as a *modern* painter; he would no more paint a Christmas tree with its commonly acknowledged shape than he would write a poem about a Christmas tree (he has such a poem) in that shape. Now, the choice of shape, among the poets interested in them for their poems, is relevant to the general ideas of shape in the visual art of the time. I don't know enough to say which art movements influenced Cummings most, dadaism, say, or surrealism, or cubism, or . . . ? Though from what I have seen of his painting, I would suppose cubism had. In any case, I am concerned here with the aesthetic of his poems, not of his paintings, and that could well be different.

What I wish to note is equally true of the three modern movements I named: they share with the baroque (which so influenced Herbert) an interest in dissolving surfaces. Applied to poems, this means that they must not look as we *expect* poems to look. The aim, of course, is different in each case; the baroque wanted to transfigure, to analyze toward mathematical and theological infinity; it had a *positive* interest in the dissolution of surface. The dadaist had a *negative* interest; he wanted not to transfigure but to disenchant, to debunk, and the cubist to disorganize (though in the best only to reorganize more perfectly). The relevance of dadaism and cubism to Cummings' poetics goes far beyond the surface of his poems; one thinks of the disenchantment of the language of the American-English lyric accomplished by his many poems reproducing the speech of prostitutes and the various idioms of workingmen, or one thinks of the positive perfections of verse he achieves out of fractured forms. But I wish to emphasize here that even so far as the *appearance* of the poem is directly concerned, it is not itself the end of the interest in shape for Cummings (as it was not for Herbert): rather the language of the poem is the end of this interest, as it must be for a poet— whether or not he is also a painter.

We have still a great deal to learn about just how Cummings uses appearances to serve the ends of language art, though some studies exist, as I have indicated; my own spotty investigation has led me to three conclusions. First, the typographical inventions are instruments for controlling the evocation of the poem in the mind of the reader; they are organic and essential where they are successful and are only ornamental and precious where either the poem or the reader fails. I emphasize that Cummings' techniques of punctuation, word breaking, and word placing are means of exorcising the temporal necessities of language with its falsification of the different temporal rhythms of experience; the latter rhythms are often quicker than those of language and may be doubled, occurring simultaneously or else in some kind of conflict, on the one hand, or reinforcing phase, on the other. This is a traditional problem, and it is especially great in lyric poetry, which cannot put to use the time lag of language in the way that epic poetry can. Rhyme, counterpoint techniques like alliteration, stanza periods, and other smaller or larger units of rhythmic control are all aids for solving the problem of the disparate times between language and experience; each of them was invented by somebody.

Second, the orthographical inventions—altered spellings, irregular use of lower case, and so on—are expansions of the ancient poetic method of connotation, where a single word is pressed for richness latent in it, but unrealized in the common spelling and appearance of it. Third, the grammatical inventions (or reintroductions such as the use of Latin word orders) are designed, some of them, to break up the usual patterns of response so that the reading *can be* brought under the control of the poet, allowing him to do his work (this is a rhetorical function shared to a certain extent by typographical and orthographical inventions as well); others of them are designed to bring that possibility into act. A prime problem in accomplishing the latter is (following Pound and Fenollosa) to secure the maximum number of active verbs and to place them most effectively within the period. One of Cummings' achievements has been to gain the *effect* of the active verb, with its closeness to elemental dynamic reality, in other parts of speech (thus: "disintegrat i o n" and "stic-ky" and "onetwothreefourfive"); and again, to make verbs themselves apparently more active (thus: "SpRiN,k,LiNg" and "kIss" and ".press" and "ex:ten:ded" and "swallow)s" and "stiffenS"). Many of the examples seem exceedingly simple; that is characteristic of discovery.

I have mentioned the rhetorical function of Cummings' language. Let me add again that each of the methods above acts rhetorically to prevent the reader from resting in what he thinks he knows and what he expects; without this, poetry would be impossible, and as humans become more and more self-consciously and self-satisfiedly "knowing," as more and more they "smash . . . why . . . into because" (No. 77), the means for bringing this about will have to be more and more radical. I should say that is a central meaning of Cummings' work. He himself has described the attempt to create a dynamic and moving expression, like that of life itself or laughter, in the following anecdote: In response to an inquiry about his understanding of his own method, Cummings said, "I can express it in fifteen words, by quoting THE ETERNAL QUES-TION AND IMMORTAL ANSWER of burlesk, viz. 'Would you hit a woman with a child?—No, I'd hit her with a brick.' Like the burlesk comedian, I am abnormally fond of that precision which creates movement."

The precision goes with exacting labor. In this regard, Cummings once answered a high-school editor who wrote to him: "As for expressing nobody but yourself in words, that means working just a little harder than anybody who isn't a poet can possibly imagine. Why? because nothing is quite as easy as using words like somebody else. We all of us do exactly this nearly all the time—and whenever we do it we're not poets." Cummings has set himself so satisfactorily to the task of using words in his own way that he is a despair to all young poets who could learn from him. They can't use his ways in their own ways. It is mildly consoling to discover that Pound was using some of Cummings' ways before Cummings; but then one remembers Pound was doing things most of his contemporaries do, and before them—and one despairs again.

Illustrative of the effects of this hard-worked precision in Cummings' poetry are the impressions induced by "that melan-choly," the poem about the organ-grinder and the cockatoo (No. 25 of 95 Poems). First, we observe that the poem is written in what we may call free-verse stanzas, separated by single, free lines. To say that the blocks of verse are stanzas means they follow a certain pattern of regularity, which might be signified by a set number of metrical feet and/or a recurring rhyme pattern, but which here (as often with Cummings) is limited to a fixed number of lines—so that we may call the pattern free. The single, interspersed line brings to mind the refrain or repeated line of many traditional lyric forms, and therefore the over-all visual *effect* of the poem on the page is that of a traditional stanzaic construction with a refrain. This effect is reinforced by the presence of full end rhyme in the first stanza (play / say). But the facts that the stanzas are free and that actually there is no pattern of rhyme throughout and that the single interspersed line is really a repeated one make the poem a departure from tradition; that is, the traditional surface appearance disappears on examination, a characteristic one associates with the baroque, or, when it is combined with a burlesque element, the dada.

We notice, too, how Cummings' punctuation works to add movement to the poem: a meaningful disregard of grammatical rules toward this end occurs in two or three places. First, Cummings' use of a period at the beginning of the second stanza serves to anticipate the sense of the line, a stopping of the hand organ, a silence. In the reality which the poem conjures, actually the stopping would follow immediately upon the statement, "I want a fortune." Omitting the grammatical period at the end of the previous line (which a reader would *not* take expressionally) allows Cummings to juxtapose this *feeling* of stopping in a dramatic fashion when he begins the next line with a period. (".At which (smiling) he stops:"). Thus the temporal sequence of actions in the fantasy of the poem (the utterance of the statement, followed by the stopping of the organ) is caught more realistically than would be the case if grammatical propriety were observed. Again, omitting the hyphen after the divided word "pick" in the second line of this same stanza draws attention away from the two-syllable nature of the *word* "picking" and, instead, places it on the immediate, simple, or so to speak "one-syllable" character of the *action* which the word signifies. Finally, the illegal insertion of commas between the letters of "taps" ("t,a,p,s") makes use of the tentative pause signified by a comma to simulate (again, I would like to say "dramatize") the action signified by the word.

There are two places in the poem where a final *s* is separated from a word at the end of the line to be placed at the beginning of the following line. A particular ghostly quality of attenuation or stringing out (hence, *thinning* in a line containing the expression "windthin") is the functional effect of this technique in the first instance. In the second, we have a rendering of the abrupt action signified by the word "tweaks" through emphasis of the *feeling* of tweaking by collapsing it, as it were, into the one final letter capitalized to accomplish this effect, as well as separated ("tweak / S"). The special intensity provided by the use of the capital distinguishes this usage (though it appears to be so similar) from the former instance, where attenuation rather than abruptness is achieved. The treatment of the word "slowly" in the fourth stanza shows us another creative use of capitals—one of Cummings' trade-marks. Here it results in the expressional deceleration of the pace of reading by drawing attention to the spelling (or literal composition) of the word as opposed to its meaning, which one perceives rapidly. Breaking the word at its middle and including it in parentheses are further delaying techniques, which expedite (paradoxical expression here!) the feeling of slowness ("SlO / wLy").

When one considers how much energy is conserved beyond that which one expects to expend in reading, in order to reconstruct from inert words the dynamic qualities of action or feeling, one is prepared to appreciate why Cummings gives so much pleasure as a writer, even apart from his extraordinary wit. This additional energy which one (working from his earlier experience as a reader) is prepared to bring to the mental activity of reconstruction, but which remains uncon-

sumed, becomes freed and escapes as a kind of smile, or perhaps, indeed, as explicit laughter. Cummings' technique thus
may be analyzed as a special case of Freud's theory of humor,
which is stated in terms of the economy of energy. Much
could be learned by applying some of Freud's discoveries about
dream mechanism as well. For instance, it is clear that what
Freud calls "synthesis" and "tmesis" are operating in the
following cases, respectively: "sob-cries" and "dis(because my
tears / are full of eyes)appears."

Two other practices of Cummings in this poem may be
commented on. First, the contraction of the elements of "fellow
will" into "fellow'll" accomplishes a musical gain around the
assonant sounds (chol/low'll/til) in the first stanza. Second, the
printing of the name "Polly" as "Paw lee" not only recreates
the effect of the name spoken with a tentative and mournful
emphasis but gains through a syllabic pun (Pol-Paw) an
emotional richness around the senses of "father," which resonate
about the figures both of the organ-grinder and of his oracular
cockatoo, to whom the speaker comes for wisdom and guidance,
seeking his "fortune."

A number of the poems in 95 Poems show Cummings in his
most virtuoso mood and consequently at his most intellectual,
most abstract. The statement of "n" (No. 53), for instance,
separated from its spacings and word arrangements, is simply,
"Note the old almost lady feebly hurling crumbs one by one
at two three four five and six English sparrows." But the words
of the statement are broken up and the letters regrouped
successively according to an arithmetic pattern, which issues
on the page—because of the way in which the numbers of
letters, and hence the lengths of lines, vary—as two proportionate isosceles triangles, or a broken diamond.

In poem No. 53 of 95 Poems the principle of composition has
to do with the counting of letters. In many others, a syllabic
principle is employed: not only the classic decasyllabic or octo-
syllabic line, but often a line of four syllables is employed, as

in the trivial poem No. 65 ("first robin the;") and No. 79 ("whippoorwill this") or the elegant and elaborate poem No. 44 ("—laughing to find") and No. 85 ("here pasture ends—"). As one of our most accomplished masters and adapters of the sonnet form, Cummings adds here several pieces, including the sweet religious lyric poem No. 76 ("these from my mother's greatgrandmother's rosebush white") and the beautiful love sonnets No. 92 ["i carry your heart with me(i carry it in"] and No. 94 ("being to timelessness as it's to time,"). One of the sonnets (No. 42) contains the lines "mind without soul may blast some universe / to might have been, and stop ten thousand stars." One is reminded of his famous lines from an earlier poem, "I'd rather learn from one bird how to sing / than teach ten thousand stars how not to dance" (No. 54 of *Selected Poems*). Having seen somewhat through the mask of his anti-intellectuality (which is actually aimed at technology with its void of feeling), I doubt that Cummings really misses the role of the astronomer as separate choreographer to the stars or the role of the poet as singing master to the birds. What would the nightingale be without Ovid and Keats? Or the robin and whippoorwill without Cummings?

The mentality of Cummings not only takes us back to the Pythagoreans and their concern with the numerical roots of language; it takes us, more than that of any other American poet, forward to the Existentialists, with their concern for catching the quality of feeling in the subject as something of greater "authenticity" than the quality of intelligibility in the object. Cummings is a scientist of the affect, a doctor of the person. He also takes us immediately, more than any other American poet except Whitman, to the idiom and subject–matter concerns of the so-called beat generation poets. The beat generation is closer to the Village mode of Cummings than to the farming of Robert Frost, the insurance selling of Wallace Stevens, the librarianship of Marianne Moore, the doctoring of W. C. Williams, the banking and editing of

Eliot, or whatever it was he did, of Pound. The celebration of the body in Cummings (in such a poem as "i like my body" [No. 16]) is superior to that in the litanies of Allen Ginsberg (for example, "Footnote to *Howl*"). Cummings is the least Manichaean of all the good twentieth-century poets, English and American. At the same time, the vocabulary, power of shock, and apparent antipatriotism of such a poem as "i sing of Olaf glad and big" show him peer to the beat generation in these matters, and he is far their superior in craft.

Comparing him with members of his own generation, a golden age in poetry, one finds that Stevens is more genteel and gorgeous, Eliot more reflective and religious, Williams more perfect in eye and in cadence, Marianne Moore more scholarly and prettier, Pound more versatile and outrageous, Frost more violent and pastoral. But Cummings is the most provocative, the most humane, the most inventive, the funniest, and the least understood. When Yvor Winters wrote that Cummings "understands little about poetry," he missed the point. It is not Cummings' job to understand poetry; it's his job to write it; and it is up to the critics to understand and to derive whatever new machinery they need to talk about the poems; for Cummings— cockatoo, organ-grinder, lover—is himself a father whom a whole generation of poets have already taken to themselves. Hard as he is to imitate, he has led them naturally to look for their own voices. They know he has best described in *i: six nonlectures* the subjects of the poet as "ecstasy and anguish, being and becoming; the immortality of the creative imagination and the indomitability of the human spirit." He has also best described in "no man,if men are gods;but if gods must" (No. 76) the nature of the poet:

> fiend . . . angel . . .
> coward,clown,traitor,idiot,dreamer,beast—
>
> such was a poet and shall be and is

—who'll solve the depths of horror to defend
a sunbeam's architecture with his life:
and carve immortal jungles of despair
to hold a mountain's heartbeat in his hand.

In the last pages of *i: six nonlectures,* Cummings quotes Keats's "Ode on a Grecian Urn" with its enigmatic close which I cited earlier. In my opinion the enigma offered by Cummings' white cockatoo casts light on that given us by Keats's urn, and a second oracular utterance of Cummings illuminates both. Speaking to the creative side in each of us, he said: "Only the artist in yourselves is more truthful than the night."

Hart Crane's Poetics of Failure

JOSEPH N. RIDDEL

I

Hart Crane's last poem, "The Broken Tower," is so confused with the sensational events of his last days that it is hard to consider the poem apart from the man. On the whole, it seems wise not to try to, for this is a poem which dramatizes, once and for all in our time, the pathetic gesture of a man dying into his work. In other words, it seems to do just what Crane's life was dedicated to—it turns the self into a poem, or almost so. For like so many of Crane's visionary poems, it renders not apocalypse, but the failure of vision. To purify the self that has fallen into a "broken world," the poet wills a new "tower" in which his being is reconstituted: a purified inner space, a marriage of self and other, the fulfillment of his subjectivity in the object, an escape from time. Yet Crane ends not by creating that "tower"—or at least, not by achieving it as a visionary poet must, in the style of the poem—but by reconfirming his role as poet and hence affirming the future possibility of creating that new "tower." In short, like all of Crane's poems, it catches the poet in his act of being a poet, pursuing the dream that lies always before him. Its true subject is the viability of the poet's means, his language, by which alone he and the vision are to be fulfilled as one.

Aspiring through language ("My word I poured. But was it cognate . . . ?") to transcend the "broken world," to achieve the "pure" in the "crystal Word," Crane realizes once again the difference between his words, which are the world's, and the "crystal Word," which seems always just beyond his grasp. Yet the triumph of failure attends the willed vision at poem's end, where Crane finds momentary consolation in the meaning

272

of his search, his quest through words, which has become his life. He finds himself buoyed up once more by his faith in his method, by his capacity to be possessed by language and purified by it. But he discovers, too, why he must forfeit his hope of ever achieving that purity; why, as he had hinted to himself in earlier poems, the visionary poet was destined to fail and thus was condemned again and again to "pour" forth words that hold him to the world even as they hold within themselves logos. To put it another way, Crane's desire to transmute the temporal self into pure space—to purify himself virtually into the form of a poem—is rewarded by a vicious yet vital irony, in which the poet finds himself to share the ultimate failure of his method because he is condemned to repeat it incessantly in time.

This is, I think, the crucial paradox that explains Crane's limitations and answers for his alleged visionary style. It is no less a quality which separates him from the optimum vitality of Whitman and from the apocalyptic style of Rimbaud, both his acknowledged masters. But recently, a group of critics, trying to revive so-called "Cosmic Poetry," have more or less apotheosized Crane for qualities he more desired than possessed. This critical reaction, though by no means dominant or persuasive, has formulated a poetics, or a critical stance, which cannot be ignored because it is so symptomatic of a modern problem. The reaction is predominantly against Eliotism, and in general against a formalistic, intellectual poetry; these critics have come to accept Crane, in terms which he himself set forth, as the direct heir of Whitman and the immediate forerunner of the "New Paganism." His style, formed so deliberately in opposition to Eliot's and, ironically, so unquestionably influenced by it, becomes the norm of a poetry that is at once "religious, physical, passionate, [and] incantatory." [1] More important, what Eliot and Pound had created as the "official" style of their age, the hard and dry and impersonal, is replaced by a new "official" style, no less contrived for its appearing spontaneous. It is a style measured not by wit or sharp paradox, but by orderly constellations of incoherent images, by highly condensed and vaguely orphic metaphors, and by personal symbols which emerge into public meaning only by the very fact that they ascribe to some achetypal significance. It is a style that "starts with the sun," yet uses words of the world, though as if to admit Nietzsche's prophecy that language could be purified of the world's appearance only by turning it into music. If Crane's is taken to be its norm, however, then there is more of a priority on recurrent patterns, image clusters, and internal linkages of a mathematical and mechanical kind than anything the Eliotics conceived. For all the talk about organicism, the "New Paganism," at least in the mode Crane represents, produces something more like a machine or a formula.[2] In any event, Crane's poetry is less Whitmanesque than Poesque, less organic than mathematical, in Valéry's sense of what Poe's poetics reveals. That Crane presumes to be an orphic poet, in the profoundest mythical sense, is one thing; the self-consciousness with which he goes about playing that role, and creating its style, is another.

There is, then, another and I think necessary way of looking at Crane's poetry than as "cosmic." For however much Crane talked of vision, of myth, and the like, however much he aspired to discover the pure language latent in the world, his poems are basically post-Romantic and post-symbolist: they are poems in which the poet rehearses the act of creating the poem, poems in which life is explored and virtually lived by holding it within the intense focus of the moment of its creation—poems, that is, which create a world rather than discover one. If the poet lives his life, as Crane seems to have, for the single purpose of transforming himself back into the pure moment of his origin, then the poem may well become a doubly transformative act. The poet seeks self-transcendence by willing a return to his beginning. In fact, Crane's theme, like Poe's, would seem to be nothing less than the creation myth itself, to which his own poetic act is analogue. Whatever, the poem becomes a quest for permanence, which is achieved only in the achievement of the perfect poem, hence never. The poet may presume to set himself at the cosmic center, and like Orpheus to speak with the power of the cosmic urge out of the no-thingness of the One. He is more likely to be involved in a very human enterprise, conducted at a higher intensity than is ordinary: the pursuit of himself, the definition of himself in his role as poet and, in Crane's particular case, as shareholder of the primordial mysteries. Like Orpheus, he is the victim of those he presumes to serve; or in other words, his role is that of victim to the very mysteries he harbors and sings.

Crane's poems do often achieve a constellated structure of recurrent images—the curve and circle imagery of *The Bridge*, for example [3]—but what kind of vision these manifest patterns represent is, to say the least, ambiguous. Surely it is more something desired than something possessed and known; surely Crane's "new" language, admitting its occasional brilliance, is anything but pure, his universe of images anything but apocalyptic. L. S. Dembo, in a most thorough reading of *The Bridge*, has shown how the pattern of imagery as well as the thematic progress of the poem leads his poet-quester not to vision, but back to the world that defiles visions.[4] The quester's vision sustains him not because it is grasped, but because it remains tantalizingly always before him, as possibility; it is his only when he has shared it with the world, that is, when he, like Columbus in "Ave Maria," has introduced it into history and thus exposed it to inevitable corruption and travesty. In *The Bridge*'s several sections, the vision invariably precedes the poem or is to follow it. A great many of these individual pieces spring from the anxiety (like Columbus') over whether the glimpsed vision can be communicated at all. For the poet's role is not so much to have the vision—Crane would seem to say with Blake that the poet by definition has had it in that he is poet—as it is to convey it to a world that must corrupt it. Crane's poet-quester lives to be sacrificed in his role, for he is to be destroyed with his vision. The enemy is history. And yet, to go one step further, he restores the vision, purifying it of history, in his act of sacrificing himself to it, in the suffering that attends the rejection of the Word by the world.

Crane's poems confess the torture of the poet who, to articulate the Word, must contend with history and its words. He has to restore the Word, then, by becoming it in his own sacrificial act. Crane's search for a language has its analogue clearly in the metaphor of Christ: the Word given, betrayed, and subsequently left to the world in words. The poetic vision he expressly desires to evoke—it is, in effect, identical with his new language—inevitably turns back upon itself, for the desire is never to be fulfilled. Dembo points up the analogy between Crane's distraught poet and Nietzsche's tragic vision of the poet-hero who fulfills himself only in his defeat.[5] Here is the crucial passage from *The Birth of Tragedy:* "Tragic myth, through the figure of the hero, delivers us from our avid thirst for earthly satisfaction and reminds us of another existence and a higher delight. For this delight the hero readies himself, not through his victories but through his undoing." [6] Yet it is not simply, as Dembo says, that Crane's frustrated quester celebrates his undoing by an indifferent but redeemable philistine world, though he does this; nor that in adapting, for his later poetry, the mask of the Nietzschean hero and discarding that of the impotent clown, Crane desired to give stature and dignity to the poet as modern hero, though above all he longed for a dignity befitting the exalted role of poet. The paradox runs deeper and is to be explained perhaps only by determining why in the mythical strategy of his poems the sacrifice of Dionysus had to be superimposed upon the sacrifice of Christ. And beyond that, why it is the sacrifice and not what should plausibly follow it, resurrection, that ultimately engages Crane; why, that is, Crane's poetry, which so passionately aspires to redeem history, by way of denying it, ultimately takes the only life it has from the pathos of the poet's failure to redeem it.

Crane aspires, in short, to write the poem that reaches beyond poetry; and yet it is in poetry, which clings tenaciously to history and its corruptions, that the poet claims his sacrificial identity. His defeat becomes necessary not so much as an affirmation of his dignity as poet, as the very act of his being. He is a seeker and sufferer, rather than a finder. And while Crane may, even must, cling to his belief that the Absolute exists not only in the particulars of the world but beyond (just as he clings to a belief in his ability to articulate it and hence to join the two in One in the poem), he is like Poe in respect to his doubt over the price one must pay for the act, the sacrifice of self. And, like for Poe, that act becomes his real theme, in which the marriage of subject and object implies the loss of subject. But the subject in Crane insists on surviving even in its own nothingness—surviving, that is, in the faith of its ultimate reconciliation and apotheosis: the clown in "Chaplinesque"; the lover in "Voyages"; the quester in "For the Marriage of Faustus and Helen"; the poet in "Praise for an Urn," whose poem aspires to its own apotheosis and fails of self-confidence; the bedlamite, the pariah, Columbus, Maquokeeta, the drunken sailor, his fellow American artists, and a host of other masks in *The Bridge*. But the end of these poems deliver, instead of vision, only the desperately renewed faith that it is still possibly available. They redeem the poet's vocation and return him to his proper role, as voice of the Absolute he feels within himself and as seeker after the Absolute that exists in the world. In other words, his role is to reunite the two in one, in poetry. The end for Crane's poems, it seems, was to justify the need for further poems, in which, ultimately, self and world might become one.

What Crane had finally to confront, perhaps unconsciously, was the fact that his failure lay in his method—the very method that had become his identity. The creative act itself is the true subject of these poems, the life of the poet-quester-visionary-lover-seeker whose role is as futile, yet as necessary, to himself as Sisyphus'. Like the Poe of the *Symbolistes*, who reappears in the "Tunnel" section of *The Bridge*, to have lost oneself to the world in quest of a way beyond it gives one a meaning and a purpose, in that it affirms alienation as prelude to transcendence. In the poet, as Crane idealizes him, resides the power to recognize the Word become flesh; his role is to transform that flesh back into the Word. But the transformative act, in that it will not yield to the easy explanations of dogma, is a suffering and a sacrifice of his own self. The flesh will not let go easily, and neither will the poem, for the poem, like life, is painfully real, and the vision, though glimpsed in that it is felt, remains problematic. The danger for a poet like Crane, however, is not that the vision may not be realized, but that his faith in it, and hence in himself, may wane. For then the very thing that sustains him, the need to pursue the vision, the need that calls forth the poem and verifies the poet's identity, betrays him to the enemy—history.

The poet's role in history (or better perhaps, his obligation to history) has a paradoxical effect on Crane's form. For the visionary poet, while he expressly denies history, must acknowledge it in the very act of trying to transform it. Crane's talent, almost every commentator on his poetry has remarked, was essentially lyrical. Yet it was virtually certain that, given his obsession with temporality, Crane would aspire to write an epic—or more accurately, to turn history into myth, to collapse the epic and the lyrical forms, by way of presenting not only the ideal that must *in*-form history but the very act of transformation by which the ideal is purified of history. *The Bridge*, clearly, is neither epic nor, as Crane suggested, a myth of America.[7] It is aptly described, as Poe described the *Iliad*, as a series of lyrical poems, each one rehearsing a basic pattern of the poet's defeat by and sacrifice to an indifferent world which will not receive his word.[8] But Crane's aspiration was, nevertheless, to transmute history into myth, by way of proving that the myth subsumed history. One method, pointed up by Eliot in his essay on *Ulysses* and by the practice of *The Waste Land*, was to telescope the individual quest with the archetypal: witness Crane's explanation of the Faust-Helen parallel in the essay "General Aims and Theories" and his various rationalizations, in letters to friends and sponsors, of the uses of mythical-historical archetypes in *The Bridge*.[9] As he moved from the short, intense lyric toward the cluster of lyrics stretched upon a mythical-historical frame, he had to create a persona (of the poet-quester) who could be involved in both time and eternity, or who, in other words, was at once personal and archetypal. Circumscribed by history, this persona was nonetheless cognate with the poet-hero-victim of all time, archetypes of the poet in the guise of mythical or historical antiheroes: with Faust, with Columbus, with Whitman and Poe and Emily Dickinson (fellow victims in the same sequence of history), with Rimbaud—in short, with the artist-*diabolus* whom history betrays because he denies history its privileges and priorities. The archetype of poet-quester becomes the archetype of visionary-victim, Dionysus-Christ. (Crane no less than Eliot could not really abide nor trust in the single, separate self of Whitman; Whitman soon became Poe, betrayed, perhaps self-betrayed, and denied by history. Unlike Eliot, he had only the archetypal self of artist-outsider to fall back on. Similarly, poetry for him was a method of telescoping personal history with the recurrent or mythical event in which history transcends itself. The distinction might be that Eliot preserves the illusion of historical time in his "tradition," while Crane is impatient with particular events that make up the logos except as they, like Columbus' voyage, can be reduced to the one truth they symbolize.) What the modern self shared with his prototype, however, was not vision so much as the commitment to pursue vision. The poem itself—*The Bridge* in particular—rather than elevating historical events into epical elaboration, thereby admitting the purposefulness of the many within the One, reduces history to a primary mythical pattern, thereby bespeaking the poet's distrust of history. This accounts, I think, for the confusions which attend Crane's very personal use of American history. He is not interested in history as such at all, except in that it offers evidence of the recurrent and universal pattern that obsessed him. American history was not so much a myth to him as an ur-myth, not history so much as a cosmic syndrome of the Absolute. In that sense alone did his particular involvement with it, and victimization by it, have meaning.

If Crane's use of history is arbitrary, therefore, this is just as it must be; for his role as he assumes it is to transform history into its absolute form before it transforms him into anonymity. This is what, in effect, Roebling had done in manifesting his vision of the bridge, which for Crane was a work of art, the marriage of form and power, even if it was destined to be received by a skeptical world only as a technological feat. The power of transformation rests, Crane would insist, with the poet, not as in Eliot with history. And therein is revealed Crane's true theme and problem. If the transformative act is history's, the poet is forced at one and the same time to acknowledge history and deny his creativity. But if the act is his, or through him, he may grasp his identity even in his undoing. For it is only through him that history can have meaning. The poet's identity rests in his method—a method which he must exercise in history, but which he hopes will lead him beyond, to the meaning of history's dynamics; which is to say, he finds history in himself alone.

His method, as a mode of his being, exists as I previously indicated to reach beyond and thus to deny itself—a paradox Crane appears to have lived to the end. The paradox is perhaps more evident in Crane's early, short lyrics. Poems like "Praise for an Urn" and "Legend" explore the sacrificial nature of the creative act and the anxiety of almost certain failure. "Black Tambourine" identifies the poet with the "black man," exiled in "some mid-kingdom, dark," which is bounded on one side by the transcendent world available to his imagination, "his tambourine," and on the other by his primordial "carcass," the origin and end of his mortal self. But to the world (of self-consciousness) he is outcast and slave, neither accepted by it nor willing to accept it, isolated by time (like the Negro by history) in an absurd space. "Chaplinesque" regards the artist's pratfalls and evasions as a kind of sacrificial gesture, the compromise of one face to preserve another—an inner integrity set against the world the poet disdains (because it is one he never made), yet aspires to purify. Even *The Bridge* celebrates at its very center the quester's ultimate triumph in his withdrawal from and return to the history that destroys him; in "The Dance," which makes the poem's completest retreat into the mythical past and back toward the primal moment, the sacrifice of Maquokeeta is at once an end and a beginning. It is fulfillment of his role, the moment in which he is given to history, which in turn will obscure and defile his meaning.

Beyond those early minor poems which state the condition, however, lay the necessity for vigorous response, evident certainly in *The Bridge* but likewise in several poems written at about the time Crane was formulating his large work. The response is manifest, as Dembo points out, in the shift of masks from impotent clown to engaged poet-quester, from the comic to the tragic vision.[10] But in the end, one has to argue, the tragic vision returns to the comic or seriocomic, as is curiously evident in two poems I should like to explore in depth: "The Wine Menagerie" and "Lachrymae Christi." They are more truly poems in Crane's proper mode than is *The Bridge,* and they reveal clearly the problems he would face, and fail to overcome, in trying to write a poem that presumes to deal with history as apocalypse.

II

Harriet Monroe, closing off her correspondence with Crane about the obscurities of "At Melville's Tomb," testily observed that the poem "reeks with brains." [11] Crane has seldom been accused since of an excess of brains, though it should be evident that the affected spontaneity of his poetry is outweighed by self-conscious contrivance and intellectual allusiveness. But Crane's allusions, whether indebted to Eliot or, more plausibly, derived from the quasi-intellectual mysticism of writers like Ouspensky, whom he was reading with careless fervor, intends something quite opposite Eliot's. If for Eliot the myth of history (that is, tradition) may be an analogue (if not the Incarnation) of the divine order, for Crane it must be made, in and through the poet's words, to distill the pure Word. History, for Crane, is simply the energy of the Word issuing into particular forms. If for Eliot allusion is the method by which the individual talent delineates that enduring past to which the present self is heir and on which it modestly builds, for Crane it is the process by which the poet searches the fragments of history for its Absolute. If for Eliot allusion manifests an escape from personality, for Crane it is the apotheosis of personality, his version of cosmic personalism in which the Word is seen to realize Itself as person and poet. Eliot's history takes on perspective and the illusion of chronology and movement; it is authentically historical, even if in the end it proves to be immediate rather than continuous. Crane's history, on the other hand, is always subsumed by the ur-myth, the ideal of Unity. Eliot's history is at once corrupt and redeemable; Crane's is not so much corrupt as corrupting.

The effects on form and style are corollary. Crane's long poems do not develop; they recur. They pivot on the eternal event, which the poet is constantly reliving. The persona of *The Bridge* is no protagonist, is involved in no agon except the recurrent event of his quest and failure. The compressed images, the ellipses, the forcefully collapsed syntax and metaphors— all reveal a poem which tries to deny the temporality of language, to distill the pure logos from the dross of the world's words. At the same time, this style calls attention to its own processes and the stresses of its effort. If Eliot's language, especially in his later poetry, orders itself toward the formal rhythms of music and points forward to the ultimate stillness upon which all is centered, Crane's aspires toward spontaneity and the illusion of creative release into the dynamics that pervade all meaningful forms—for example, the Bridge as still motion. Paradoxically, it is acutely self-conscious; it "reeks with brains" at its most illogic extremes. But—and this is the crucial point—it achieves, or seeks to, an intensity of rhythm and movement that overrides intellect and purifies it. The poem aspires toward the tranquillity and silence of "belle isle" (monistic union), but the language ironically will not let go and ultimately disdains the end in which it would consume itself. The new language, that is, reconciles subject and object, id and ego, in that it is the bridge by which alone the self passes from one world to the other, from alienation to home and back again.

In "The Wine Menagerie," for example, stylistic compression vies with some rather indirect allusiveness to evidence this process. The telescoped metaphors just fail to conceal the obvious scene, a bar, even as they fail to render adequately the dramatic evolution of vision. But that is just the point. The heady release, under the inspiriting effects of wine, leads to a new freedom and wholeness that is in itself a wrapt confinement.

The images of the opening two stanzas turn upon this paradox, the transformation of time into space. For the redemption of sight frees an interior self which is at the same time pure and violent (the id that is both creative and destructive) and in turn transforms the impurities of real things into the purity of images. Yet the poet is "conscripted," even enwombed, by the very bottles that contain the wine of his release:

> Invariably, when wine redeems the sight,
> Narrowing the mustard scansions of the eyes,
> A leopard ranging always in the brow
> Asserts a vision in the slumbering gaze.

> Then glozening decanters that reflect the street
> Wear me in crescents on their bellies. Slow
> Applause flows into liquid cynosures;
> —I am conscripted to their shadows' glow.

Indeed, this lacerating paradox controls the entire poem. The redemptive wine releases a Dionysian self that is "conscripted" by its own dual nature.[12] Not only the "leopard" but the "glozening decanters," which contain the poet's image in their womblike "bellies," point forward to the new "thresholds" he will affirm—"thresholds" in which "freedom" is circumscribed by "Wine talons." Stanzas 3 through 6 extend the paradox of the opening two: the refracted images of the dance are animal and violent, yet surely Dionysian, and they suggest, in a painful way, the sacrifice of self attendant upon the transformative act. The scene manifests all the violence of a rape, contained within a drabbly sham interior (space) and attended by the nightmare image of the serpent (time, but no less the destructive-creative primal force that is the union of subject and object), which circumscribes the speaker's vision. If on one level the scene does violence to the vision, it is no less the arena of the "I's" necessary act. In other words, the redemption implied in the poem's first line, this release from one kind of seeing (common-sensical) into another, is a freedom to undergo the agony of a generative act. The "urchin" who enters the scene in stanza 5 comes like a supplicant to the mysteries of the revel to which he is likewise victim. The dance contrasts rudely with his innocence, but is nonetheless the complement of it. For the "urchin," like the poet, is an outsider whose innocence must be sacrificed if he is to be an insider. What he knows, or is to know, is the revelation imaged in stanza 6, in which "roses shine" between "black tusks," a metaphor of the Dionysian season, spring, and the paradox of creation in destruction.

What, then, are the "New thresholds, new anatomies!" of the two succeeding stanzas?

> New thresholds, new anatomies! Wine talons
> Build freedom up about me and distill
> This competence—to travel in a tear
> Sparkling alone, within another's will.
>
> Until my blood dreams a receptive smile
> Wherein new purities are snared; where chimes
> Before some flame of gaunt repose a shell
> Tolled once, perhaps, by every tongue in hell.

The poem may be remotely connected with the love affair Crane described so ardently to Waldo Frank in a letter dated April 21, 1924.[13] "Lachrymae Christi" certainly is: it was written a short two months before the letter and incorporates the ambiguous guilt and idealization of that "affair." But "The Wine Menagerie" was completed almost a year and a half afterward. The ecstatic (but no less conscripting) transport within "another's will" is to be understood only in the context of the tear-smile imagery. In *The Birth of Tragedy* Nietzsche describes the dismemberment of Dionysus in terms of the agony of individuation, the division of the One into the many, like the "separation into air, water, earth, and fire." Individuation, he continues, "should be regarded as the source of all suffering, and rejected. The smile of this Dionysos has given birth to the Olympian gods, his tears have given birth to men." [14] He remarks further that individuation was in the Eleusinian mysteries the "root of all evil," while art signified reintegration. The movement in the stanzas above, through a "tear / Sparkling alone" toward the "new purities" of a "receptive smile," re-enacts the Dionysian cycle, which Nietzsche speaks of as a special kind of transformative act: "No longer the *artist*, he [in the ecstasy of his dance] has himself become a *work of art*," [15] and in turn he becomes for his worshipers, like Orpheus, the object of violent desire. From the individuation and consequent suffering that gives birth to the poem, through the agony of the creative (re-creative) act which destroys the self, to the ecstasy of the "receptive smile," the imagery records an act of recomposing the self into a work of art: the reuniting of subject and object, self and other. But in this poem the "smile" only beckons, is not fully achieved, and the momentary "freedom" distilled in the sacrificial act exists but to be destroyed—again like Dionysian wholeness. The compressed and highly oblique metaphors of the last two stanzas can only suggest other forms of fragmentation, and particularly, in the images of beheading, the new cycle of Dionysian frenzy which must lead endlessly from wholeness to individuation and back again.

Yet the tragic rhythm, as the last couplet suggests, is more aptly comic. The freedom achieved in the moment of the poem— those "New thresholds, new anatomies"—is betrayed by the world's ruddy "tooth" and the "treasons of the snow," by time. And the poet becomes an "exile," an individual, once more in order to fulfill himself. Inevitably, the poem ends on the note of individuation and exile, not of ecstasy. While the symbolist poem should ideally conclude with vision or silence, with "new anatomies" evoked, the modernist poem must celebrate victory in defeat. The cycle of Crane's poem is not from the One to the many back to the One, but from fragmentation toward ecstasy and back again. The "new purities" of the Dionysian smile are not the poet's possession, but his compulsion. They are dreamed, not realized, except in the sense that one knows them only in the moment he knows he needs them. Unlike the symbolist poem, Crane's moves toward a threshold (the verge of unity) within the self rather than beyond the self; the ecstatic moment for him—at the center of the poem—is a moment of integration desperately grasped, in the act of making the poem, which precedes betrayal and exile. The "new purities" are "snared"; the "freedom" is built up around him by "Wine talons." His moment of integration is attained by transforming the kind of violence that marks stanzas 3 and 4 into pure form, "a shell." He aspires toward "new purities" of a "receptive smile," while the masculine actor of the earlier stanzas "takes her" with the "forcepts" of his smile, an act in which "an instant of the world" is *unmade*. But the one act precedes the other; the time-space tomb must be unmade if the self is to be released into a womb of "new purities," from which, of course, must follow another birth or individuation. Confined by one world (time-space), the poet must dream new ones, to be "snared" only at the expense of self. But the "tooth implicit of the world" pursues and destroys the wholeness of vision and of the self, giving the self back itself and its agony. Like Dionysus, the poet must not possess but be possessed, and realize himself in losing himself. He can "travel" in a "tear," "within another's will," but only for the instant of his poetic act, his "dream." Yet even that for the poet means he must lose himself. The smile is earned at the price of tears, to which there is an inevitable return; at poem's end, the poet is once more an alien in reality, the exile.

The mark of a Crane poem is almost always this kind of turbulence and violence. It turns not on the language of paradox, but on the paradox of his act which anticipates the undoing of the actor. The Dionysian smile of rapture (which gives birth to the Olympian gods) is achieved in the agony of his fragmentation; the recognition of wholeness lies in our recognizing how far we have fallen from it, and yet how the poem returns us to it. Similarly, Crane's exile, a wondering Aeneas returned to the hellish world and its betrayals, pays the price of vision, which is not had except that it is lost. Was Marianne Moore so wrong, we might ask, to change the title of the poem to "Again" when she published it in the *Dial?*

Within this kind of context it is possible to understand the larger rhythms and some of the obscurer particulars of "Lachrymae Christi." Crane's most incoherent poem, stylistically his most outrageous, "Lachrymae Christi" is to be understood primarily in the sense of its being only one more version of the one poem Crane could write. The imagery is at once more blatant and more inward than in the usual Crane effort; and unlike *The Bridge,* it is not long enough for motifs, images, and symbols to recur into coherence and clarity. Preceding "The Wine Menagerie," and less open than that poem, "Lachrymae Christi" is illuminated, at least in part, by the later piece. It moves from smile to smile through the agony of sacrifice and tears and ends in the ecstatic moment of anticipated self-transcendence. The concluding image of Dionysus' "Unmangled target smile" is a vision of wholeness anticipated in the moment of fragmentation, and the image in the opening stanza of the "unyielding smile" is the blank expressionlessness of a sterile world into which the fragmented self is born, another kind of death. Between the two, between his birth into the modern landscape (a figure of absolute dualism) and his release into the ecstatic unity of death, lies the poet's creative ground. He must generate the one out of the other; he must, as Crane puts it in his most notorious essay, "acclimatize" the machine (of time). The middle of the poem is just that generative and purifying yet self-destructive act.

If the tears of Christ (and by metamorphosis, of Dionysus)

are the wine which redeems agony, the "benzine / Rinsings" of the opening stanzas are anything but sacramental. They are venomous, sterilizing, death-rendering; they negate the ground of life and compel the sacrifice of the creative act. It is difficult, given the syntactical dislocations, the parenthesis, and the stanza break, to respond to the poem's opening sentence, which runs halfway through the second stanza. The analogy between the "Rinsings" and the "Immaculate venom" must certainly image, however, the impotent landscape in which the generative energy is contained—the body of the creative soul, the dualism of id-ego. And this energy is frankly, if obliquely, imaged as sexual. The illogic of the metaphor "venom binds" manifests the tension between vital and sterile, organic and inorganic. The imagery of evolving spring, which follows, is the imagery of sexual violence, a destruction of the virgin innocence (a sterility in itself) that is paradoxically necessary to the fulfillment of that virginity. (Similarly, the crucifixion of Christ and the riving of Dionysus are essential to their fulfillment, the former an Apollonian illusion, the latter the stirrings of ecstatic transcendence; likewise, the analogy between poet and his fulfillment in the poem.) Here, then, we can possibly understand the metaphor of the "Immaculate venom" which "binds / The fox's teeth"; [16] for if the violence of sexual energy fragments in order to generate life, that which "binds" this energy is at once pure (immaculate and Apollonian) and sterilizing (venomous). Moreover, the complex associations of the immortal serpent, the sexual serpent, the serpent of intellect and time, and the serpentine dance of Dionysus begin to accumulate upon the double vision of the sacrificial and the generative act.

The agony of the creation not only results from the act of making the Word flesh (though that birth is agony enough) but anticipates the further consequence of regaining the Word from the flesh, the crucifixion. Thus the initial birth, the coming

of the many out of the One, the individual self out of nature
into isolation, is both fulfillment and betrayal. Here, in the
paradox of the Nazarene's tears which distill "clemencies" even
as they evidence the violation of innocence, we have Crane's
variation on the fortunate fall. The poet, like the Nazarene, is
given to the world, sacrificed to it; he does not assume his role;
it is thrust upon him. He is the world's innocence and its
redemption. But in his suffering and death, there is not "peni-
tence / But song," the perpetual flow of redemptive waters by
which alone the world survives the ravishments of its birth.
Death (or the tunneling worms of time, again associated with
"venom" and "vermin") is fulfillment in that it frees the self
from time into the work of art.

Hence, the poet (and the poem) survives his betrayal by
resolving the paradox of it. The resolution is once again, as in
"The Wine Menagerie," locked parenthetically in the poem's
center:

> (Let sphinxes from the ripe
> Borage of death have cleared my tongue
> Once and again; vermin and rod
> No longer bind. Some sentient cloud
> Of tears flocks through the tendoned loam!
> Betrayed stones slowly speak.)

Paraphrase is difficult, but not altogether impossible. The con-
densation of images, indeed, is explicable both within the
development of the poem and within the context of Crane's
intellectual habit. Clearly enough, the passage turns upon the
release of a submerged or pent-up energy, a primal force, into
articulation, the freeing of the self into words, the surge of id
into ego forms. For the first and only time in the poem, Crane
uses the personal pronoun, underscoring the identification of
poet with Nazarene. But more pronounced is the explicit association of the mystery with death, the analogy with the Chris-

tian paradox and the sexual pun of the death that is a birth. Oneness, then, is death, which binds and completes life; and death is power, potential life.

The clarification of particular images or symbols, however, is no easy task, in part because the strategy of the poem is to distill a new language: the language of primal force residual in the baser elements of the world's words. One can only pick at the parts, describe the arrangements and the possible relationships into which the parts coalesce. "Borage" must be read in the context of the title. A medicinal herb, it is likewise the source of a cordial wine, thus linking with the ambiguities of the title. The "sphinxes," on the other hand, combining in their dual nature both the spiritual and the animal, are the proper source of the mystery of the One that issues into the violent dualism of life. They are at once containers ("Let" in the sense of concealing) of the elemental and the elemental itself (that from which all is "Let," the pent-up source that must be released). They contain the mysterious and sacred energy (on the level of the poem's sexual metaphor, the id) which being released (individuated) is at once creative and destructive. But released it must be, and through the poet and at his expense—for that is his role. The full explanation owes something, no doubt, to a passage in *Tertium Organum,* where Ouspensky quotes from Mme. Blavatsky to the effect that "Adam Kadmon is *humanity,* or humankind—Homo Sapiens—the SPHINX, i.e. 'the being with the body of an animal, and the face of a superman.' " [17] But it may likewise call to mind Emerson's "Sphinx" (as well as his use of the figure in *Nature* and the essay "History"), who manifests at once nature's mystery and the poetic mind which will free her by unlocking her enigma. Surely the metaphorical pressure here implies a oneness of the vital mysteries and the self which in giving them voice frees both, the life emerging from death at the expense of the primal Unity, but no less at the expense of the Christian myth of death.

Similarly the metaphor of the binding "vermin and rod," which picks up the earlier "venom" even as it suggests the caduceus and its multiple associations: both curative and releasing (Christ the Physician), but also emblematic of the sexual bifurcation and violent reunion that are the paradoxical source of creation. Crane's intellectual preferences may once more provide a clue, this time a passage out of a book he had earlier read with enthusiasm, Remy de Gourmont's *Physique de l'Amour:* "I don't know whether anyone has ever remarked that the caduceus of Mercury represents two serpents coupled. To describe the caduceus is to describe the love mechanism of ophidians. The bifurcated penis penetrates the vagina, the bodies interlaced fold on fold while the two heads rise over the stiffened coils and look fixedly at each other for a long time, eye gazing into eye." [18] In the generative moment the paralysis is broken: the creative release issues into a flow (a "cloud / Of tears") at once spiritual and sentient, the metaphor of natural rebirth (of individuation, but literally of the nature's coming to life in the spring). The things of nature fragment Nature, yet fulfill Her wholeness only by destroying it; or in Nietzsche's terms, nature rises to celebrate her reconciliation with her lost child, man.

Indeed, the subsequent movement of the poem implies nothing else but the process of individuation. And the poem turns back in the end to fulfill the Nietzschean process almost to the letter. For individuation, which is a necessary manifestation of the Word, portends betrayal, but no less the reunion of man and nature. Rather than rounding off the poem in terms of the Christ analogy (as he did in an earlier version),[19] Crane metamorphoses Christ into Dionysus, and for a very good reason. For the one signifies the necessity of history, and its Apollonian dream, the other the transformation which denies history. Analogously with Dionysus' tears, which in Nietzsche's version of the myth give birth to man, Christ's symbolize the fortunate fall, the simultaneous betrayal and rationalization of individuation. But Dionysus' smile is the fulfillment of himself, not of the Father, and a triumph of the One. The vision of Crane's poet is not to be redeemed by divine fiat; the betrayal of our birth must be its own redemption. Thus Dionysus' "Unmangled target smile," that rapture or ecstasy which as Nietzsche indicates emerges "at the shattering of the principium individuationis," becomes the emblem of wholeness, of art, toward which life aspires. In betrayal lies the necessity of vision. Yet the smile of Dionysus, one notes, is not an achieved and communicated vision in the poem; it is the ecstasy of anticipated fulfillment. For the moment of the poet's betrayal and dismemberment is, like Dionysus', as inevitable as his transcendence, and indeed is essential to it; the moment, in truth, is his fulfillment. It is not just that one must precede the other in sequence; the one is the other. The tears of Christ (history's betrayal) are redeemed by Dionysus' smile (which denies history). But the fulfillment of the "smile" is always a "target," the unmangled or unmediated vision always the promise of suffering and its balm.[20] The poem, like *The Bridge*, would confront Spenglerian pessimism, an enduring problem for Crane, by transforming history's incessant motion into the myth of an ongoing cycle, realized through the voice of the Dionysian self. Crane indicates, thereby, that the cycle (and history) is manifest only in the coming and going of the individual self— the poet as word and as flesh, the poet as sufferer returned again and again to the deathly landscape of history's changes and the perfidies attendant upon his role as keeper of the Word, the ground of being.

III

The consequences of Crane's vision are as obvious in his life as in his style. The method arrives at an impasse, condemning the poet to a repetition that can only be sustained by a heroic expenditure of energy upon intense and forced moments. There was not in Crane's poetics, so like his temperament, the economy that allowed a conservative expenditure of that energy—like Wallace Stevens' "violence from within" that would adjust itself to contain and counter rather than deny the "violence without." [21] What finally happens to Crane, one wants to say, is that he became the ultimate victim of history, and the constant cycle of renewal-defeat upon which his poems turned led finally to an exhaustion rather than a revival of his energies. What is victimized is his faith in the inexhaustible energy of self; in effect, the failure of *The Bridge* to articulate in some vague way the principle of the conservation of energy in recurrence suggests pathetically his own exhaustion. But this is no less a failure of method—a method, again paradoxically, contrived like Poe's upon what I should like to call, tentatively, the "poetics of failure."

The "poetics of failure" may be manifest in two different but complementary effects. The poet may posit an idea of the visionary poem as self-transcending and hence aspire toward a poetry which either denies itself or destroys itself. Or he may get hung up on the paradox of the poem which wills its own end, because he and the poetic method have become one. These are two kinds of symbolism in effect: Mallarmé's on the one hand, Poe's on the other. The Poe of *Symbolisme* wills the former, the poem as dream, but most often achieves the latter, the poem as a quest which leads the poetic self through the terrifying landscape of its mortality. The one wills the ecstasy of silence; the other experiences the darkness of blackness. And in a sense, the two represent the dilemma of American poetics. Even Emerson's unruffled cosmic optimism issued in a poetics of failure. Confronted by the contradiction that the poet should be "the man without impediment," but that history had never yet and never could produce that man, he had to fall back upon the poem which anticipated what it could not yield: "Thus journeys the mighty Ideal before us; it never was known to fall into the rear. No man ever came to an experience which was satiating, but his good is tidings of a better. Onward and onward!" [22] Poe reveals his consequences of reflecting too long on the ungraspable, though he too takes it as the true impetus for poetry: "There is still a something in the distance which he has been unable to attain. We have still a thirst unquenchable, to allay which he has not shown us the crystal springs. This thirst belongs to the immortality of man. It is the desire of the moth for the star. It is no mere appreciation of Beauty above." [23] Still, Emerson's cosmic optimism, admitting that "poetry was all written before time was" and the fault of any one poem lies in man's translations, had to confront the limitations of language. He had to live in the faith that his poetics would someday have its poet. But in the meantime, if the pure poem was not yet to be written, the poet's responsibility was to prepare himself to write it.[24] For his own part, Emerson wrote poems which almost literally were dedicated to defining what this poet must *be*, not to rendering what this poet does *see*. They are essentially verse essays in poetics, poems which explore the role of the poet but never dare to assume that role. And this is as true of poems like "Woodnotes" and "Monadnoc" as of those explicit poems about ideal poets like "Bacchus," "Saadi," and "Merlin." In a sense, Emerson was writing Poe's "Israfel," an optative poem, in the optimum mode. But in so doing he made poetry as large as life, in that he made it a mode of preparing for the end. Between what his poet could and should do lay an abyss Emerson never really crossed or even confronted.

The point is this: the only possible solution to the poetics of failure, which is essentially the minority report upon symbolism, is some kind of post-symbolist adjustment. One possibility is to substitute the process of the poem for any transcendental end it may aspire to reach. Resolution, in other words, is available in a poetics like Whitman's, in which the seeking self and the end sought become the same thing, contained as they are within a Hegelian faith in the rightness of whatever is, in the rightness of history as mythic process. In short, it is the resolution which disclaims the problem. Or resolution may lie in a posttranscendental, humanistic poetics like that of Wallace Stevens, which, denying resolution, throws the poetic self back upon the resources of an all-to-human imagination that can discover its identity only in the act of relating itself to otherness. There, at the center of himself, the poet must learn to live in the act of creating not the Word but himself. Either that, or retreat into a myth of history that does not so much absolve the self as subsume it to the larger purposes of history. This is Eliot's response, which begins by denying that poetry can redeem us, except by teaching us to sit still in the eternity of history.

For a poet like Crane, however, there is ultimately no resolution: neither the broken world into which he falls nor the pure world he envisions is convincingly real for him, and hence no reconciliation of the two suffices, even were it possible. The poetic self, trapped in one and longing for the other, finds itself and its methods denied by both. For not only is the self betrayed: the poetic method is betrayed; or better, it betrays itself at every turn. The betrayal is manifest on several levels. The recurrent event demands an ever-renewed language; the language of the "broken world" must be constantly repurified, until at last the poet betrays himself into ingenuity. It is not, and cannot be, as he says, that there is *a* language to be discovered. For once it is had and given to the world, the world corrupts it, as well as the giver. The language must constantly be renewed, and this finally becomes the poet's onus. He might begin with the enthusiastic proclamation that he is possessed by language and with a faith that this language is the revealed truth, that the Word is the force *in* the world. But the fact that came home to Crane very early was that each embrace of the unknown, even if it brought him momentary ecstasy, was consummated in loss. He was always returned to his one responsibility: to the words of the world which repeatedly obscure the true Word they severally contain.

The history of *The Bridge* is a history of renewed assaults upon his theme, until finally, as Crane was to admit in moments of despair, the writing of the thing became an exhaustive burden rather than, as it was to be, the ultimate of transport. Characteristically, he wrote the last section first, the section which carried him to the threshold of vision. Then he got down to his true theme, the quest and its ultimate frustration. He might have recognized something very like this within the individual sections. In the guise of searching history for its idea, he was celebrating his own method, by which alone, his poetics insisted, history could be cleansed. And since the method fulfilled itself only in defeat, it failed ultimately to sustain him, demanding re-engagement to the point of diminishing returns. In the end, his resources of energy were rapidly exhausted, even before his resources of language, if we are to judge from "The Broken Tower."

Unlike Eliot, Crane could not adapt his method to his life, to make the process of searching a discipline of waiting; nor could he, like Stevens, find his method an end in itself, the act of the mind in search of the supreme fiction which finally discovers that the supreme has being only in the mind seeking and hence creating it. Perhaps in "The Broken Tower" Crane caught a glimpse of that possibility. But when that poem fell, as he mistakenly thought, on deaf ears, Crane suffered the ultimate betrayal of his method. For if the need to communicate his vision to the world had always been his one compulsion—and in effect, the essence of his vision—the threat of utter solipsism was intolerable in that it would cut him off once and for all from the world he disdained. Yet here alone, in isolation from the world, could the Word be pure. In the end, ironically, he needed the very world he and his language denied, and in revenging himself upon it, he betrayed himself into the silence his method at once paradoxically sought and feared. What is left, the very tentative new language of his canon, displays enough of the corruption, and of the purity, to remind us of his heroic pathos.

NOTES

1. James E. Miller, Jr., Karl Shapiro, and Bernice Slote, *Start with the Sun, Studies in Cosmic Poetry* (Lincoln, Neb., 1960), p. 4. This book in effect constitutes the academic defense of the "New Paganism," which embraces at one pole the lymphatic personalism of Shapiro's most recent verse, and at the other the mystique, vagaries, and bombast of the so-called Beats.

2. One crucial problem in assessing this style is that of distinguishing between the assertion of vision and the process of evoking it; another has to do with the "uses" of myth, whether conscious and structural or spontaneous and natural or mystical. The first problem is similar to the contradiction within Poe's theory which calls at one extreme for a language that is music and at the other for a poem that subscribes to an ideal, predetermined, mathematical form (the notes without the sensuous sound).

3. See Bernice Slote, "Views of *The Bridge*," *Start with the Sun*, pp. 137–165.

4. *Hart Crane's Sanskrit Charge: A Study of The Bridge* (Ithaca, N.Y., 1960).

5. *Ibid.*, pp. 12–22.

6. *The Birth of Tragedy and the Genealogy of Morals*, trans., Francis Golffing (New York, 1956), p. 126.

7. See Roy Harvey Pearce, *The Continuity of American Poetry* (Princeton, 1961), pp. 101–111, for a concise discussion of why the poem is neither epical nor, except in the very broadest sense, mythical.

8. Dembo, pp. 10–12.

9. The essay is published as Index I in Philip Horton's *Hart Crane, The Life of an American Poet* (New York, 1957), pp. 323–338, originally published by W. W. Norton, 1938. For the letters, see Brom Weber, ed., *The Letters of Hart Crane* (New York, 1952), *passim*.

10. Dembo, p. 19.

11. The exchange is included in Brom Weber's *Hart Crane, A Biographical and Critical Study* (New York, 1948), pp. 416–422. The quotations from Crane's poems in this section and elsewhere are from *The Collected Poems of Hart Crane*, ed., with introd. by Waldo Frank (New York, 1933, 1946).

12. See *The Birth of Tragedy*, pp. 66–67: "In his existence as dismem-

bered God, Dionysos shows the double nature of a cruel, savage daemon and a mild, gentle ruler. Every hope of the Eleusinian initiates points to a rebirth of Dionysos, which we can now interpret as meaning the end of individuation."

13. *Letters*, pp. 181–183.

14. Nietzsche, p. 66.

15. *Ibid.*, p. 24.

16. One cannot avoid suggesting here the possible source of Crane's imagery in the most appropriate of biblical sources, The Song of Songs 2:15, and the parallels in Ezekiel 13:4 and Luke 13:32. Preceding the figure in the Song of Songs is a verse which must have fascinated Crane, who was known to have speculated on the ambivalence of his sexual nature and his name: "My beloved is like a roe or a young hart."

17. *Tertium Organum,* trans. Nicholas Besseraboff and Claude Bragdon, with introd. by Claude Bragdon (New York, 1922, 1944), p. 201.

18. See *The Natural Philosophy of Love,* trans, with a postscript by Ezra Pound (New York, 1940), p. 67. This translation was first published in the early twenties. Crane read and commented on it specifically in a letter to Gorham Munson, dated June 18, 1922, offering comparisons between de Gourmont's description of sexual sacrifice and the ceremonies of Dionysus (see *Letters,* p. 91).

19. See Weber, *Hart Crane,* pp. 225–227, for two early versions of the poem.

20. Interestingly, and relevant to Crane's imagery in this and other poems, Nietzsche suggests that the Dionysian dithyramb introduces "an entirely new set of symbols. . . . First, all the symbols pertaining to physical features: mouth, face, the spoken word, the dance movement which coordinates the limbs and binds them to its rhythm. Then suddenly all the rest of the symbolic forces—music and rhythm as such, dynamics, harmony—assert themselves with great energy" (*The Birth of Tragedy,* pp. 27–28). The predominance in Crane's poetry of just this kind of imagery, and the manipulation of it to suggest movement from static to dynamic, leaves one to speculate on whether Crane consciously or intuitively fulfills Nietzsche's observations. In any event, as Nietzsche observes, the votaries of Dionysus alone can understand this symbolic force and participate in its life. That seems to be the inarguable rationale by which critic-votaries of the "New Paganism" ignore their critic-adversaries who would reject symbolistic incoherence and obfuscation.

21. "The Noble Rider and the Sound of Words," *The Necessary Angel, Essays on Reality and the Imagination* (New York, 1951), p. 36.

22. The first quotation is from Emerson's "The Poet" and idealizes the role of poet as seer, while the second is from his essay "Experience," which assesses the exigencies of living amid dualism. The second immediately precedes the famous "Fall of Man" passage.

23. In this section of "The Poetic Principle" Poe admits the self-absorb-

ing abyss between the poet who must sing in the common language of mankind and the hypothetically divine poet who sings beyond the tensions of the lyre. The poet as person, he admits, knows the divine poet, Israfel, only in his desire for and in his struggle toward transcendence.

24. One might, it is true, argue that this dilemma, of seeking what is not to be found, has been the enduring theme of poetry—in fact, the very thing that prompts the need of poetry. Pope put it very well:

> That something still which prompts the eternal sigh,
> For which we bear to live, or bear to die,
> Which still so near us, yet beyond us lies.

Yet the very serenity and control of Pope's lines—the decorum that manifests the revealed order of his world—suggest the differences between a poetics which imitates the metaphysics of its world and one which veritably creates that metaphysics. The differences between Emerson's brahmin acceptance (and rationalization) of his limitations and Poe's schizophrenic response to the abyss is to be accounted for perhaps in Emerson's own Unitarian (and, in part, Deistic) background and in his ability to adapt that sense of the universal in the particular to the more open and organic version of Romantic thought. Poe, on the other hand, could not embrace both worlds, nor resolve contradictions. He could only stand, now above the battle in philosophic superciliousness (as in *Eureka* and his theory of poetry), now within it, as in his haunted epistemological voyages.

Theodore Roethke:
The Poetic Shape of Death

FREDERICK J. HOFFMAN

The poetry of Theodore Roethke describes four stages in the development of what he intended it to say. While this may not be a sensational truth, the intensity with which Roethke engages in each of the stages marks both it and him as exceptional. From the second volume (*The Lost Son*) on, Roethke made his verse his own, inscribed it with the signature of his inimitable temperament and fancy.

We might as well define these stages at the very beginning: they relate to a prenatal condition, to childhood, to the move toward maturity, and to the contemplation of the conditions and implications of death. Throughout, there is an overlapping of one upon the other, a spiral turning back, a reach for self-definition. More than normally, Roethke was overtaken by the fancies of childhood and by the fear of being forced out of that state, with no reliable surrogates for "papa" and "mama." The poems therefore abound in talk comparable to a semi-intelligible child's garble, a language in itself designed to induce security (because of its identification with a time when he *was* secure):

> Mips and ma the mooly moo,
> The likes of him is biting who,
> A cow's a care and who's a coo?—
> What footie does is final.

> My dearest dear my fairest fair,
> Your father tossed a cat in air,
> Though neither you nor I was there,—
> What footie does is final.

> Be large as an owl, be slick as a frog,
> Be good as a goose, be big as a dog,
> Be sleek as a heifer, be long as a hog,—
> What footie will do will be final.
>
> ("Praise to the End!")

Roethke's poetry is one of the most exhaustive, vital, and vivid reports we have of a soul in the several agonies normally recorded in one human life. The intensity results from an absorption in a form of subliminal nature, a deep sense of the most elementary agonies attending the process and the necessity of living. But it has other causes as well. Roethke impressed both his friends and readers profoundly as a human being, almost overwhelmingly "present," in his person as in his poetry. When I saw him in the summer of 1957, I had been teaching a seminar at the University of Washington on the subject that led to the publication of *The Mortal No*. He told me then that he was much concerned with the mysteries and paradoxes of death, and that his new poetry reflected these concerns. It did just that; and the meditative poems that appeared in *Words for the Wind* and, recently, in *The Far Field* demonstrate this interest remarkably. Nowhere in modern American poetry are the metaphysically speculative and the naturally commonplace so well balanced, so reciprocal in effect.

I want especially to notice these two aspects of Roethke's verse: the "metaphysical fusion" I have spoken of and the effect upon it of the puzzle of death—not so much the expectation of it, but the exhausting contemplation of its curious nature and the struggle to define it in public terms.

Roethke was at the beginning so engrossed with the wonder of his origins—and of the origins of life—that his poetry described a spiral of flight, fear, and return; the place itself can be characterized as the condition of "underness," which exists "everywhere." In *Open House* (more formally written and imitative than his other work) there is little we may call characteristic of

Roethke. Like most first volumes, it offers only clues as to his future direction, though it scarcely even serves for this purpose. Like a hundred others, the poem "Death Piece" states a general condition of insentience, without localizing it or investing it with emotional energy:

> Invention sleeps within a skull
> No longer quick with light,
> The hive that hummed in every cell
> Is now sealed honey-tight.
>
> His thought is tied, the curving prow
> Of motion moored to rock;
> And minutes burst upon a brow
> Insentient to shock.

Only with *The Lost Son* were his characteristic rhetorical gestures revealed. These have, of course, been much discussed: as a "peculiar balance of the natural and the artificial . . ."; [1] as describing the "agony of coming alike, the painful miracle of growth . . . "; [2] as a form of "Noh" monologue, in which, "wearing a mask painted with a fixed smile of pain, he visits a pond in a wood which is haunted by a nymph-like ghost, and performs a very slow and solemn pirouetting dance, . . ." [3]

Of course, the greenhouse provides the scene and source of all the poems in this volume and of many others. Roethke shows a remarkable awareness of the scene, as well as a sensitivity to its every conceivable affective meaning. He always reacts precisely and meaningfully to it, as a person deeply committed to it in memory and making it the basis of all meditations. The greenhouse has a peculiar usefulness as a microcosm of subhuman life. Within its vivid forms, a number of effects reside: the specially created climatic conditions, the *schwärmerei* of plant life awaiting the "knock" of attention and the flow of warmth which help their growth, and the artificially created "edenic" conditions which guarantee that freshness, beauty, and purity (the rose, the carnation) will survive.

Most of all, the image of "papa" dominates:

> That hump of a man bunching chrysanthemums
> Or pinching-back asters, or planting azaleas,
> Tamping and stamping dirt into pots,—
> > ("Old Florist")

As God, "papa" gives life and endows it with order, separating the good from the expendable nongood, "weeding" impurities from this floral Eden:

> Pipe-knock.

> Scurry of warm over small plants.
> Ordnung! ordnung!
> Papa is coming!

> > A fine haze moved off the leaves;
> > Frost melted on far panes;
> > The rose, the chrysanthemum turned toward the light.
> > Even the hushed forms, the bent yellowy weeds
> > Moved in a slow up-sway.
> > > ("The Return")

Roethke believed the "papa principle" to be indispensable to a forthgoing knowledge. Many of the poems in the volumes beginning with *The Lost Son* characteristically struggle to escape the "slime," the "loam," the level of prenatal existence; in short, they offer a portrayal of what Roethke called "an effort to be born, and later, to become something more." [4] Both being born and becoming "something more" are disturbed by the agonies of self-assertion and of separating the self from its prenatal associations. The language at this point is almost without abstraction, as indeed that of a small child is: full of long vowel sounds, one-syllabled words which label, questions for which there seems to be no answer. But the poems show a progression nevertheless. Roethke spoke of the need "first to go back," in order eventually to go forward ("Open Letter," p. 69). The poems move chiefly from dark (the "underness" that exists everywhere) to light: or, from the dark recesses of the almost entirely quiescent self, to the world where the light requires an activity of the mind, what he called "spirit" or "soul."

The basic natural origin is defined in terms of "Shoots dangled and drooped, / Lolling obscenely from mildewed crates"; "Even the dirt kept breathing a small breath." The leaf gives us a primary natural image of life; extended, it suggests the hand, and when the body dies, the hand has the appearance of a leaf deprived of its source of life. This deprivation resembles the kind of separation suffered by a leaf cut away from its tree, a flower taken from its sustaining soil. The title poem of *The Lost Son* describes the full experience of struggling to be—in this case, to be born, then to be, then simply once again to return to the being of the nearly born. The imagery describes the fear which accompanies the spiral movement; the agony of Part One is described in terms of a "going forth" in doubt and fear, like the birth of any organic being. The "under" side demonstrates its reality even more powerfully and persuasively than the outside.

> Where do the roots go?
> Look down under the leaves.
> Who put the moss there?
> These stones have been here too long.
> Who stunned the dirt into noise?
> Ask the mole, he knows.
> I feel the slime of a wet nest.
> Beware Mother Mildew.
> Nibble again, fish nerves.
> ("The Pit")

But, along with these apparently simple queries, the poet suggests a growing awareness of the outer world. We stand "out there" when we look back upon the minimal life we have left. Ultimately, Roethke's protagonist (his "I," who comes very close to being himself) sees the natural world formally, as in the beginning of winter, when we so often acutely sense the quality of forms and surfaces, since the "underness" is quieted.

> Light traveled over the wide field;
> Stayed.
> The weeds stopped swinging.
> The mind moved, not alone,
> Through the clear air, in the silence.
> ("It was beginning winter.")

In time, this condition of silence will become symbolically contained, like and yet very different from the various stillnesses of T. S. Eliot's *Four Quartets*. Roethke's achievements of silence always indicate a move out of the noise, the thickness, the confusion of life (or a meaningful pause in it), while Eliot's seem forever to dominate life and to force it into a subsidiary and symbolic *ménage*.

These movements occur in much of Roethke's verse: the move outward ("Mother me out of here . . ."); the desire to return, for reinforcing sustenance, the occasional sense of quiet "at the centre" ("A rose sways least. / The redeemer comes a dark way."), and not always, but with increasing frequency—a feeling of perfection, in which the noise of living lessens and one may contemplate the condition of life as a symbolically "free" condition:

> To know that light falls and fills, often without our knowing,
> As an opaque vase fills to the brim from a quick pouring,
> Fills and trembles at the edge yet does not flow over,
> Still holding and feeding the stem of the contained flower.
> ("The Shape of the Fire")

The movement in Roethke's verse becomes more complicated, as the poetry itself becomes more meditative, more "metaphysically extended." It reaches out beyond the greenhouse world, but always with a sense of the need to return. *Praise to the End!* reminds us of the full cycle. Roethke's mind and sensibility were formed by the greenhouse experience, and

most of his poems remind us of the poet's memories. He
chose the title of his next book not so much to call our attention to Wordsworth's view of nature as to emphasize his own
uniquely separate position. I cite enough lines from the 1805–
1806 version of *The Prelude* to give some sense of the strange
relationship:

> . . . Praise to the end!
> Thanks likewise for the means! But I believe
> That Nature, oftentimes, when she would frame
> A favor'd Being, from his earliest dawn
> Of infancy doth open out the clouds,
> As at the touch of lightning, seeking him
> With gentlest visitation; not the less,
> Though haply aiming at the self-same end,
> Does it delight her sometimes to employ
> Severer interventions, ministry
> More palpable, and so she dealt with me.

The phrase which begins this quotation denotes a happy
gratification over the sense of being that Wordsworth enjoys
through the act of Nature upon his being; he is surprised
that he should have "come through" so well, that the fears he
suffered in the past should have anything to do with the making of "The calm existence that is mine when I / Am worthy of
myself! . . ." [5] In one sense, Roethke's use of the phrase suggests a stage in his growth, though his sense of nature strikes
us as far more "intimate," direct, and imagistic than Wordsworth's. The formalities of Roethke's verse and attitude, however, did increase with the publication of *Praise to the End!* [6]
He was more and more drawn to a consideration of "last things,"
and the title phrase (as did Wordsworth's use of it) expressed
surprise that nature should have permitted him to meditate
about them seriously.

The verse bespeaks a genuine maturing. Beginning with
Praise, Roethke followed the practice of combining selections
from earlier volumes with new poems, to suggest the spiral

or cyclic progression he had mentioned in his "Open Letter." But "progress" showed more obviously in the new poems, and the quality of memory changed. With the death of "papa" ("He was all whitey bones / And skin like paper"), a change occurred in the image of Godhood ("God's somewhere else"), which came more and more closely to resemble an independent self ("I'm somebody else now"). The responsibilities of the new self are seen everywhere. The echoes of childhood phrases slowly give way to the need of being—without regret—independently oneself. "There's no alas / Where I live" recalls the blessed simplicities of a childhood he finds it hard to give up. But the image of himself as "standing up" and alone ("When I stand, I'm almost a tree") appears more frequently than before. He defines himself in a new status through many devices:

> We'll be at the business of what might be
> Looking toward what we are. . . .

> I've played with the fishes
> Among the unwrinkling ferns
> In the wake of a ship of wind;
> But now the instant ages,
> And my thought hunts another body.
> ("Give Way, Ye Gates")

The other body offers both another meaning of self and another self. Roethke is involved both in his own maturing and in his finding another person, whose love will illuminate his own identity. His Dante must also know a Beatrice. He needs to take a long and fearsome journey to "somewhere else," but he is willing to assume the risks.

> Has the dark a door?
> I'm somewhere else,—
> I insist!
> I am.
> ("Sensibility! O La!")

"Praise to the End!" provides an especially revealing and

significant statement of his new role, his "progress." The
elements of nature (not Wordsworth's respected, capitalized
Nature) remain, as do the childish sounds (moo–who–coo;
frog–dog–hog); but the poet speaks mainly of the need to
"separate": "I conclude! I conclude! / My dearest dust, I can't
stay here." In his escape from the "under world" of the greenhouse, the poet retains the belief the natural world has given
him. But he is also aware of the crisis of separation, the threat
to childhood security:

> I have been somewhere else; I remember the sea-faced uncles.
> I hear, clearly, the heart of another singing,
> Lighter than bells,
> Softer than water.

The experience with nature now demands a transition to
"somewhere else." "I can't crawl back through those veins, / I
ache for another choice." Roethke calls to the small things of
his past, to "sing" as symbols. Nature must become "A house
for wisdom; a field for revelation." He has, in other words,
found the need for other meanings, for ways of defining himself
through others than "papa," in a world wider than Woodlawn.

The poet needs also to find another vocabulary, to reinforce
the old one. The respect for life remains, but he approaches it
obliquely, sometimes even with the aid of "literary" and
"metaphysical" reflections. The famous sequence, "Four for Sir
John Davies," refers to a sixteenth-century English poet, whose
Spenserian poem, "Orchestra" (1596), attempts to present
nature in a universal dance, or a solemn, orderly motion.[7] The
importance of the sequence depends primarily upon its full
commitment to sexual involvement. Roethke sees the sexual act
as both a move away from the simplicities of childish "aloneness" and "an harmonious" recovery of life. The third step
is now achieved. The poet sees love at the moment as not weari-
some but rich in pleasure and delights. Moreover, we are

aware of a "standing with"—a dancing with, a partnership. The "I" changes to "we" in this maneuver; the delights are not unmixed with doubt and wonder, but they seem to be a profitable means of sending the self toward that "somewhere else" that Roethke had earlier called "far away."

> Incomprehensible gaiety and dread
> Attended what we did. Behind, before,
> Lay all the lonely pastures of the dead;
> The spirit and the flesh cried out for more.
> We two, together, on a darkening day
> Took arms against our own obscurity.
> ("The Wraith")

Roethke uses a new vocabulary, even a newly formal verse pattern. The end pauses usually remain; but, the idea being more complex, the phrase which includes it enlarges. For at least a moment in his time, he pauses to speculate upon love, as later he will meditate upon dying, in the fashion of the modern "metaphysical poet," a John Crowe Ransom, probably more than an Allen Tate. Having chosen "desire" as a device for extending the range of self-definition, he must now define the word and overcome his doubts concerning its value. It is scarcely reassuring to know that "two" are more than "one" in the effort to shut out "our own obscurity," unless the "two" can become permanently a One in the economy of life. Beyond the dissolution of the two lies death; the danger of annihilation is already genuinely present, even in the most pleasant conditions. At least momentarily the union seems to hold:

> Did each become the other in that play?
> She laughed me out, and then she laughed me in;
> In the deep middle of ourselves we lay; . . .

The fourth poem of the sequence speaks even more confidently of the ministering effectiveness of love. Speaking of Dante's being blinded by the inner light of the Paradiso, Roethke defines it as the light of love, reducing it to love itself and to the verbal trickeries by which it is embellished and exalted. "All lovers live by longing, and endure: / Summon a vision and declare it pure."

The lovers "undid chaos to a curious sound"; the "I" of Roethke's world hopes now to give "thought" to "things," to work on the assumption that "We think by feeling . . .": that is, that we endow things, and acts, with ideal virtues by living and feeling them (or, by acting in a "necessary conjunction," in the spirit of Eliot's "East Coker").

Love assists in our fight to postpone death; it is also a testimony of Godhood. As a form of dying, love at least momentarily pushes the threat of dying out of mind. The protagonist concludes the *Waking* volume in a simple, calm assertion.

> Light takes the Tree; but who can tell us how?
> The lowly worm climbs up a winding stair;
> I wake to sleep, and take my waking slow.
> ("The Waking")

Love remains an important human gesture in *Words for the Wind*. The lover speaks again and again of the newly achieved confidence his love has given him. His cries are no longer prompted by fear, but by delight: ". . . I know / The root, the core of a cry." The title poem, from which this quotation comes, continues in a mood of frankly innocent confidence:

> I kiss her moving mouth,
> Her swart hilarious skin;
> She breaks my breath in half;
> She frolicks like a beast;
> And I dance round and round,
> A fond and foolish man,
> And see and suffer myself
> In another being, at last.

The open sensuality remains a prominent element in the wit of "I Knew a Woman":

> She was the sickle; I, poor I, the rake,
> Coming behind her for her pretty sake
> (But what prodigious mowing we did make).

The thought of death is not precluded by the performance of love; it is only postponed, if even that. The sacrifice of the self to another yields much pleasure; but the Roethkean "I" eventually allows death to intrude: at first, by reconverting what was once a pure pleasure into a human gesture of dubious value. "The Sensualists" suggest a surfeit of love—in other words, the conclusion that it cannot always, entirely, put aside the thought of death. The lovers are, in fact, like Ransom's of "The Equilibrists," doomed to live in a prison of their love:

> "The bed itself begins to quake,
>   I hate this sensual pen;
> My neck, if not my heart, will break
>   If we do this again,"—
> Then each fell back, limp as a sack,
>   Into the world of men.

With the apparent failure of love, the old questions return; only, now they seem more importunate, and the answers cannot be disguised in sentiment or in fantasy. Loving offers the last barrier to the thought of dying. The protagonist more than ever despairs of his power to define life and himself; he needs to do the first to prepare for death, the second in order personally to bear it. His thoughts return briefly to "papa"; his intellect inquires if "form" will help to limit himself. "Papa" had once been sufficient to pull the weeds from what the poet as God principle had wanted to survive. Now Roethke's "I" needs some formal way of saving himself from sensual chaos:

> I know I love, yet know not where I am;
> I paw the dark, the shifting midnight air.
> Will the self, lost, be found again? In form?
> I walk the night to keep my five wits warm.
>   ("The Renewal")

Such a failure should now appear inevitable, a consequence of the physical circumstances of love. For, in the true "metaphysical" consensus of love, the individual dying was always associated with the final thrust of death, as in John Donne's "Canonization" ode. But in Roethke's poems the particulars of love are almost always linked to the past: to the warm, moist, subliminal world of the womb that sponsored all living and the "papa" who sustained it. He can only cry, "Father, I'm far from home, / And I have gone nowhere," and "I fear for my own joy." The failure is accompanied by the recurring imagery of the past and by the son's renewed fears. Father had been "Father of flowers"; but the son combines "several selves" which reflect at first "Lewd, tiny, careless lives / That scuttled under stones," and he eventually becomes "myself, alone."

He has finally to persuade himself of death. The poem "The Dying Man" is dedicated to Yeats, but actually the Roethke persona looks firmly at "Death's possibilities." Now, he sees dying as a continual becoming; this knowledge, of growth as a move toward mortality, is indispensable to the adjustment. The great poem of *Words*, "Meditations of an Old Woman," combines gracefully and skillfully the two vocabularies Roethke had developed, the "natural" and the "metaphysical." Once again, "The weeds hiss at the edge of the field"; but the old woman can no longer claim a superiority to the small natural particulars (when they do not frighten her, they bore her):

> I've become a strange piece of flesh,
> Nervous and cold, bird-furtive, whiskery,
> With a cheek soft as a hound's ear.
> What's left is light as a seed;
> I need an old crone's knowing.
>   ("First Meditation")

This remarkable poem admits all types of encounter with

mortality. The old woman, on the edge of death, has only her "meditations" to help her tolerate the expectation. She must, finally, learn to "sit still," in the spirit of Eliot's "Ash–Wednesday," but without theological assurances. For, in her extremity, she must seek in the familiar details of nature the substitute for a god. "In such times," she says, thinking of the sights and smells and sounds of her past life, "lacking a god, / I am still happy." Yet she finds it difficult to speak of a soul, because in Roethke the soul must always somehow be activated; it cannot rest merely on a theological premise.

> The soul knows not what to believe,
> In its small folds, stirring sluggishly,
> In the least place of its life,
> A pulse beyond nothingness,
> A fearful ignorance.[8]
> ("What Can I Tell My Bones?")

In the end, the old woman lives only in dread of the rational view of death, and hopes that she may find some escape from its implications.

> I rock in my own dark,
> Thinking, God has need of me.
> The dead love the unborn.
> ("What Can I Tell My Bones?")

She expresses a sense of renewal in her final observations: as though nature will reclaim her in allowing others to be born, as though she were for a valiant moment "Anna Livia Plurabelle." Roethke is a poet who finds it unimaginable to rest with any large denial of life.

The Far Field demonstrates the extent to which Roethke had defined death to himself before the summer of 1963. The poems, or some of them, also testify to the agony of moving toward the threshold of death. I do not mean to say that the thought of death was constantly with him, but only that he

suffered a type of "dark night" and that it was partly caused
by his being unable to will a transcendence that he could also
will to believe in. The "congress of stinks" of *The Lost Son*
here becomes

> A kingdom of stinks and sighs,
> Fetor of cockroaches, dead fish, petroleum,
> Worse than castoreum of mink or weasels,
> Saliva dripping from warm microphones,
> Agony of crucifixion on barstools.
> ("The Longing")

There is reason to believe that Roethke suffered these
agonies because (1) the world of "papa" no longer enlightened or assured him; and (2) he failed to secure consolation
in the pleasures of what he called ". . . the imperishable quiet
at the heart of form." But I also suspect that, occasionally at
least, he saw—perhaps forced himself to see—the possibility of
the flesh's assuming the role of the spirit. The image of water,
which in *The Lost Son* was made equivalent to "Money
money money," now more frequently takes on the conventional
symbolic aspects of death and the soul:

> Water's my will, and my way,
> And the spirit runs, intermittently,
> In and out of the small waves,
> Runs with the intrepid shorebirds—
> How graceful the small before danger!
> ("Meditation at Oyster River")

However improvised this metaphor appears to be, it will
certainly play an important role in the ultimate critical assess-
ment of Roethke's work. With much of the evidence in, he
appears to me to have alternated between the fear of death
which his doubt of immortality forced upon him and the speculative pleasure in his own power of transcendence. I do not
think this is an "aesthetic" power solely, or entirely, because
much of the prospect of transcendence had to be willed;

that is, his pleasure in the metaphors of transcendence undoubtedly was earned by a strong effort of the will.[9]

Ultimately, Roethke seems to have come back to a peculiarly American "stance," the Emersonian confidence in *seeing* the spirit in matter, also, in a sense, in *creating* matter (or forming it) through the power of the transcending will. Much more than Emerson's,[10] Roethke's mind was drenched in particulars. He had at the beginning to move away from them, in order to notice his own identity, to "be himself." The "papa" principle had eventually to yield to the search for adequate limits of self, simply because "papa" had died. Momentarily, he found a surrogate definition in the physical nature of love; when his confidence in this ceased, he was forced alternately to meditate upon the end of a temporal process and to will transcendence of it.

"In a Dark Time" illustrates the conditions persuasively. The "dark time" has several applications: to the darkness of "underness" which he found everywhere; to the darkness of despair that came to him when he found that he had alone both to define and to defend himself; and, of course, to the time of death, of what he calls "the deepening shade" and "the echoing wood." He conceives of himself as both creating (as in the poem) and living in the world of nature. Such a union of living and "making live" may surely be considered an act of voluntary creativity, in which the creator exists, surrounded by his creatures; the latter survive partly in his memory, but are refined in his having remembered them. As he has said in his "comment," the heron and the wren, the "beasts of the hill and serpents of the den," ought not to be thought of as either emblematic or strange, but rather as a part of his own experience. One may do too much by way of endowing Roethke as a "son of Blake," or of Yeats, or whomever.

The "madness" is a condition of the soul. One nurses his idiosyncrasies at his own peril, but there is nothing "mad" about his accommodation to the fact and the necessities of "the dark time." He is on the "edge" of meaning, looks out upon "that place among the rocks. . . ." Naturally, in consequence of the evidence we have already examined, he is assaulted by, not only a "congress of stinks," but "A steady storm of correspondences!" These are not unlike Baudelaire's "vivants piliers," which "Laissent parfois sortir de confuses paroles"; but Roethke does not want to be thought either "theoretical" or pompous about them. In fact, the analogical necessity is derived not from them in themselves, but from his need to stand apart from them and to strengthen both his facility of inference and his power of implication.

Ultimately, the issue becomes one of maneuvering within the circumstances of his mortality.

> A man goes far to find out what he is—
> Death of the self in a long, tearless night,
> All natural shapes blazing unnatural light.

The beautiful simplicity of these lines is convincing because they come at the end of a long career of defining self, a time during which the quest of the "I" has been dramatized brilliantly again and again. But the poet indicates not only a quest for "self-definition," despite the question, "Which I is I?" He as much strives to escape the multiplicity of selves, the "storm of correspondences," as he does to steady himself for the prospect that *all* selves disintegrate, that death happens to all of them.

So, we have the brilliant final stanza, with its quizzicality of Emily Dickinson ("My soul, like some heat-maddened summer fly, / Keeps buzzing at the sill. . . ."), and its apparent Emersonian affirmation:

> A fallen man, I climb out of my fear.
> The mind enters itself, and God the mind,
> And one is One, free in the tearing wind.

As Roethke has said, these lines are far from the forced improvisation they have been accused of being:

The moment before Nothingness, before near annihilation, the moment of supreme disgust is the worst: when change comes it is either total loss of consciousness—symbolical or literal death—or a quick break into another state, not necessarily serene, but frequently a bright blaze of consciousness that translates itself into action.[11]

The "fallen man" is the self that has gone the long way toward deprivation; he recalls not only "the lost son" but the son of a dead father, and he must therefore find a way of making significant use of himself. He climbs "out of [his] fear," in the manner that we have watched so often in Roethke's books. He is that loathsome thing, the fly, what he has called "a disease-laden, heat-maddened fly—to me a more intolerable thing than a rat." [12] Surely no one will hesitate to grant him the choice. In any case, the fly is Emily Dickinson's only in being a fly; for her the insect is not loathsome because it serves as the décor of mortality.

If we grant Roethke the right to his first metaphors, we find it difficult not to permit him the concluding ones—despite the fact that these are more suddenly (or at least, more unexpectedly) grasped. The mind's entering itself seems to me to be Roethke's steady concern. Far from a solipsistic condition, or a madly egocentric one, what we have is the process of self-examination which all of us come to when we need to "stand aside," when we abandon the "papa principle" or it abandons us. We are less certain that God enters the mind. Roethke points out that God is not customarily supposed, by the "hot-gospelers," to enter the mind, but rather invades the heart.

In any case, the final line offers a neat possibility: if, after God enters the mind (not the heart or the liver, or even the soul), "one is One," then we may assume that the mind (with the help of God, perhaps) changes the "one" to the "One." To conceive of this change requires both creative ingenuity and daring. For the soul is "free in the tearing wind," and this freedom can scarcely be envied or ideally desired.

At least in terms of the evidence, Roethke has come the long way, to climb out of both his fear of chaos and his trust in easy and comfortable confidences, and to stand in the place of "papa," ministering not so much to the many as to the One he has himself created. Perhaps the idea strikes us as fanciful; but one can, I am sure, be too much handicapped by logical or even eschatological necessity, to see the neatness and convincingness with which "In a Dark Time" stands as a genuine resolution of the mazes caused by life and the problems created by the expectation of death. Roethke's death, seen in the light of this *mort accomplie,* most properly sets the seal to his life, in terms of the imaginative brilliance and the moral courage which dominate and direct his poetry.

NOTES

1. Kenneth Burke, "The Vegetal Radicalism of Theodore Roethke," *Sewanee Review,* LVI (Winter, 1950), 82.

2. Stanley Kunitz, "News of the Root," *Poetry,* LXXIII (January, 1949), 225.

3. Stephen Spender, "Words for the Wind," *New Republic,* CXLI (August 10, 1959), 22.

4. "Open Letter," in *Mid-Century American Poets,* ed. John Ciardi (New York, 1950), p. 68.

5. William Wordsworth, *The Prelude,* ed. Ernest de Selincourt and Helen Darbishire (Oxford, 1959), p. 22.

6. I do not mean that the verse became "classical." If anything, the use of the free line, controlled almost invariably by either end punctuation or caesural pause, increased; and the characteristic vigor remained much in evidence.

7. See Ralph Mills, *Theodore Roethke* (Minneapolis, 1963), pp. 31–35, for a discussion of this indebtedness.

8. Ultimately, in these "Meditations," Roethke arrives at the biblical phrase, "Do these bones live?" which Eliot made prominent in Part Two of "Ash-Wednesday." Roethke's woman is concerned not so much with the promise of resurrection which they originally suggested but rather with the old woman's power to speak *to* them. The title of this, the last section of the long poem, is "What Can I Tell My Bones?"

9. I should maintain this despite his statement that the last two lines

of "In a Dark Time" were the product of pure inspiration. "This was a dictated poem," he said in 1961, "something given, scarcely mine at all. For about three days before its writing I felt disembodied, out of time; then the poem virtually wrote itself, on a day in summer, 1958." "The Poet and His Critics," ed. Anthony Ostroff, *New World Writing*, XIX (1961), 214.

10. Whom he might well have had in mind when he wrote "Prayer Before Study":

> A fool can play at being solemn
> Revolving on his spinal column.

> Deliver me, O Lord, from all
> Activity centripetal.

11. "The Poet and His Critics," pp. 217–218.
12. *Ibid.*, p. 217.

Robert Lowell's Early Politics of Apocalypse

JEROME MAZZARO

Robert Lowell's first volume of poems, *Land of Unlikeness* (1944), presents itself as a collection with a clear perspective on history. This perspective seems as much "millennial" in its outlooks as the poetry of the nineteenth century had been "progressive." For Lowell, Western culture, despite its mechanical successes, was not in some evolutionary drift toward perfection, but in a spiritual decline. The world was not daily getting better in every way. Yet, if it were not getting better, how else was one to understand, control, and account for the changes that obviously did occur? One answer had been offered by the ancient Greeks, who had developed a belief that the earth was not itself eternal, but was modeled on an eternal pattern and that time, imitating eternity, moved in a circle measured by number. In "Cratylus," "Statesman," and "Laws," Plato had evolved upon this notion of a circle the idea of a Golden Year wherein the course of history would begin again, and in his Fourth Eclogue, the Roman poet Vergil speaks, too, of a return to greatness. Although philosophers like Aristotle had allowed in this circular motion of time for the possibilities of contingency and free will, the more common view became that of a determinism which claimed the exact return of events. There would be a new Troy, a second Helen, another Ajax. Out of this sensibility a typological view of history evolved, and by the second century B.C., the ideas of decline and rebirth had invaded Jewish thought in the Book of Daniel (*ca.* 165 B.C.). According to Daniel, there were to be five kingdoms, the last of which would be a permanent golden reign lasting a thousand years. It would be preceded by a reign of chaos.

The ideas in the Book of Daniel were repeated for Christians in about 93 A.D. in the Book of Revelation, which spoke of the millennium as the Second Coming of Christ and the fourth kingdom as Babylon. By this repetition, there developed in early Christian times a view of the Old and New Testaments as containing a typal pattern of all history beginning with Genesis and ending with Revelation. Here, the Fathers of the Church had denied exact renewal, but claimed to varying degrees interpretations of events which showed their correspondences to typal patterns revealed by the Prophets. Moreover, they took up positions in regard to this Kingdom of Christ, whether it was to be of this world or not. With the appearance of Constantine, an equation arose of the Kingdom of Christ with the Roman Empire and, in the wake of Rome's invasion by the Huns, Augustine attempted to deal again with the question in *The City of God* (413–426 A.D.). He indicated, first, that the Kingdom of Christ on earth would never be objectively realized and, second, that it was ever being realized subjectively. In the sixteenth and seventeenth centuries, radical Puritans, accepting an apposite notion of a New Canaan on earth, sought to discover this state in reforms of the English government and in their founding of American colonies. Behind these efforts was a belief that Babylon and world destruction could be forestalled by living godly lives, and, if this were not possible, they individually might be saved.

At the turn of the twentieth century, the *Action Française*, decrying the loss of Christianity and nationalism in France, began a movement to restore a Catholic framework to her "declining" culture. In 1917, W. B. Yeats spoke in *A Vision* of a process of history outside of human control causing civilization's decline, and he was followed a year later by Oswald Spengler's similar beliefs in *The Decline of the West*. Subsequent writers like Christopher Dawson in *Religion and the Modern State* (1935) and T. S. Eliot in *The Idea of a Christian Society* (1939), following in the tradition of the radical Puritans, showed how the need to believe in a millennium was a human need and how the dialectic of Karl Marx was in a way understandable only as an attempt to substitute for that need an economic view of the millennium. They insisted that the Christian nations of the world were in danger of losing their Christian cores by giving in to such secular notions and, further, of forcing upon themselves world destruction and everlasting Judgment. However seemingly Calvinist this active role of Christianity in politics was, as Dawson explains in *The Judgement of the Nations* (1943), it was really medieval Catholicism and Gregorian: "Though Calvinism has always been regarded as the antithesis of Catholicism to a far greater extent than Lutheranism, it stands much nearer to Catholicism in its conception of the relation of Church and State and in its assertion of the independence and supremacy of the spiritual power. In this respect it carries on the traditions of medieval Catholicism and the Gregorian movement of reform to an even greater degree than did the Catholicism of the Counter-Reformation itself."

For Lowell, who began his awareness of social action in the thirties at Harvard and at Kenyon College among friends and followers of Ezra Pound and T. S. Eliot, magazines were alive with such notions of civilization's decline, and radios boomed with the voices of Father Charles E. Coughlin and others telling America the reasons of her Depression and corruption. Pope Pius XII was speaking of "Darkness over the Earth," and armies were being marshaled into new wars. If the end of this fourth kingdom which underlay their views was not being portrayed as religious, it was being portrayed as political, with Fascism, Communism, and Democracy offering the world the "comings" of Benito Mussolini, Josef Stalin, and Franklin Delano Roosevelt. Under such circumstances, it was difficult not to form a view of Apocalypse, and, in 1963, Lowell admitted to Alfred Alvarez and the readers of the London *Observer* that he had indeed begun his career with such a view: "My first book was written during the war, which was a very different time from the thirties. . . . The world seemed apocalyptic at that time, and heroically so. I thought that civilization was going to break and instead *I* did." Although he disclaims a connection of this apocalyptic view with writers of the thirties, one has merely to survey their works to find a number of people whose views were identical. In fact, as Allen Tate suggests in his Introduction to *Land of Unlikeness,* the view is to be associated with Dawson, whose books, *Religion and the Modern State* (1935), *Progress and Religion* (1938), and *Beyond Politics* (1939), had already influenced Eliot's *The Idea of a Christian Society* and whose later book, *The Judgement of the Nations,* was to go through the publishing house of Sheed and Ward at a time when Lowell was a reader there (1941–1942). Moreover, as I demonstrated in *The Poetic Themes of Robert Lowell* (1965), the view of an Apocalypse was being espoused by Jean C. de Ménasce in the pages of *Commonweal* during the winter of 1942–1943 when, as Lowell indicates in a *Paris Review* interview (1961), he and his wife were with the Tates in Monteagle, Tennessee, "reading Catholic writers" and writing most of the poems for the volume, "though some," as he remarks, "were earlier poems rewritten."

What Lowell derived generally from these other contemporary expressions of Apocalypse can be easily seen. They offered him, first, a separation of the City of God from the City of Babylon so that progress toward one did not necessitate progress toward the second. In fact, as Dawson had suggested in *Religion and the Modern State,* progress toward the City of God was often called in Babylon "a failure." This progress of the soul would involve not the fatalistic, morphological transformations of Spengler, but, as E. I. Watkin was to suggest in *Catholic Art and Culture* (1944), a coming age of contemplation associated with the Holy Ghost. In the Middle Ages, the idea had been propagated by Joachim of Floris and the Spiritual

Franciscans, and earlier in the twentieth century it had been revived in the work of D. H. Lawrence. This Age of Contemplation would relate to the Second Coming of Christ and evolve a community which, by its theoretical exclusion of non-Christian elements, might be described practically as anti-non-Christian. Second, as part of the imminence of an Apocalypse, they evolved a view of contemporary society as the collapse, rather than the realization, of liberalism. Modern man was caught in a method, not an ideology of totalitarianism, where, through the devices of mass propaganda, he was being bombarded into soullessness. According to Dawson, the methods of the totalitarianism which hold him were employed first by the leaders of the French Revolution, but became as well a part of the strategies of men like Mussolini, Hitler, Lenin, and Roosevelt.

In addition, the tendency of these writers, in speaking of the collapse of democratic liberalism, to associate the failure with capitalism and control of government by the financier supported such views of money as those which were being circulated during the thirties by Pound and Coughlin and which had been complained of earlier in the century by Henry Adams and the *Action Française*. In the nineteenth century, they had been the concerns of John Adams, Thomas Jefferson, and Martin Van Buren. The tendency led many of the writers to attack what they called "the international Jew," and vestiges of these attacks occur in the "hog-fatted Jews" of Lowell's "Christ for Sale" and in his general attacks on bankers and capitalists. In this connection, the writers tended to view World War II as an unjust war connected with these "bankers" and as employing methods which would turn man into a counterpart of Cain. As Dawson suggests in *The Judgement of the Nations*, "The great conflict, that had divided Europe . . . and has produced two world wars, is the result of . . . science and mechanization being used, in the one case, in a commercial spirit for the increase of wealth; in the other, in a military spirit for the conquest of power." This "military spirit," he notes elsewhere in the book, "is no longer the pastime of kings and the trade of professional armies, it is the death-grapple of huge impersonal mass Powers which have ground out the whole life of the whole population in the wheels of their social mechanism." These views led to the creation of a "politics" of Apocalypse, which, like the radical Puritanism of the seventeenth century, would reform current governments over the world to forestall world end by restoring godly virtues and, if this were not possible, to permit man to be saved again individually. In *Land of Unlikeness*, this "politics" remained generally concerned with spiritual reformations.

More specifically, these writers gave to Lowell's poetry and life at the time certain attitudes and phrases which he admits to indirectly in his *Paris Review* interview by his being "much more interested in being a Catholic than in being a writer." Imagery directly related to the Book of Daniel and the Book of Revelation occurs in poems like "The Park Street Cemetery," "In Memory of Arthur Winslow," "The Bomber," "Concord Cemetery after the Tornado," "Salem," "Scenes from the Historic Comedy," "Christ for Sale," "The Crucifix," "The Wood of Life," "Satan's Confession," "Christmas Eve in the Time of War," "Cistercians in Germany," and "Leviathan." In addition, Dawson's works seem to lie behind "Children of Light" and may have contributed also to "Concord" and "Dea Roma." Besides its parable of the unjust steward (Luke 16:8), its echoes of John Milton's "On the Late Massacre in Piedmont," and sentiments like the Quaker John Easton's toward the Indian, the ten-line "Children of Light" seems to owe as well to remarks in *The Judgement of the Nations* wherein Dawson states: "Thus the new international order of Versailles and Geneva was doomed to failure from the beginning since every year and every fresh political and economic crisis made the contradiction between nineteenth-century ideals and twentieth-century realities more palpable and obvious." Earlier in *Religion and the Modern State*, Dawson had remarked: "The peace-makers of

Versailles sowed dragons' teeth in the furrows of war and to-day we see the outcome of their well-intentioned efforts in a world bristling with national antagonisms and economic rivalries." It is true that in using the quotations Lowell adds Calvinism to the meaning of Geneva (the world court) and a hint of the French and American Revolutions to the "hall of mirrors" (Versailles) as well as a touch of mechanization (searchlights) to the "light" of the scene, but these additions all accord with sentiments that Dawson had himself expressed.

"Concord" uses the town whose name ironically belies its having marked the place of the start of the disharmonious Revolutionary War to extend attacks on the mercantilism, exploitation, and the unchristian attitudes of American industry. In the poem, Lowell speaks of a search in the present chaos for a continuity. This continuity, as Dawson suggests in *Religion and the Modern State,* without Christian principle becomes Heraclitean:

> It [a moral and political system made relativist and historically materialistic by the undeifying of Christ in Unitarianism] would recognise that revolution was not, as the liberals believed, the vindication of absolute rights and the liberation of humanity from the bondage of superstition and injustice, but a part of the necessary cycle of change which governs the life of society, the destruction of the old order giving birth to the new one which will in turn pass away when its time is ripe. . . . And the philosopher himself would cease to share the naïve passions of the mob and would turn like Heraclitus to the contemplation of the unseen harmony which runs through the apparent strife and confusion . . . since "strife is justice" and "war is the father and the king of Gods and Men."

The poem attacks specifically Henry Ford's attempts through the restoration of landmarks to step again into the "river" ("Heraclitus' stream") of American heritage while at the same moment, through his mass-production techniques, he is contributing to the soullessness about. He has ignored Heraclitus' famous example that one cannot step into the same river twice, for the second time it is not the same river. The statement of Dawson is prophetic, moreover, of the direction which Lowell would take in and after *Life Studies* (1959) as a result of his disaffection from Catholicism. There "the necessary cycle of change . . . the destruction of the old order giving birth to the new one which will in turn pass away when its time is ripe" becomes his major theme.

The opening stanza of "Dea Roma" owes perhaps more tenuously to Dawson's "St. Augustine and His Age" (1930), which appeared in *A Monument to Saint Augustine.* There Dawson described the "misrule of the capitalist oligarchy and the tyranny of military adventurers" which Julius Caesar and Augustus "mended" by returning Rome "to the Hellenistic ideal of an enlightened monarchy." In the essay, Cicero's rebuke of Brutus for charging forty-eight percent on his loans to the impoverished cities of Cilicia is mentioned, but Lowell may have derived the incident directly from Cicero's *Epistles ad Atticum,* though his corruption of it to "forty-six percent" remains odd. From then on, a variety of sources are used in the poem to delineate Rome's history from the "city of gold and marble, a worthy incarnation of the *Dea Roma* whom her subjects worshipped," to her attack by St. John in Revelation as "the great harlot enthroned upon the waters, drunken with the blood of the saints and the blood of the martyrs of Jesus" and her becoming in Canto II of Dante's *Purgatorio* the shore from which the souls of the faithful leave to meet Christ, albeit there they are fetched not by Christ but by an Angel of God.

Lowell's decision to resist going into military service in 1943 on the grounds that total bombing was wrong may additionally have gained support from these apocalyptic writers, particularly from statements like Eliot's in *The Idea of a Christian Society* that "The man who believes that a particular war in which his country proposes to engage is an aggressive war, who believes that his country could refuse to take part in it without its legitimate interests being imperilled, and without failing in its duty to God and its neighbours, would be wrong to remain silent (the attitude of the late Charles Eliot Norton in regard to the Spanish-American War of 1898 is to the point)." As Lowell explained to the newspapers, "when he felt that the country was in danger of invasion he tried to enlist in both the Army and the Navy," but now felt "the intention of bombing Japan and Germany into submission is a 'betrayal of our country.'" The danger of invasion to which he alludes may be to the description of a "defenseless" New England coast "with the German fleet just over a black horizon," which Bill Cunningham drew for readers of the Boston *Herald* in February, 1942, and which was followed shortly by a Japanese submarine attack on the West Coast. The article prompted Senator David I. Walsh to propose on the floor of the United States Senate the possibility of the need "to bring back from the four corners of the world our depleted navy to be a source of defense for our own shores," and the Coughlinites in particular took up the cry. Lowell's action would be in direct opposition to their intent. He also objected in his 1,000-word "declaration of responsibility" to a war which might leave Europe and China "to the mercy of the U.S.S.R., a totalitarian tyranny committed to world revolution." Coupled with the statements of his poetry, these sentiments seem unquestionably to ally the direction of his politics with that of Dawson's.

The need to pin down the precise natures both of this apocalyptic vision of *Land of Unlikeness* and of its practical consequences which act mutually as metaphoric vehicles for Lowell's objectifying the tenors of the modern world and of himself is important, for they both shaped and misshaped what he saw in that volume, and, as vehicles, they represent the frameworks out of which he has tried subsequently to move. But even if this were not so, they are, as Glauco Cambon has suggested in *The Inclusive Flame* (1963), vehicles which of necessity a reader must understand, for a poet's function is not only to be in time with his age but also to be a witness to it. Since Lowell is, as Cambon rightly asserts, "one of the most history-conscious American writers . . . precisely because he has a quarrel with history," an understanding of the exact nature of that quarrel and consciousness becomes especially essential. It is, as Cambon concludes, finally "eschatological and not, properly speaking, 'historical.'" Lowell "speaks like an angry prophet, not like a Hegelian historicist or hopeful humanist." This, as George Herbert Mead indicates in *Mind, Self, and Society* (1934), is expected of one who "goes against the whole world about him": "To do that he has to speak with the voice of reason to himself. He has to comprehend the voices of the past and of the future. That is the only way in which the self can get a voice which is more than the voice of the community." Nor are these vehicles of Apocalypse and prophet, as Lowell seems to suggest, things he holds only in the forties. They return in the dialogue of *The Old Glory* (1964) and in remarks like the one he made on America in a second interview with Alvarez shortly after the assassination of President John F. Kennedy: "I think of Jefferson and the whole idealism [of American culture]—there are very few countries founded on a declaration the way ours was. There's something biblical and Jewish about that—Messianic. It is both what is unreal about America and what's noble about America." Lowell then goes on to assert, "Violence and idealism have some occult connection. . . . It's deep in us that the man who draws first somehow has proved himself."

In the sense that in order to communicate all art must repeat structures with which an audience is familiar, all art becomes cyclical and any poet becomes a cyclical writer, and that any experience to have significance must be seen in relation to previous and projectable experiences, the whole significative system of man's thinking may be seen as repetitive. In these connections, writers have always had at their disposals the typological frames of classical and early Christian thought. But more recently, depth psychologists have, in their notion of human archetypal behavior, suggested that the structures of self-consciousness are repetitious as well—the phylogenetic must be repeated ontogenetically. In the twentieth century, a revived typal literature, based on this idea of symbolic or exact renewal, grew to prominence in "mythic" writers like James Joyce, Yeats, Lawrence, Pound, Eliot, and Thomas Mann. Mann explains its method in "Freud and the Future" (1936) as a convergence of typical and mythical events so that "lived myth" becomes "lived life." It is a reconstruction of the primordial mind of myth in flesh and blood so that a Napoleon "mythically" confounds himself into Charlemagne, announcing not that "I am like Charlemagne" nor "My situation is like Charlemagne's," but that he *was* Charlemagne. For Lowell, this reconstruction consisted in a portrayal of experience in terms of an Augustinian duality of the City of God and the City of Babylon. The first, he, like Dante, associated with the spirit, Rome, Aeneas, and the Tiber; the second, like Augustine, he associated with the world, Babel-Boston, Nimrod, and the Charles. The spirituality of this City of God made its earthly localization impossible, however much it was ever within the reach of the virtuous. These virtuous were either saved contemplatives like Dante's St. Bernard, or Christians capable of salvation like John Bunyan's Christian Pilgrim. Their counterparts nearing or inhabiting the City of Babylon were either lapsed Christians, imaged in terms of Goethe's Faust, or damned souls, seen as correlatives of Cain. The nature of one's expiation from this immoral City was envisioned as love.

Biblical and classical allusions more than psychological referents are used by Lowell to present modern culture on the brink of the Last Judgment. Approximating the "decline" or "winter" of biographic cyclical theories of history, the world of the early forties was rife with what must be seen as a parallel to the chaos of the fourth kingdom of Daniel or to the Babylon of Revelation. It was awaiting "spring," the fifth kingdom, or Parousia. In his role of prophet, Lowell would have to distort the experiential, temporal, operative world about him into an immediately significative, atemporal, and thematic one. Rather than encountering a literal or realistic art, his readers would be kept reacting to significances. These reactions would obscure for them the essentially cyclical nature of art by forcing them out of their usual thinking in terms of analogues to other art works into readings whose energies would be primarily consumed in translating words backward from their significances to their sometimes highly incredible realistic images. Thus in Part IV of "In Memory of Arthur Winslow," which derives partly from François Villon's "Ballade—Que Villon Feist à la Request da sa Mère, Pour Prier Nostre Dame," partly from Revelation (18:22), and partly from Pound's Usury Canto (XLV), the source and person of the Virgin Mary in her "scorched, blue thunderbreasts of love" is obscured by her significative function. As mediatrix, she is to drown and rebaptise the warring world in the Flood of Revelation in order to prepare it for Christ's Second Coming. As critics of Lowell have insisted, the image is "appalling," "incredible," and "grotesque," but by so being, it creates the impression of an eschatological, rather than a historical voice.

The traditional example of this kind of obscuring in English is Edmund Spenser's *The Faerie Queene*, which reverses the normal order of levels of interpretation by deliberately projecting an unbelievable literal level. The reader is forced as a consequence into the significative levels particular to that work. This is the reverse of the way in which signification is established by Albertus Magnus and Thomas Aquinas, who both had insisted in their writings that the literal level of an art work be credible if significative levels are to be drawn. By seeming to by-pass the inherent cyclicisms of form and interior reflection as a means of deriving signification and by seeming to make significance intuitive or prereflective, this reversal of interpretative levels pretends to avoid the cyclical pitfalls of normal patterns of experience. By dealing with words that convey transtemporal signification, not with words that convey realizable (that is, temporal) things, it achieves a sense of prophecy. This sense differs from the vision of utopian literature, whose potentials are realistic and realizable in time, however unlikely it is that they may be brought about. It differs, too, from the significations of nonsense literature, whose meanings are present or past and where a reader can refute them, not as facts, but as demanding the kind of commitments which Jean-Paul Sartre in *Literature and Existentialism* (1949) establishes for thematic literature: "Rousseau, the father of the French Revolution and Gobineau, the father of racism, both sent us messages. And the critic considers them with equal sympathy. If they were alive, he would have to choose between the two, to love one and hate the other." Thus, in Lewis Carroll's "Jabberwocky," the reader is not asked to act upon what he reads; but alter the poem's verbs into a future tense and immediately a choice must be made:" 'Twill be brillig and the slithy toves will gyre and gimble in the wabe."

However unintended the revelation may have been on Lowell's part, what he contributes as the past and future to the techniques of prophecy in *Land of Unlikeness* can be seen in "The Park Street Cemetery." The poem inaugurates the volume, opening it in back of the Athenaeum, that "nostalgic temple of literature and art," over which for a century, as members of its board of trustees, the Lowell family had been the moving spirits. There, in this modern approximation of Hades or Avernus, the reader is told that "only the dead are poorer" and that "dusty leaves and frizzled lilac" liven the grounds with "baroque and prodigal embellishments." The Golden Dome of the Statehouse is now held by the Irish Catholics, and the New World eschatologies that once fascinated the Puritan founders have dwindled with the loss by the modern mind of its spiritual imagination, its ability to transform the self-realizable potential of Boston's Golden Dome into St. Peter's Golden Dome as the place for the faithful to embark upon their new journeys to God. The operative metaphor of the poem is art, couched in its dominant adjective, "baroque," and John Frederick Nims, in reviewing the book for *Poetry* (1945), seized upon the word to describe Lowell's general manner of writing as "a kind of inverse baroque." The profusion of its detail and allusion was held together not by exuberance and sympathy as they might be in normal baroque, but by ratiocination and analysis.

It was as if, by choosing the metaphor, Lowell were unconsciously embracing a view similar to that expressed by Oscar Wilde in "The Decay of Lying" (1889) that life imitates art: "At present, people see fogs, not because there are fogs, but because poets and painters have taught them the mysterious loveliness of such effects. There may have been fogs for centuries in London. I dare say there were. But no one saw them, and so we do not know anything about them. They did not exist till Art invented them." To this view, Lowell seems to have added the view of Matthew Arnold in "The Study of Poetry" (1880): "We should conceive of poetry worthily, and more highly than it has been the custom to conceive of it. We should conceive of it as capable of higher uses, and called to higher destinies, than those which in general men have assigned to it hitherto. More and more mankind will discover that we have to turn to poetry to interpret life for us, to console us, to sustain us. Without poetry, our science will appear incomplete; and most of what now passes with us for religion and philosophy will be replaced by poetry." The "leaves and lilacs" of "The Park Street Cemetery" can be "baroque" because, in the manner of Wilde, art has taught Lowell what "baroque" is, and because, in the manner of Arnold, Lowell is intent in his art to show his readers what "morality" is. The view does not differ radically from that expressed in "The Fiction Writer and His Country" (1957) by the equally apocalyptic Flannery

O'Connor, who is cited by Lowell as a "favorite writer": "The novelist with Christian concerns will find in modern life distortions which are repugnant to him, and his problem will be to make these appear as distortions to an audience which is used to seeing them as natural; and he may well be forced to take ever more violent means to get his vision across to this hostile audience." In both cases, the relation of the believing writer to his society is that he must try to redirect that society, and art becomes one of the ways of comprehending the past and the future so that, in going against the world about him, he may speak to himself with the voice of reason.

As Søren Kierkegaard pointed out in *Either / Or* (1843), one danger of such a position is that, on the reader's part, the choice may become aesthetic rather than ethical. As opposed to ethical choice, which is an absolute choice between good and evil, "The aesthetic choice is either entirely immediate and to that extent no choice, or it loses itself in the multifarious. . . . When one does not choose absolutely one chooses only for the moment, and therefore can choose something different the next moment." The existence of this danger was borne out in reviews of *Land of Unlikeness,* which demonstrated that the concerns of the readers were more aesthetic than ethical. Conrad Aiken, for instance, told the readers of *The New Republic* (1944) that the book was "intellectually embarrassing and retrogressive at times" and the poems often "either turgid and strained or merely heraldic." R. P. Blackmur in the *Kenyon Review* (1945) chose to view the work as violating the organic relationship of form and content: "It is as if he demanded *to know* (to judge, to master) both the substance apart from the form with which he handles it and the form apart from the substance handled in order to set them fighting . . . and the fight produces not a tension but a gritting. It is not the violence, the rage, the denial of this world that grits, but the failure of these to find *in verse* a tension of necessity." In reviewing Lowell's next book for *The New Leader,* Leslie A. Fiedler sums up the situation in "The Believing Poet and the Infidel Reader" (1947): "It is the poet's skills, he will insist, his music or his honest eye that is the source of his pleasure; or, a trifle condescendingly, the unbelieving reader will confide that a particular 'false and partial' view is, at the moment, 'useful.' At worst he will pretend to discover 'heresies' that have slipped past the poet's orthodoxy, and that only the properly heterodox can relish."

A second danger is that in writing mythically "lived myth" can degenerate into "lived metaphor" in what Wilde cites as a tendency of consciousness to find its "self" in the metaphors of art. In acquiring his understanding of "the voices of the past and of the future," the individual too often neglects the voice of the present, so that the metaphor of identity becomes an outmoded Apollonian self. This self, as Friedrich Nietzsche points out in *The Birth of Tragedy* (1872), calls into being a Dionysian urge to destroy what is created as proof of the individual's freedom. In such circumstances, one must pay careful attention to certain distinctions between the two forms. Chief among them is that in "lived metaphor" one brings his image of himself into line with himself in terms of will rather than in terms of love. In contrast, in "lived myth" one unconsciously aligns his being and mentally recognizes upon reflection the confusion through love and understanding of typical and mythical lives. In the first instance, the self becomes a static image which is independent of the subject and recognizable beforehand. In the second, the image is unified, dynamic, and open to contingency and free will. Like the imitation of Cicero in the early Renaissance, "lived metaphor" fulfills only part of the total personality and does this by making the tenor subservient to the vehicle. One establishes not oneself but one's model. In contradistinction, "lived myth" completes the entire personality by allowing the individual to undergo the stages outlined by Mead in the full development of the self. In the first stage, the self organizes its identity from the particular attitudes of other individuals toward it and toward one another in the specific social acts in which the subject participates with them. In the second, it organizes not only these particular individual attitudes but also the social attitudes of the generalized other or the social group as a whole to which one belongs. Thus, Christ and Napoleon preserve their identities as Saviour and Charlemagne independent of the archetypes they complete. Lowell's complaint in the *Paris Review* interview that he found his poetry "was getting increasingly stifling" and that "he couldn't get his experiences into tight metrical forms" seems to suggest that as early as this volume he was tending toward "lived metaphor."

These failures of getting his experiences into poems become more apparent as Lowell's indebtedness to the visions of writers like Dawson and Eliot extend beyond *Land of Unlikeness* into the poems written shortly after: "The Quaker Graveyard in Nantucket" and "To Peter Taylor on the Feast of the Epiphany." In his Note to *Lord Weary's Castle* (1946), he openly acknowledges the debt which "The Quaker Graveyard" owes Watkin's *Catholic Art and Culture*. The study contributes most of the details of Part VI of Lowell's poem as well as the idea implicit in its conclusion that one day Walsingham "will return to the Church." To enforce the eschatology of this return, a sailor "whistling Sion" about the shrine of the Virgin is introduced to offset the lamenting sailors about the Whore of Babylon in Revelation (18:17–21). Though not cited, the debt to Dawson in "To Peter Taylor on the Feast of the Epiphany" is as considerable. By its allusions to Armageddon, Whore, Beast, and Dragon and its metaphor of the hero's "skating on thin ice," which promises, in turn, to thaw into the waters of the Last Judgment (Revelation 17:15–18), the situation of the poem is allied to the situation of the modern world as described in *The Judgement of the Nations:* "It [the modern world] has reversed the whole hierarchy of spiritual values so that our civilization has been turned backwards and upside down, with its face toward darkness and nonentity and its back to the sun of truth and the source of being. For a short time—whether we reckon it in decades or centuries is of small importance—it remained precariously skating on the thin ice of rationalism and secular humanism. Now the ice has broken and we are being carried down the flood [for Lowell the Flood of the Apocalypse], though we may delude ourselves that the forces that have been released are of our own creation and serve our will to power." This eschatological view, as H. A. Reinhold was reminding readers of *Commonweal* in "Parousia, 1943" (1943), is embedded in the very Gospel associated with Epiphany: "Two thundering Sundays (the last after Pentecost; the first of Advent) . . . have as their Gospels the announcement of the Parousia [Christ's Second Coming]. They are prophecy, spoken by Christ. January 6th and its companions in this constellation are the 'pre-reality,' the pledge that the Parousia is true, is real, because God has already manifested Himself, and His Godhead shone through one human Life in four symbolic visions."

These broader views of Apocalypse remain seemingly unrestrictive so long as Lowell wishes to remain eschatological and prophetic, but as soon as he enters history and the political significance of the collapse of King Louis XVI into the French Revolution in "1790," the constrictions begin to be manifest. Though not necessarily royalist, the poem relies upon anti-populist sentiments like those suggested in "Dea Roma" and contained in Dawson's *Beyond Politics:* "Democracy and dictatorship are not opposites or mortal enemies, but twin children of the great [French] Revolution." Dawson goes on to note, "Anyone who studies the history of the First French Republic in the light of recent political developments cannot fail to be impressed by the way in which the Jacobins anticipated practically all the characteristic features of the modern totalitarian regimes: the dictatorship of a party in the name of the community, the use of propaganda and appeals to mass emotion, as well as violence and terrorism, the conception of revolutionary justice as a social weapon, the regulation of economic life in order to realize revolutionary ideals, and above all the attempt to enforce a uniform ideology on the whole people and the proscription and persecution of every other form of political thought."

Dawson sees Europe dividing in the thirties into three opposing totalitarian ideologies—Fascism, Communism, and Democracy (total rule by the majority to the persecution of the minority)—and adds in defense of monarchy: "We react instinctively and emotionally to the great pageant [the coronation of an English king] that flatters our national pride and yet at the same time appeals to something deeper or higher, some vague numinous conception of the State as a holy community and of political power as a sacred God-given office which transcends the limit of utilitarian and nationally selfish ends, and binds man by a golden chain to the order of heaven." The sentiments as they relate to Democracy and the advantages of Kingship over popular government are not too different from those expressed by Eliot in "The Literature of Fascism" (1928): "Now it is manifest that any disparagement of 'democracy' is nowadays well received by nearly every class of men, and any alternative to 'democracy' is watched with great interest. . . . I cannot share enthusiastically in this vigorous repudiation of 'democracy.' . . . It is one thing to say, what is sadly certain, that democratic government has been watered down to nothing. . . . But it is another thing to ridicule the *idea* of democracy. A real democracy is always a restricted democracy, and can only flourish with some limitation by hereditary rights and responsibilities. The United States of America, for instance, were more or less democratic up to 1829, when Andrew Jackson became President, when the system which is euphemistically known as *la carrière ouverte aux talents,* and more exactly as the Pork Barrel System, became powerful."

After acknowledging a personal attraction to the views of Charles Maurras, Eliot goes on to note, "The *Action Française* insists upon the importance of continuity by the Kingship and hereditary class, upon something which has some analogy to what the government of England was, formerly, at least supposed to be; it would protect the humble citizen against the ambitious politician." In addition, the views of both Eliot and Dawson are close to those expressed for readers of *Commonweal* by de Ménasce in "Leviathan Come to Pass" (1942): "The French Revolution also played the dictator's game. In attacking the theory of the King's divine authority, the men of the revolution did not know exactly what they were doing. They wanted, simply, to limit the King's power, to assert the peoples', but what they did actually was to render limitless the power of the state. . . . For my part I prefer an authoritarian 'I' who is competent only to build roads to a democratic 'we' who is competent to decide whom I must marry, what profession I must follow, what city I must live in and to what school I must send my children."

Unquestionably this link between the King and Christian government was in Lowell's mind when he decided to begin "1790" with a Maundy Thursday episode, which, as Victor Doyno pointed out in "Poetic Language and Transformation" (1968), was part of the poem's original source in *The Memoirs of Baron Thiebault*. On Maundy Thursday, the King, in imitation of Christ at the Last Supper, washes the feet of twelve "guests" as Christ had washed the feet of his disciples. As in the parable in Matthew (22:1–14), which likens the Kingdom of Heaven to a king giving a marriage feast, few of the many called to the ceremony are "chosen." These linguistic and ritualistic links of the King to God are broken at the poem's close by the mention of the Champs de Mars, where on July 14, 1790, Louis was made to agree to the constitution demanded by the revolutionaries. The agreement led subsequently in 1793 to his own painful death, foreshadowed for the reader by the dog whose back the King breaks in the course of the poem. The proximity of this death spatially to the Maundy Thursday rite, echoing the proximity of the Last Supper temporally to the Crucifixion, emphasizes a second connection of Louis with Christ. The poem thus moves from Christian government (Maundy Thursday) to the New Paganism (Mars), which both Dawson and de Ménasce associate with the effects of the French Revolution. In relation to the real Baron, the poem's narrator is far more sympathetic with the King and suggests the whole political movement has reduced the French populace to "dog's lives."

The yearnings in both "Concord" and "Salem" to step again into the stream of American history to fetch back the New England spirit that "fought the British lion to his knees" suggest that, like Eliot, Lowell would approve of the kind of restricted democracy that existed in the United States prior to 1829. But that a reader of Lowell not mistake the form of government in these poems for its function, one should mention here that in "The Fens," based upon social reformer William Cobbett's *Rural Rides* (1830), the loss of Catholicism hastening the world's end occurs under the kingship of Henry VIII, who has erred not in a break from Christ, but in his break from the Catholic Church. Thus, Lowell's politics become not a matter of royalism per se, but a matter of Catholicism, as the *Action Française* conceived it, as "essential to civilization" if civilization is to continue, or as de Ménasce and Dawson conceived it, as a necessary framework if man is to escape his imprisonment "in the network of an immoral society," or as Eliot saw it, as a "natural advantage" of Christian over pagan values.

The constrictions force Lowell in these political poems to enter what Fiedler was to call the "ambiguity of the dramatic." Using the dramatic monologue technique of Robert Browning, Lowell presents these currently unpopular political views in a manner which he may, in truth, deny as his own by virtue of his having skillfully fitted them to personages who might well have spoken them. Thus, in "Mr. Edwards and the Spider" and "After the Surprising Conversions," Jonathan Edwards' works are used to present the need for a moral society (radical Puritanism) and to attack materialism (the devil-peddler). The poems doubtlessly derive from Lowell's intent in going to the Tates' house in 1942 to do a biography of the New England divine. He had tired of the work, and owing to "reading particularly the Sixteenth and Seventeenth centuries," had begun instead to write poems. The stanza form of "Mr. Edwards and the Spider" is indebted to John Donne's "A Nocturnal of St. Lucy's Day," as is the stanza form of "The Ghost." So is the technique of disturbing the normal regular fall of the verse stresses by forcing rhetorical stress on syllables which the metrical pattern leaves unstressed. In "Mr. Edwards and the Spider," he has altered the last line of each stanza into a Spenserian alexandrine, but connection of the poem with the Tate visit is unquestionable. Still, as Baron Thiebault did not intend his *Memoirs* to become a defense of kingship, nor Cobbett his *Rural Rides* a boost for Catholicism, one might argue that Edwards had no intention in his sermons and "Personal Narrative" of returning, in the face of Christianity's having left New England, to the oligarchies of the Puritan founders. Obviously the contexts are to reflect Lowell's personae, his trying on masks to define himself and achieve his self's full development, as Pound suggested in *Gaudier-Brzeska* (1916) his translations were to relate to him: "In the 'search for oneself,' in the search for 'sincere self-expression,' one gropes, one finds some seeming verity. One says 'I am' this, that, or the other, and with the words scarcely uttered one ceases to be that thing. I began this search for the real in a book called *Personae,* casting off, as it were, complete masks of the self in each poem. I continued in long series of translations, which were but more elaborate masks." But these contexts lead Lowell in *Lord Weary's Castle* and *The Mills of the Kavanaughs* (1951) only to other masks and never to a sincerity of self.

Interesting in this connection because, while reaffirming the royalist politics of "1790," they continue in *The Mills of the Kavanaughs* Lowell's use of masks, are "Mother Marie Therese" and "Falling Asleep over the Aeneid." The *Action Française,* which forms half of the Mother's main reading in the first poem, is, as Michael Curtis has pointed out in *Three Against the Third Republic* (1959), both antidemocratic and anti-Semitic. Its leading writers, Georges Sorel, Maurice Barrès, and Charles Maurras, ranged from syndicalist to monarchist. They had in common the notion that the French government suffered weaknesses from within from immigrants who had been given French citizenship, but who were not truly Frenchmen, and from a conspiracy of "the big Jew bankers." They felt that only the Catholic Church, the army, an agrarian tradition, and, for Maurras, a monarchy or at least a hereditary aristocracy could bring government back to its true purpose and stability. Their views on certain points, being no different from those expressed by Henry Adams in *The Education,* the Boston Brahmins against the Irish Catholics, Pound in *Mussolini and/or Jefferson,* and Father Coughlin in *Social Justice,* are therefore not idiosyncratically imposed.

"Mother Marie Therese" discusses in particular the effects of monarchy. Its first political reference is to Pio Nono (Pius IX), who held the pontificate from 1846 to 1878. During his reign, the doctrine of Papal infallibility was defined, church and state were finally separated with the authority in the church centralized in Rome, and the lands of the Vatican were seriously diminished. He became the Vatican's first "prisoner," having like Louis XVI conceded to constitutional government and having then been victimized by the forces of revolution. He began his reign as a liberal and moved in the 1860's to oppose the liberal view of a "free church in a free state." A victim of the Franco-Prussian War (1870–1871), he lost his territories when Napoleon III, no longer able to maintain a garrison in Rome, removed his troops and left Rome to the revolutionists. He stands for Lowell crucially both negatively at the beginning of the decline of Papal authority by its removal of the Church from politics, and positively, at the beginning of her attacks on liberalism for being antireligious and the foe of true freedom. Thus "the strangled grouse and snow-shoe rabbits . . . fresh in their blood and color," matching the royal glint of his vestments, color those vestments so that he shares a fate with them and the physically maimed of the Franco-Prussian War. The idea is enforced by the image of the Papal tiaras and the Bourbon crown (Louis XVI), fluttering down so that under Pio Nono, Church (priest) and state (prince), now separated, might stand opposed until Michael and all his angels repel Satan's advances (Revelation 12:7–9).

The idea of the opposition is reinforced a few lines later when the Mother's enticement from the state into the Church is depicted as an echo of Proserpina's seduction by Dis:

> Christ enticed
> Her heart that fluttered, while she whipped her hounds
> Into the quicksands of her manor grounds
> A lordly child, her habit fleur-de-lys'd
> There she dismounted, sick; with little heed,
> Surrendered. Like Proserpina, who fell
> Six months a year from earth to flower in hell;
> She half-renounced by Candle, Book and Bell
> Her flowers and fowling pieces for the Church.

Yet this "émigrée in this world and the next" prefers reading Rabelais and spouting the royalist stands of the *Action Française* and honors more her letter from the "soi-disant French King" (Philip VIII) than the golden wedding ring that signals her own marriage to Christ. The tension echoes the position of Leo Ward in *The Condemnation of the "Action Française"* (1928) regarding the movement. He contends that Maurras sought the organization of Catholicism to stifle the possibility of individual mystical union with Christ, and certainly the Mother's "Hohenzollern standards," which lead to her "chiding novices and plucking them by the ears for gabbling in Canuck," are more organizational than mystical Catholicism. Yet, as Eliot argues in "A Reply to Mr. Ward" (1928), he could see no real conflict between mystical and organizational Catholicism, merely a cautious discrimination by the Church which acted as a "safe-guard against Johanna Southcotts." The idea of Mother Marie Therese's being organizational Catholicism is foreshadowed in Father Turbot's calling her "a sword" rather than "a saint," and a reader is doubly aware of this activism when he stops to com-pare her conversion of gifts which the Indians bring her to food as opposed to St. Francis' protection of all life. Already spoken of by the narrator in metaphors of Proserpina's rape into the world of the dead, the Mother's renunciation of the world in her nun's vow is given further emphasis by the priest who celebrates her memorial mass on August 25: "N-n-nothing is so d-dead as a dead s-s-sister." The day is appropriately the feast day of Louis Neuvième (Louis IX, Saint Louis), who is the patron saint of the Bourbons. It suggests that her serving cake at the opening of the poem is meant to be pregnant with echoes of Marie Antoinette's reply to the populace's cry for bread: "Let them eat cake."

But, as if this already complex point of view were still too constrictive, Lowell presents the poem through the voice of a second nun, who seems influenced not by the Action Française, but by William Shirley's rhetoric in enticing a war between the New England colonies and New France. Shirley (1694–1771) was Governor of Massachusetts (1741–1756) and tenaciously held that "Carthage" (New France) must be destroyed. Ac-cording to Francis Parkman's Montcalm and Wolfe (1884), the cry, Delenda est Carthago, from Cato, became the cant not only of Shirley but also of William Livingston, of New Jersey, and of Massachusetts clergymen like Thomas Foxcroft, pastor of the "Old Church in Boston." Foxcroft's sermon preached from the text, "The Lord hath done great things for us, whereof we are glad," asserts: "Long had it been the common opinion, Delenda *est Carthago,* Canada must be conquered, or we could hope for no lasting quiet in these parts; and now, through the good hand of our God upon us, we see the happy day of its accomplishment. We behold His Majesty's victorious troops treading upon the high places of the enemy, their last fortress delivered up, and their whole country surrendered to the King of Britain in the person of his general, the intrepid, the serene, the successful Amherst." In the poem, the nun describes the setting of the Maris Stella House as "Carthage," and the order as "friends of Cato," bringing upon the establishment destruction like that of weather and time. Shirley's expeditions against the French echo the unjust King Philip's War (1675–1676) of "At the Indian Killer's Grave" and "Children of Light," a war prompted by Lowell's forebear, Josiah Winslow, then governor of Plymouth. John Winslow and John Stark, other forebears of Lowell, accompany Shirley in his campaigns.

Of the gifts which the Mother has received from the Indians, only the "billy goat, or its descendent" remains as an exception to bleat into the current Atlantic squall atonement for James Wolfe, who, as Eli Forbes told his congregation in Brookfield, gave Massachusetts "the downfall of New France, the North American Babylon, New England's rival"; the Hurons, who were "systematically impelled to use their tomahawks against the enemies of the Church" (that is, non-Catholics); and the priests, who in the settling of Canada had, according to Parkman, systematically excluded all non-Catholics to the detriment of the colony. Their combined religious fervor has meted them a place in Hell like that meted Dives in Luke (16:22) so that M. de Montcalm, like Lazarus, looks down on them, not from the Plains of Abraham, but from Abraham's bosom. That sleep characterizes the state of both Mother Marie Therese and Montcalm suggests that she, too, may lie in Abraham's bosom for her having heeded the parable in Luke by feeding the Lazarus-like sisters in her charge. The suggestion, which is part of the active life of her Martha role, is strengthened by the associations with the Apocalypse, baptism, and ultimately salvation which the Atlantic Ocean has set up both within the poem and in other Lowell poems, like Part IV of "In Memory of Arthur Winslow" and "The Quaker Graveyard in Nantucket."

At peace, she looks down upon the convent, which finds itself giving ground "little by little." Against the triumph of the natural man of Jean Jacques Rousseau, which the images of the billy goat and the buck ruffed grouse evoke in a year which, over the protests of the *Action Française*, commemorated the bicentennial of Rousseau's birth, the sisters see their stern virginity "contra naturam." Inside the convent, piling more driftwood on the fire and stoking it with a poker, the reminiscing nun images her action as "swording at her fears," fears of being "burned into lime, like thorns cut down, that are burned in the fire" (Isaiah 33:12). The image and reference is identical to that used by Lowell in "Mr. Edwards and the Spider." Moreover, the suggestion that the Mother twitches at the nun's shoulder, as earlier Heaven's Prince was believed to have whispered to the Mother, contrasts with the devil-peddler groaning in the ear of Josiah Hawley in "After the Surpising Conversions" to advise him to cut his own throat. These whispers, as the *venite* reference suggests, are salvific. Over the failure to heed them is an image which foreshadows the weeping Black madonna at the close of *The Old Glory*. The Mother's "hollow sockets fill with tears." Thus, Lowell seems to be saying in the poem that the organization of Catholicism as opposed to the delusive Calvinism of Edwards is necessary to salvation and that this Catholicism, in opposition to what Ward indicates is a single-mindedness of the *Action Française* and in the more traditional distinctions of St. Bonaventure, is realizable in three forms—Martha, Mary, and Lazarus: Martha as abbott "faithfully discharges our temporal affairs"; Lazarus as novice "goes in fear of judgment till the assurance of Christ's pardon rolls away

the stone"; and Mary is the contemplative. Though not dis-
counting the contemplative, Lowell is here more concerned
with the active role of Martha.

"Falling Asleep over the Aeneid" deals with hereditary class
in what Eliot called "a restricted democracy." The poem outlines the efforts of one family, the Lowells, to "protect the
humble citizen against the ambitious politician." It is a dream
narrative of Vergil, "an old man in Concord," who has forgotten
to go to morning service. In his sleep, he dreams of Pallas,
whose death was described by that more famous Vergil, Publius
Vergilius Maro (70–19 B.C.) in Book XI of the *Aeneid.* The
death merges with the death of his heroic Uncle Charles, who,
as Dudley Fitts points out in *Furioso* (1951), has become, in
turn, a confusion of Charles Russell Lowell and Robert Gould
Shaw. "The Boston purist may be forgiven," Fitts goes on to
note, "for doubting if the Negro regiment [the 54th Massachusetts Infantry] ever did parade through Concord—but how rich,
how evocative, the verses are!" The confusion of Charles Lowell
and Shaw is understandable when one recalls that the two were
almost brothers-in-law, and both served the same idealistic
cause of freeing the Negro slaves. Charles married Shaw's sister
Josephine shortly after Shaw's death, and he himself died in
1864 before the end of the Civil War. Most of Charles's service,
as Ferris Greenslet notes in *The Lowells and Their Seven
Worlds* (1946), was seen with the Second Massachusetts Cav-
alry. Consequently, the whole idea of Lowell's coffin being
frowned upon by a separated Church (Phillips Brooks) and
state (Ulysses Grant) and the parade of "his colored volunteers"
is meant to be seen more as an echo of the *Aeneid* (and art)
than as a description of an actual historical event. It is perhaps
even a foreshadowing of Michael's angelic forces in Revelation.

In this connection, the enormous debt of the poem to the
Aeneid (XI:59–61, 67–68, 70–77, 89–92), which was in part the
result of Lowell's effort to try a translation of the *Aeneid*, takes
on new meaning. The sword which in his dream the dreamer

inherits "to keep from falling" blurs into the sword with which Dido killed herself (IV:633–635) as well as the sword with which Aeneas, in the name of Pallas, kills Turnus (XII:984–952). As a bridge between these two figures of strong love and strong manhood, Pallas, whom Turnus kills, has been buried in coverlets woven for Aeneas by Dido (XI:72–75). The weapon becomes the objectification of familial responsibility. In this light, the incidents of the dream blur into a necessary effort of the latter-day Vergil to construct out of his family history an image of a new Augustan age. The image of this age does not pierce through the pupils of Vergil's eye into his heart, as images of love are wont to do in classical and Renaissance poems. Rather, it reflects off his glasses at itself, reminding the reader of Lowell's own sense of constriction in his efforts to objectify himself in poetry and of his earlier position regarding Augustus in "Dea Roma."

Nevertheless, the failure of Vergil to equal his forebears does not constitute an attack by Lowell on the effort. Throughout his poetry, Lowell has maintained a strong emphasis on family obligation in upholding proper standards and shaping culture. In fact, his refusal to be inducted into World War II was based, by his own admission, upon his "responsibilities to myself, my country and my ancestors who played responsible parts in its making." In fixing sentence, Judge Samuel Mandelbaum, falling into the same imagery, told the poet: "You are one of a distinguished family and this will mar your family tradition." Certainly, this view of one's familial obligation accounts for the strong presence of ancestral voices in the early poetry. They make Lowell's speakers responsible either to atone for the sins of their forebears or to live up to the traditions of their successes, and generally they provide the continuity Eliot finds necessary for democracy. But underscoring their strong Apollonian traditions by being the metaphors of their descendants' selves-consciousness are the haunting Dionysian urges to break these metaphors and to set up lives independent of such traditions. Family obligations, then, form one of the communities to which Lowell listens in his going against the larger community about him, as the *Action Française* and other views outlawed by this community form another, and art and the Bible form still others. In all these communities Lowell in many cases rejects more than he accepts from his listening; yet none of the communities sways him from his view that civilization is in danger of breaking if it does not reform, and none provides him with the proper methods for achieving the fullness of his self or with an archetype which might naturally bring his image of himself into line with himself and his age in terms of love. It seems it required collapses both in his poetic technique and in his life to accomplish these ends.

Fishing the Swamp:
The Poetry of W. D. Snodgrass

WILLIAM HEYEN

I

What W. D. Snodgrass has written of John Crowe Ransom's early poems in *The Contemporary Poet as Artist and Critic* (1964) is true, to a large extent, of his own: "Those first poems quite defeat criticism—one can only point to them, with perhaps a few sentences of explication, and say, 'See? He's done it again!'" For Snodgrass' Pulitzer Prize-winning first volume, *Heart's Needle* (1959), communicates feelings stronger than thoughts. It is not that the reader senses anything like what T. S. Eliot called a "dissociation of sensibility." Call it "thought," or "theme," or "idea," or "intelligence," or "mentality"—this abounds in a Snodgrass poem. But the communication is almost wordless, subliminal.

What we come to know, for example, from "April Inventory," one of the nineteen poems preceding the "Heart's Needle" sequence, we come to know, as Theodore Roethke puts it in "Journey to the Interior," "As a blind man, lifting a curtain, knows it is morning." A young man in one of my classes read "April Inventory" aloud, and when he had finished, a hush fell over the room. Snodgrass' gentle, wise, hopeful speaker had turned all of us deep inside ourselves, and the kind of classroom talk inspired by many other poets, talk that had nothing finally to do with poetry, was unnecessary. But for the rest of the semester we used no other poem as an illustration of the mysterious ways in which poems *should* work more than we used "April Inventory." Snodgrass' lyrics are here, at this time, and are undeniable and touching. He captures what he has described as

351

the "spooky, modern quality" of Christian Morgenstern and
Eliot. Reading *Heart's Needle*, I feel somewhat the way A. E.
Housman's first audience, at least the young men, must have
felt reading the plaintive but hard songs of the eternally sad
lad from Shropshire.

Snodgrass is commonly associated with the "confessional"
school of verse, given its main thrust, in our time at least, by
Robert Lowell's *Life Studies* (1959). Snodgrass' major effort—
no small task—is to write from and of the self beneath the several masks—to write poems "more personal and so more universal," as he describes his final version of Section VI of "Heart's
Needle." The Romantics would not have batted an eye at this
credo; indeed, they felt that to write poetry of social value, one
had to release the stirrings of the universal man within the self.
And they would have considered Lowell's and Snodgrass' work
a continuation of the great tradition at the same time that they
would have considered the belly-laced-up-like-a-football poetry
of Anne Sexton and the daddy-I-hate-you-love-you poetry of
Sylvia Plath a misdirection of the credo, a misinterpretation.
Somehow, the two women never emerge from what, in "A
Decade of American Poetry: 1957–1967" (1968), Judson Jerome
calls the "self's swamp." Snodgrass does. He knows he has to:
"Stick in the mud, old heart, / what are you doing here?" ("The
Marsh").

II

In general, *Heart's Needle* is a poetry of experience, of present
tense and present tension; *After Experience* (1968), as its ambiguous title implies, is at once a poetry of the poet's meditation
on past happenings and a poetry of his determination to experience new ways of seeing, acting, and feeling. By the time of its
appearance—though some of the poems date back to when
Snodgrass was composing *Heart's Needle*—the poet has survived

certain experiences and is out, after these, looking for others that will continue to make him feel alive. Snodgrass tells us again and again that one can exist only by living the passionate life, by freeing the soul, though this action itself will inevitably bring grief to those we love the most.

In *Heart's Needle* both the world men had some part in making and the natural world—the world of seasonal ebb and flow —dominate the poet-speaker. He is caught up in, and not a little stifled by, what seem to be inexorable cycles of existence. There are occasional pauses, moments of permanence, as in "The Operation" when "In my brandy bowl / Of sweet peas at the window, the crystal world / Is inverted, slow and gay." But there are no new directions. Monotonous patterns remind us only of the fact that we are moving closer to old age and death.

In "Ten Days Leave," the opening poem, the poet expects, returning home, that the war would have changed something:

> But no; it seems just like it seemed. His folks
> Pursue their lives like toy trains on a track.
> He can foresee each of his father's jokes
> Like words in some old movie that's come back.

And in the final section of "Heart's Needle," visiting the park with his daughter, the poet says that "our seasons bring us back once more / like merry-go-round horses," and he again fastens on the image of the train—"and the miniature painted train / wails on its oval track." Snodgrass' universe is oval and largely determined, but just as there may be room in Ishmael's woof-and-warp world for free choice, Snodgrass suggests that we can choose our fate. He tells his daughter: "Child, I have another wife, / another child. We try to choose our life" ("Heart's Needle," vi). And she, too, must still learn to choose the unavoidable.

The social protest and the uncomfortable feelings associated with the cyclic existence hinted at in "Ten Days Leave" are deepened in "Returned to Frisco, 1946." The speaker, one of those who had "scrambled like rabbits / Up hostile beaches," fears the land to which he is returning, "this land / Intent on luxuries and its old habits." The poem concludes:

> Off the port side, through haze, we could discern
> Alcatraz, lavender with flowers. Barred,
> The Golden Gate, fading away astern,
> Stood like the closed gate of your own backyard.

This is a brilliant stanza. Its ironic central images of prison and golden bridge become revelation, pierce the "haze" of the problem, posed by an earlier line, that we are "Free to choose just what they meant we should." We know from Nathaniel Hawthorne's *The Scarlet Letter* (1850) that our country's earliest immigrants had considered it a necessity to allot a portion of the soil for a prison. Here, then, is the American Dream. The Golden Gate stands barred from view and fades away astern. Alcatraz is lavender with flowers. Choice is always, perhaps, a matter of illusion. And the reality of the Dream: "Beyond, jagged stars / are glinting like jacks hurled / farther than eyes can gather" ("At the Park Dance").

Having lost his individuality during the war, having forgotten his name, the poet returns to what he calls "No Man's Land." In his "Home Town" he learns he is "no one here." To be a personality instead of a statistic, to have a name and to be able to sing it—these things are matters of life or living death. After, in "A Cardinal," cursing this bird for devouring an insect, the poet realizes he is being absurd. He hears the bird's indisputable song: " 'I music out my name / and what I tell is who / in all the world I am.' " And he comes to realize that "Each trade has its way of speaking, / each bird its name to say." In "These Trees Stand . . ." he assures himself that "Snodgrass is walking through the universe." In "April Inventory" he tells us how, though "In thirty years I may not get / Younger, shrewder, or

out of debt," he can afford the "costly seasons": "I taught myself
to name my name." If, as in "A Cardinal," the noises of free
enterprise are a "devil's Mass"; if, as in "The Campus on the Hill"
(with its ironic echoes of E. A. Robinson's "The House on the
Hill") and "April Inventory" even academia is shot through
with twisted, nonhumanistic values; if the necessities to name
his own name and beat out his own rhythms estrange him from
others—he can still, as he writes in "Orpheus," be "Rich in the
loss of all I sing."

Many of the lyrics in *Heart's Needle* are lasting achievements, but the title sequence of ten poems, one for each season
over a period of two and a half years, is one that makes
Snodgrass' volume as important as, perhaps, only a half dozen
others during this century of American verse. The poet-father's
voice here is unique: urgent but controlled, muted but passionate, unassuming but instructive. Snodgrass manages a
poetry that moves from his own psychological problems to
suggest what it feels like to be a man and to live in the mid-
century world. The frequently reiterated charge that Snodgrass
offends "aesthetic distance" is nonsense and is made by those
who feel it necessary to group the poet with certain other
flagrantly abusive autobiographical poets. We are likely to hear
more talk about the women in Snodgrass' life and about his
Iowa City background than we are about "Heart's Needle"
as poetry.

The poet refuses, though he could so easily have fallen into
sentimentality, to cry in his beer or look for the reader's
shoulder. His verses are tightly rhymed and are rendered, with
some variation, in accentual syllabics. Underneath the form
is the recognition that there is to be no letting go, no back-
sliding into bathos. One of the stanzas that keep echoing in my
mind is from Section IV, perhaps the tenderest and most passionate, and therefore the most aesthetically dangerous, of the
sequence:

> No one can tell you why
> the season will not wait;
> the night I told you I
> must leave, you wept a fearful rate
> to stay up late.

The rhythmic poundings, the broken lines and full rhymes, make for an emotional music, but one with an edge of rage. These are the fourth, fifth, and sixth stanzas of the same poem:

> But the asters, too, are gray,
> ghost-gray. Last night's cold
> is sending on their way
> petunias and dwarf marigold,
> hunched sick and old.

> Like nerves caught in a graph,
> the morning-glory vines
> frost has erased by half
> still scrawl across their rigid twines.
> Like broken lines

> of verses I can't make.
> In its unraveling loom
> we find a flower to take,
> with some late buds that might still bloom,
> back to your room.

What is apparent here is the speaker's self-control. His teeth, so to speak, are on edge with tenderness. The "twines" of "Heart's Needle" are rigid, and there is a dramatic irony that makes the sequence come alive. The poet is talking to himself and to us more than he is to his daughter. As he says to her in Section IX, "I write you only the bitter poems / that you can't read."

The title of the sequence comes from "The Frenzy of Suibne," an old Irish story. Even the epigraph adopted by Snodgrass suggests that what is to follow is to be no soulful, melancholy outpouring of grief: " 'Your daughter is dead,' said Loingsechan. 'And an only daughter is the needle of the heart,' said Suibne. 'Dead is your son who used to call you "Father," ' said Loing-sechan. 'Indeed,' said he, 'that is the drop that brings a man to the ground.' " The loss of an only daughter is, indeed, a needle of the heart, but it is the loss of a son that kills. And although the poet-father of the sequence finds that his daughter, separated from him because of his divorce, has changed, he concludes, addressing her, "And you are still my daughter."

The first section of the sequence consists of six quatrains, one sentence, a form that suggests that neither the enunciation of the conflicts begun when "I could not find / My peace in my will," nor the resolution of these conflicts is to be an easy matter. If the Korean War—in *Heart's Needle* war is as constant as the seasons—"fouled the snows" of Asia, his child's mind, "a landscape of new snow," is also likely to be marked by what he sees as his own "cold war." The speaker seems to realize that his passion, his heart's will, had to take him toward the "love I could not still," that his head's will had to lose. As he does in "The Operation," Snodgrass associates white-ness with innocence; his divorce, a peculiarly modern aspect of alienation, will be, for his daughter, a life's lesson, a move-ment toward experience.

The second poem, a parable for his daughter, concerns her garden, one she herself seems bent on destroying, and suggests that she, too, is a sprout that will come to full flower only when (and perhaps because) he will be away. The third poem, beginning "The child between them on the street / Comes to a puddle, lifts his feet / And hangs on their hands," con-tinues the cold war theme. Here he wishes to assure his child that although he is "gone / As men must and let you be drawn / Off to appease another," he loves her: "Solomon himself might say / I am your real mother." This implies that to save his daughter he must be willing to give her up. Unfortunately, there is no wise king to decree that the two of them shall not be separated. For him the pain remains, and the rage: "what must not be seized / Clenches the empty fist."

With the fourth poem, four stanzas of which are quoted above, fall has arrived. Father and daughter walk among ghost-gray flowers and try to talk. As Donald T. Torchiana has written in *Poets in Progress* (1962), here the father's hopes "remain for his daughter's life in spite of the separation. These hopes also commingle with his fears for the halted scrawl of his own unfinished verses brought home to him by a glimpse of broken morning glories." The poem's final stanza portends grief for her and death for him, but unspoken here is also the realization that he must continue his writing:

> Night comes and the stiff dew.
> I'm told a friend's child cried
> because a cricket, who
> had minstreled every night outside
> her window died.

The fifth song of the sequence brings winter and a deadening of feeling. His daughter, growing strange to him, is happy and does not seem to mind "the squalls and storms / That are renewed long since"; he, at the same time, compares himself to a fox who "backtracks and sees the paw, / Gnawed off, he cannot feel; / Conceded to the jaw / Of toothed, blue steel." But April is the "cruellest" month. In the sixth poem "Easter has come around / Again." Memories are stirred by the spring thaw, and the father fears, because of a night he remembers when his daughter's "lungs caught and would not take the air," that she will not choose her own life. He is afraid that, letting her go as he let a pigeon go to its keeper, he has snarled her in a net. After a storm "torn limbs that could sap the tree" are hacked loose. "In the debris lay / starlings dead." The institutions of society, throughout *Heart's Needle*, are traps, prisons, tangles of branches. And destruction, perhaps, is the inevitable outcome of any attempt to live the individual life.

The push-pull of the poet's relationship with his daughter, his desire to turn her loose and, at the same time, to hold on to her, troubles him, and he weighs the destructiveness of this desire. In the seventh poem his heart's needle is seen as a force natural as gravity:

> Here in the scuffled dust
>   is our ground of play.
> I lift you on your swing and must
>   shove you away,
> see you return again,
>   drive you off, again, then
>
> stand quiet till you come.
>   You, though you climb
> higher, farther from me, longer,
>   will fall back to me stronger.

The left margin moves back and forth like a swing, and the sound-sense rhythms, as in the third and fourth lines above, attest to Snodgrass' metrical virtuosity.

In the eighth poem his daughter becomes the fox, visiting him over Halloween and not knowing what she has lost and what effect her relationship with her father has on her. He watches her sleeping. She grates her jaw, as cold war soldiers grind their jaws in the third poem, and he remarks: "Assuredly your father's crimes / are visited / on you." But it is as though, as his daughter breaks the "year's first crust of snow / off the runningboard to eat," she has accepted and chosen to live in the real world. No longer does she chew on "white, sweet clover." Her food is not to be stars cooked for dinner; rather, the meals that her "absentee bread-winner" father can prepare for her will be more earthy fare. And the father realizes that if he is to continue building "back from helplessness" she will have to visit him less often: "Indeed our sweet / foods leave us cavities."

Three months later and alone—although she is living less than a mile away it has been this long since he has seen his daughter—he visits a museum, the setting of the ninth and longest of the "Heart's Needle" sequence. The museum becomes for the poet a microcosm of the world and its passions, and this is also the darkest of the poem's movements; indeed, this is one of the darkest poems of our time. It is only in the museum that the evil and disease of the world is "arrested . . . in violent motion / like Napoleon's troops"; only here that stuffed animals "in their peaceable kingdoms freeze / to this still scene"; only here that "the malignancy man loathes / is held suspended." Outside the "world moves like a diseased heart / packed with ice and snow." The origin of the world's ills is traced back even to the "putty-colored children curled / in jars of alcohol." The poet doesn't know the answers. A return to the world, after the museum, is a return to the seasons, to cycles of both numbness and agony. The poem reads like a cynical and bitter suicide note. There is no such thing as a time that heals all wounds.

In the tenth and final poem, however, father and daughter are once more together. "The vicious winter finally yields"— not the winter of discontent, but the winter of absolute negation. It is as though the father, a prisoner of his passions, is determined to accept the bitter fruits of his life. His situation parallels that of the coons:

> If I loved you, they said, I'd leave
> and find my own affairs.
> Well, once again this April, we've
> come around to the bears;
>
> punished and cared for, behind bars,
> the coons on bread and water
> stretch thin black fingers after ours.
> And you are still my daughter.

At the end of the sequence the poet, still on bread and water, is in the same position he was in when he returned from "Frisco."

Heart's Needle remains a poetry without answers, but it is a poetry of total awareness. Inherent in its criticism of the way things are is the ability of the intelligence that informs its lyrics to accept this reality and to struggle against it at the same time. *Heart's Needle,* without caterwauling, free from what Ezra Pound calls "emotional slither," takes on dimensions of the tragic.

III

I suspect that whether or not *After Experience* is as good a book, or worse than, or better than *Heart's Needle* is a non-issue. It is a different book and moves in a different direction. If less lyrical, as some have said, it is more dramatic; if it does not have a single poem as ambitious as the "Heart's Needle" sequence, it does include several poems whose complexities and subtleties require a more intense reading; if it does not have the same sort of thematic center as does *Heart's Needle,* it still manages to encompass a world; if the voice of its first fifteen or so poems is now a familiar one, we ought not to criticize a poet because hosts of imitators have sprung up between his two volumes. To be sure, Snodgrass has not suffered a sophomore slump. Even his most virulent critics agree that *After Experience* includes many poems as fine, from any point of view, as anything in his first book.

In *Heart's Needle* Snodgrass moves out of the swamp of self-pity; *After Experience* is the record of the poet's strenuous effort to order, somehow, his sense of confusion, frustration, and helplessness within some philosophical framework. After experience his reality is what he has come to be—frequently bitter, frequently cynical; he then sounds history and his own past for suggestions of some truth that will enable him to live in the world as he is.

Maximilian, in Snodgrass' poem on Édouard Manet's "The Execution of the Emperor Maximilian," "dreamed that one day he might stand / At the top of some broad magnificent staircase." But, dead, he "Stands in an impartial iconoclastic light / That will not hint where you might best direct your sight." And what grand pronouncement is to be made on the Emperor? Of what meaning is any man or any action or any grief? This is the swamp of metaphysics in which modern man, his gods dead, founders. The statement of this problem in poetry, of course, has become one of the great clichés of our age.

What Lionel Trilling has called "residual pieties," outworn beliefs that no longer serve a creative function but are still given lip service, no longer serve the poet. It is not that Snodgrass bemoans the loss of his myths; in fact, he has said that he is tired of people who do. *After Experience* assumes the loss and attempts to build something despite it. "Powwow," perhaps, is the one poem that laments, imagistically and therefore not offensively, the poignant loss of the way things were when there were still words that were magical and meaningful. After hearing an old Indian howl,

> We tramp back to our car,
> Then nearly miss the highway, squinting
> Through red and yellow splatterings on the windshield—
> The garish and beautiful remains
> Of grasshoppers and dragonflies
> That go with us; that do not live again.

Still a Snodgrass constant, at least with the first fifteen or so poems here, is the whole syndrome of hurt and confused affections caused by his divorce and his separation from his daughter. But the poet now sees things in a colder, more objective light. He can say to his daughter, as he does in "The First Leaf," "You move off where I send you; / The train pulls down its track. / We go about our business; / I have turned my back." Although he can't remember her face or what she said ("September"), he restores her in the verses he sells to magazines ("Reconstructions"). There is a kind of unstated recognition in several poems (stated more directly in W. B. Yeats's poems on Maud Gonne) that his imperfect life has proved beneficial to his poet's work, has opened up areas of feeling that might have remained closed. Certainly, he still wants no part of the "Dullard in the nerves" that "Chicken-steers around Love's curves / Teasing the intimate abyss" ("Exorcism").

Indeed, by the time of *After Experience*, even in his serious poems, the poet is almost bemused by the paradoxical nature ("Still," he asks in "Take-off," "who would dare diminish / The loveliness or the loss?") of love. In "The Lovers Go Fly a Kite," the kite, symbol of their love, plunges and bobs, wobbles and floats, and "would spill if one chill wind coughed, / Dive down to tear, or to kiss." The poem concludes:

> It's enough to make you laugh—
> In these uncommitted regions
> Of an invisible staff
> To run up an allegiance.

But, as he says in "No Use," "No use telling us love's / No use." And in "Leaving Ithaca" (to a plastic replica of the Aphrodite of Melos), a poem with the distinctive grace and control of "April Inventory," the poet realizes that whatever poverty his "Lady" has brought him, and even though he must leave a place where things were lovelier than they will likely be again, he must take her along. A similar rededication to love and beauty occurs in "Leaving the Motel," when lovers, careful not to leave any evidence that they ever spent a night there, "Leave in their vase / An aspirin to preserve / Our lilacs."

As Snodgrass says in "Leaving Ithaca," reiterating a theme from *Heart's Needle*, "We'll try to live with evils that we choose," and *After Experience* continues to affirm, despite whatever pain inevitably results, living the passionate life. Again, self-denial drains the life force ("Mementos, 1"). We feel what we must do, and any action must proceed from feeling. People who deny themselves are objects of the poet's scorn:

> Already you can see them through the trees—
> Bulldozed lots where men will spend their lives
> In glossy houses kept by glossy wives
> That have no past or future, but will please
>
> The Company. They go for the main chance
> But always save the weekend for their passions;
> They dress just far enough behind the fashions
> And think right thoughts. They keep it in their pants.
>
> ("Leaving Ithaca")

These are the people who "fall back with the mass / Heaped in their common trench" ("Lobsters in the Window"). In "The Examination" the powers that be in our world, sinister birdmen in black robes, repack the brain of their candidate, set blinders to his eyes, and tie his genitals off:

> Well; that's a beginning. The next time, they can split
>   His tongue and teach him to talk correctly, can give
> Him opinions on fine books and choose clothing fit
>   For the integrated area where he'll live.

At the end of the poem, "Bowing away, / They nod, whispering, 'One of ours; one of ours. Yes. Yes.'"

The struggle on Snodgrass' part to denounce self-denial, to affirm the passionate life while realizing the destructiveness of the passionate existence, brings him, as it must, to the concurrent conviction (first apparent in Section IX of "Heart's Needle") that human nature has not changed since genesis, that despite our sweet illusions we are animals dirtying the beautiful but diseased world. To this extent, even our feelings of free choice may be fictions. The world is the way it is and we have made our situations what they are simply because what will out will out. In Snodgrass what is moving toward Bethlehem and light is not a new myth, but the beast in our souls. Ultimately, what the poet recognizes is that "Luck, friend, not character," makes us what we are. "We took the parts / Our time and place allowed" ("A Visitation"). He contradicts, as he must, Hannah Arendt who, addressing Adolf Eichmann in *Eichmann in Jerusalem* (1963), writes: "We find that no member of the human race can be expected to share the earth with you." The poet tells Eichmann that "Our days exact / From you, as from me, the deep faults they must." He says to the Nazi: "Close your eyes—I'll just wander off somewhere. / Or watch the way your world moves—you can look through me" ("A Visitation"). Eichmann lives in all of us, governs us: "How subtle all that chokes us with disgust / Moves in implacably to rule us, unaware." "Inquest," the poem preceding "A Visitation," satirizes those who "see no place where our own hands are red."

Stated this extremely, these sentiments are, perhaps, shocking; but *After Experience* is a book that begins deeper and goes farther than *Heart's Needle*. In the beginning of each possible world, there is "The Men's Room in the College Chapel," in which the "subversive human in his cell" shuts out his shame and "scribble[s] of sex and excrement":

> This is the last cave, where the soul
> turns in its corner like a beast
> nursing its wounds, where it contemplates
> vengeance, how it shall gather to full
> strength, what lost cause shall it vindicate,
> returning, masterless and twisted.

What "gathers to a greatness" here is just the opposite of the "dearest freshness deep down things" that Gerard Manley Hopkins saw in "God's Grandeur."

Snodgrass, however, does not present this vision of human nature nihilistically. What he dramatizes is a dynamic existence, one that balances a stoical recognition of what, genetically, we are with the determination that men go on living as though they are responsible for what, in truth, may be unavoidable. His speakers are still out looking for experiences that will suggest that the world is at least as beautiful as it is ugly and depraved. Snodgrass' "A Character," another object of his satire, "thinks the world is his scab and picks at it." This man, considering himself "beyond good and evil," looking for "some small fortress / against manifest vulgarity and worldliness," both decorates his room and dresses in white, but is strangely susceptible "to lesions / apparently of some old wound he's liable to forget." When one ignores the dark half of his soul, he joins the walking dead. When, in the volume's title poem, the poet says "I'm going to show you something very / Ugly: someday it might save your life," he means it. In this poem the poet is determined to live beyond the ultimate realization, to live in spite of it, to accept his fate, and to continue to choose it.

Just as, in his poem on Henri Matisse's "The Red Studio," a reality independent of human perception exists, there are universal, if unpleasant, truths in Snodgrass' world. "A Flat One" —on one occasion Snodgrass said he considered this his favorite poem—tells the story of an "Old Fritz" who lay a hopeless case, but insisted on life for seven months. Keeping him alive, his nurses, in effect, are keeping alive in the face of unavoidable misfortune both the world as it must be—here leveling its full woe on an old man—and human dignity. Both patient and attendant-speaker fight to choose and keep alive the imperfect world:

> Such pious sacrifice to give
> You all you could demand of pain:

Receive this haddock's body, slain
For you, old tyrant; take this blood
Of a tomato, shed that you might live.
You had that costly food.

* * * *

I can't think we did *you* much good.
Well, when you died, none of us wept.
You killed for us, and so we kept
You, because we need to earn our pay.
No. We'd still have to help you try. We would
Have killed for you today.

IV

Heart's Needle encompasses a smaller world than does *After Experience*. Snodgrass' second book is still a personal poetry, but with several poems (" 'After Experience Taught Me . . .'," "Inquest," "A Visitation," "A Flat One," "The Men's Room in the College Chapel"), we witness a widening of the poet's horizon, an increasing depth of field. More directly than before, the poet, writing a more complex poem, comes to grips with the eternal questions of evil and sin, their origins, their masks, and being in the face of them. *Heart's Needle* is done and, perhaps, need only have been done once. But the imperatives and the final question of the last stanzas of " 'After Experience Taught Me . . . .' " open a poetic world without end:

You must call up every strength you own
And you can rip off the whole facial mask.

Wishing to be, to act, to live. He must ask
First, in other words, to actually exist.

And you, whiner, who wastes your time
Dawdling over the remorseless earth,
What evil, what unspeakable crime
Have you made your life worth?

Nick, in Ernest Hemingway's "Big Two-Hearted River," must leave off, for the sake of his sanity, fishing the swamp until another day. Snodgrass already, with *Heart's Needle*, cast his line into the most dangerous waters, but it did not snag. In *After Experience* the swamp is an uncompromising reality, but the poet is more worldly, and, though often heart-deep in mud, he manages to maintain his difficult balance.